India's Changing Rural Scene
1963–1979

GILBERT ETIENNE

DELHI
OXFORD UNIVERSITY PRESS
BOMBAY   CALCUTTA   MADRAS
1982

Oxford University Press, Walton Street, Oxford OX2 6DP

LONDON GLASGOW NEW YORK TORONTO
DELHI BOMBAY CALCUTTA MADRAS KARACHI
KUALA LUMPUR SINGAPORE HONG KONG TOKYO
NAIROBI DAR ES SALAAM CAPE TOWN
MELBOURNE AUCKLAND

and associates in

BEIRUT BERLIN IBADAN MEXICO CITY

Phototypeset by Vimalson Photocomposing Centre, New Delhi 110065
Printed by Rekha Printers Private Ltd., New Delhi 110020
and published by R. Dayal, Oxford University Press
2/11 Ansari Road, Daryaganj, New Delhi 110002

India's Changing Rural Scene, 1963-1979

Contents

Introduction

Is it correct to assume, apropos the so-called green revolution, that 'the rich get richer and the poor get poorer'? Can one, as the F.A.O. states in its report prepared for the World Conference on Land Reform and Rural Development (July 1979), say whether the growth rate in Asia is fast or slow, whether poverty is increasing? Such themes are being increasingly debated in international organizations, within developing countries, and in academic circles. Let us see how they apply to India, frequently cited in connection with rural poverty.

How should one approach these issues? The usual way is to rely on secondary sources: to sit in one's office and tabulate all available data: U.N. and national statistics, special surveys, reports and so on. An alternative method is to conceive and conduct a large project with teams of surveyors who go and interview villagers with a detailed and highly sophisticated questionnaire, and feed the answers later into a computer.

At the risk of seeming old-fashioned, I have followed a more direct method, one that was already endorsed about two thousand years ago in the *Artha Shastra*, the old Indian treatise on Political Science. That is to go and see what is happening with one's own eyes. In fact, all through Indian history, the guiding principle of government has been to get into close personal touch with events in the country. This is why Ashoka and Akbar, the Hindu senior civil servants of the distant past, the *mansabdars* of the Mughals, as well as the I.C.S. officers, no matter what the colour of their skin, have followed this approach, emphasizing the importance of touring the kingdom, the provinces and the districts. Of prime importance for a sound government policy, this very simple method is equally well suited to research, not only in anthropology, but also in rural economics.

Then comes a second problem. Rural life, techniques and wages do not change in a push button manner. One needs to observe them over a period of time. My first detailed surveys were conducted in 1963-4,[1] the last ones in 1978-9.

The main focus of this book is on rural development: agricultural and non-agricultural activities, growth trends as well as the pattern of incomes, with particular attention given to small farmers and landless labourers. Some other issues have been tackled too, though less systematically: family planning, education, and relations between social classes and castes. The basic idea is to see rural development from the farmers' point of view and from the administration's. While my field studies deal mostly with villages and districts, administrative and planning problems are tackled in the second part of the book, making more general conclusions on India's rural development.

Finally I adopt a still broader perspective, comparing the findings of other scholars brought out in their field studies, and referring to visits I have made to other Asian countries: China, Pakistan, Bangladesh and Afghanistan. This leads me to the most ticklish question: why is there such a gap between studies like this one and so many books and reports of a more general nature? This raises suggestions as to how to approach the problems: to put things bluntly, should we speak *about* the poor or *with* the poor?

The manuscript of this book was completed in March 1980. The text of the chapters dealing with field surveys have remained as they were. Part II has been updated in order to include the latest trends in India's rural world and new agricultural policies.

Chene-Bougeries, Geneva
May 1982

---

[1] I started visiting India in 1952, making more general studies of the economy and the population.

Acknowledgements

The Graduate Institute of International Studies and the Institute of Development Studies in Geneva very kindly gave me sabbatical leave in 1978-9 to conduct this research. I also wish to thank the Swiss National Fund for Scientific Research for its grant.

Such a study would have been impossible without the participation of many people in India. B. Sivaraman, then member of the Planning Commission, was of particular help. He gave me the benefit of his vast experience and recommended me to the authorities of the states which I visited. G. V. K. Rao, then Secretary, Ministry of Agriculture and A. J. S. Sodhi, Joint Secretary of the same Ministry, were no less helpful. Ashok Mitra, former Secretary, Planning Commission and B. B. Vohra, then Secretary, Ministry of Petroleum and Chemicals, were, during this visit as well as on previous ones, of great help and gave me some sound advice. It was again a rare privilege to meet Professors M. L. Dantawala in Bombay and Raj Krishna in New Delhi. The authorities of the different states visited, the state capitals, the districts and the blocks received me with great hospitality. They supplied me with much information, sparing no effort to make my enquiries easier. Particular mention must be made of Dr K. C. Panda who accompanied me during most of my time in Puri.

Very warm thanks go to the large number of farmers, small and big, interviewed in the villages. Without their friendly and unsparing co-operation such a work would have been impossible.

Once again I must express my appreciation of the remarkably free atmosphere prevailing in India, without which any research would have been much more difficult. Practically everywhere I came across officials and farmers who talked to me very frankly, even about sensitive issues.

After our village and district trips, my family and I enjoyed the hospitality of very dear and old friends, who at the same time enabled

ix

us to understand their country better. I wish to thank Raghu Raj and his wife Vimal, Pran and Raksha Talwar, Aspi and Kitty Moddie, all in New Delhi, Naval and Simone Tata in Bombay, Surendra Pal Singh in Unchagaon and New Delhi.

As far as the writing of this book is concerned, Gerry Rodgers from the International Labour Office made some very useful comments on the second part. I owe a debt of gratitude to Isabelle Gerardy and Marie-Jeanne Montant for typing the manuscript. I am also most grateful to Urvashi Butalia for her painstaking work in improving my English and to Oxford University Press for editiorial assistance.

During these long months in the field, my wife accompanied me, as she has so often done before. Her advice and observations made my task easier. She was also of great assistance at the time of writing.

It goes without saying that I take sole responsibility for the views expressed in this book.

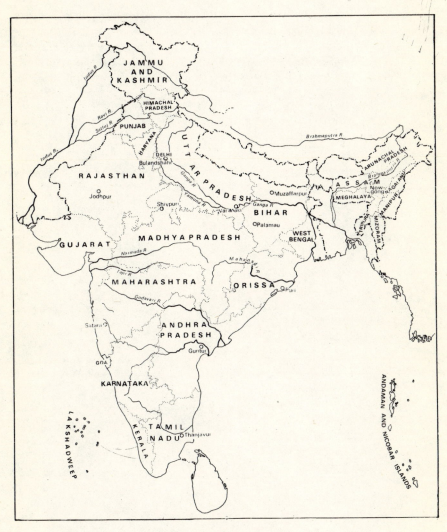

Map of districts surveyed

PART I

Meeting the Farmers

CHAPTER 1
Research Methodology

In 1963, after over a decade during which I had spent several years in India for economic studies and other projects, I felt it was high time that rural development be observed at the grassroots. At that time there was a growing concern in India and elsewhere over what should be done to speed up both economic growth and social progress in the villages.

Already in those days, two basic methodological problems were being debated. Macro-economic studies could not bring out the complexity and diversity of a rural economy, and the gradual erosion of the subsistence sector in favour of monetary transactions.[1] It was thus necessary to combine a macro approach at the national and regional levels with a micro approach at the village level. Secondly, it was already quite obvious that economic problems could not be isolated from their cultural, social and political surroundings, at both the national and local levels.

In order to tackle these complex interdependent problems, I sought to combine an economic approach (factors of growth, input-output, savings and investments, employment) with the anthropological method of research, that is to say, observing a village society, its various forces, classes and castes, at first hand. While very helpful, the anthropological approach could be followed for only a part of the research. Usually such studies are confined to a single village, which gives one a limited insight into development, especially in a country as large and diverse as India. That is why, in order to cover at least a sample of typical situations, I had to make each village study relatively brief, focusing on economic problems and only on non-economic factors which have a direct effect, positive or negative, on development.

[1] Even in ancient times, as also in pre-colonial India, many rural areas were not entirely bound to a subsistence economy. Especially in the vicinity of towns, monetary transactions often took place.

3

However, unlike anthropological studies, these surveys could not stop at the village level. It was essential to pay particular attention to district planning and operations such as extension work, credit institutions, local councils. Finally it was necessary to proceed further, to the state and central government levels where agricultural policies are designed.

Selection of Areas

Several criteria were pinpointed in order to present a sample of the most typical situations arising in India. The first of these was the historical background. Even if one ignores the differences that existed in pre-colonial times, one finds a wide range of situations prevailing today. Several rural areas entered rather rapidly into the process of growth and economic diversification by the end of the last century (and perhaps even earlier) as, for instance, the whole north-west (from western Uttar Pradesh to Punjab) or the southern deltas along the east coast. Many other regions went through a very slow growth process with few, if any, technical innovations. In these regions the main change was the increase in the area given to cultivated land, though this increase was unable, in most cases, to keep up with population growth. Such was the case in eastern U.P., Bihar, the plains of Assam and Orissa and vast stretches in the Deccan.

It is certainly not a coincidence that the areas that were already advanced at the time of Independence, have proceeded further and faster than others today. To explain the reasons for these differences is beyond the scope of this book. Here and there I have given partial explanations, but a more complete answer has to come from historians. For people concerned with contemporary development, what matters first is to realize the weight of the past, a remark which would seem a platitude if history were not so often neglected by scholars of developmental problems.

A second set of criteria covers physical or geographical conditions such as climate, rainfall, irrigation potential and soils. While many parts of India, especially the alluvial plains, enjoy very favourable growth potential, others, particularly in the Deccan, are hindered by severe constraints such as low and erratic rainfall, limited irrigation potential, poor soils and erosion. No matter how extensive the research and investment, such areas face a rather limited future in terms of agricultural growth.

No less crucial are human factors and behaviour. In India, as in most countries, certain groups, often inhabiting particular areas, are more inclined than others to undertake agricultural work and hard manual labour; for a long time they have been used to painstaking, traditional techniques. Other groups of people are less inclined to such hard work; they may be more relaxed, less careful in tending their crops. In India these differences are easily identified through the caste system. Several castes, traditionally oriented as they- are towards agriculture, have been remarkable farmers for centuries. Even those only slightly familiar with India's rural scene know that the Jats in the north-west—no matter whether they be Sikh, Hindu or Muslim—the Kammas and Reddis in Andhra and the Patidars in Gujarat are excellent farmers, whereas the same cannot be said of the Thakurs, the Bhumihars or certain—though not all—Brahmin castes in the middle Ganges basin. Here again it is up to historians and anthropologists to find explanations for these differences, since I can only analyse certain elements. For the development economist, what matters is to know that such differences exist and that they have implications for development.

It is also appropriate to have a relatively wide sample of agricultural and non-agricultural activities. On the agricultural side, crops include wheat, paddy or millet, cash crops like sugarcane or cotton, and possibly oilseeds. At the same time one should notice changes in cropping patterns such as the expansion of rice in the north-west and the penetration of wheat into the lower Ganges basin. However, while agriculture remains the main source of income and employment, growing attention must be paid to rural non-agricultural activities which may give full or part-time employment to many people. This leads us to small industries, trade and other services and the infrastructure at the village, block and district levels. In these fields also, enormous differences become apparent between regions, in that this growth process is well advanced in some and is just beginning in others.

Using the criteria just described, I selected three districts which have experienced relatively rapid growth involving a substantial process of economic diversification. These are Bulandshahr district in western U.P., the irrigated part of Guntur district on coastal Andhra, and the new delta of Thanjavur district in Tamil Nadu. Here one finds the best combination of growth factors: an early start, good agricultural castes, favourable natural conditions. Then come two districts which are examples of those that started late and did not have particularly agriculturally-minded castes: Varanasi (Banaras) district in eastern U.P., and Muzaffarpur in north Bihar. A brief visit to Assam led me to Nowgong district, also a slow-moving area with a growth potential which is still largely untapped. Puri district in Orissa offers another example of favourable natural conditions still very inadequately used. Finally comes a third category of cases: able farmers facing inhospitable natural conditions. No matter how clever the Maratha farmers may be, they are hindered by the severe constraints which were observed during different surveys of Satara district (Maharashtra). Perhaps even more difficult are the natural conditions in arid, semi-desert areas like Jodhpur district, Rajasthan, which I visited briefly in 1979.

Village Inquiries

Within each district one village was usually selected for systematic interviews with landless labourers, and small, medium and large landowners in order to have a representative sample of various classes and castes, as well as different incomes. I took care through visits to other neighbouring villages, to select places which typified the area. At the same time, local authorities from the village, block and district were interviewed. They supplied me with the statistics quoted in this book and with local records.

I have indicated in this book, as in my first surveys, the broad economic and social trends of the village. In the second round of surveys particular attention was given to small farmers and landless labourers. I have described a number of people and their families: landholdings if any, the size of the families, main and secondary occupations, sources of income, etc., using a simple questionnaire which even illiterate farmers could answer. In the case of landowners, I concentrated on cash expenses devoted to production and to sales, because other data are bound to be very approximate. For instance I saw little point in trying to convert family labour input into monetary terms or in making detailed estimates on the amortization of a tubewell or of bullocks, when the farmer himself was not interested in such calculations.

A question that may be asked is, how reliable are the data gathered in this way? Some of the data for districts or blocks were so obviously uncertain or self-contradictory that I preferred not to use them. However, those quoted can, at the very least, be relied upon as indicators of a trend. Data supplied by farmers also need some qualification. Figures on yields contain an acceptable degree of approximation and enable us to differentiate bad, medium or good yields. It is, for instance, important to know whether the wheat yield is around 2,000–3,000 kilograms per hectare or much below 2,000. The same applies to paddy: there are wide areas in eastern India which often yield between 1,000 and 1,500 kilograms per hectare, versus 3,000 or more in the Guntur and Thanjavur villages.

Wage rates are quite reliable because they were checked with many people, both the employers and the recipients of the wage. What is more unreliable is the food component. All one can say is whether wages are 'sukha' (dry), as they say in Hindi, or whether they include a meal. Figures on inputs like chemical fertilizers are rough. In fact, what matters is to know whether the applied doses approximate the recommendations of agricultural officers or are still very small. This can be partly checked by the yields obtained.

In interviewing villagers, especially the poorer ones, particular attention has to be given to secondary jobs, and subsidiary activities. The income derived from them and the number of days of employment they entail cannot be accurately measured, but one can tell by taking a look at a man's house, meeting his wife and children, or by talking to him, whether or not these additional activities enable him to get by in a state of bearable poverty. In all these cases we need to make use of our eyes and legs, which may yield better information than other sources of data.[2] This method may seem untidy. True, it does not result in clear tables on employment, income, number of men/days of work, breakdown of incomes or a detailed cost-benefit analysis, but the picture which emerges is probably closer to the actual reality than calculations which rely on too much extrapolation, or are sometimes mere guesswork dressed up as mathematics.[3]

Finally there comes the question of language. Knowing Hindi, as I do, I had no problems in communicating with people in U.P., Bihar and Rajasthan. In Orissa I was fortunate in having the help of an excellent young officer lent to me by the government. In Andhra, Tamil Nadu and Maharashtra, I relied on private interpreters or local officers.

[2]It is essential to move about a great deal in any village as well as in the fields, so that one can meet the poor away from the local *neta* (village leader), whose presence is embarrassing and inconvenient to them.
[3]We will return to that problem in Chapter 16 when discussing the concept of the poverty line.

As far as living conditions were concerned, during the 1963–4 survey, I lived (along with my family) in each village, except in Thanjavur where I commuted from the district town. I also commuted for the 1967 and 1978–9 surveys, except in the case of Mirpur (Bulandshahr district) where I settled, again with my family, in September 1978 and February 1979.

The reader will find some imbalance in the amount of information gathered on each area. The study on Mirpur is more detailed than the others. This is where I started in 1963 in order to get used to village inquiries, and stayed six months. After that experience, other surveys required less time. Secondly the consolidation of holdings having just been completed, I was fortunate in getting up-to-date land records and a precise profile of land tenure conditions. Finally, there are, of course, more things to write about in a dynamic village than in slow-moving areas.

The Time Dimension

Four villages and districts (in western and eastern U.P., Thanjavur in Tamil Nadu and Satara in Maharashtra) were first surveyed from August 1963 to August 1964 and again studied between September 1978 and the end of February 1979.[4] In between, Bulandshahr district was briefly visited on several occasions, and Satara and Varanasi districts in 1975. Muzaffarpur and Guntur districts were surveyed in July–August 1967 and October–November 1978. The other areas were surveyed only once, but data were collected for two decades in Puri district.

To visit the same area after ten or fifteen years is fascinating. One can meet a number of people interviewed during one's first visit, so that they can testify to the changes—or the lack of them, that have taken place since one last saw them. The period of time between the first and last visits is of particular importance. In the present case, the first surveys took place just before the advent of the new seeds, the last ones after a period long enough to assess the various problems involved: technical and economic factors, and social and political implications.

The National Scene

Instead of following the standard pattern whereby field studies are

---

[4]During the two main surveys, I travelled through India in my own car.

preceded by an overall view of the problems. I deliberately started with villages and districts. Prepared policies and guidelines exist in New Delhi and in the state capitals, but their crucial testing occurs at the implementation level where countless practical tasks, difficulties and troubles may interfere with plans and programmes.

Thus, it is only after trying to see problems through the farmer's and administrator's eyes that an all-India assessment can be attempted. In Chapter 13 I introduce the link between my surveys and broader information, indicating how direct information confirms general trends. Chapters 14 and 15 tackle planning and administration problems and general rural policies around the fundamental question: how to attack poverty, given the political framework. As we know, the margin of manoeuvre open to political leaders is relatively narrow in view of the prevailing balance of political forces.

In my *Studies in Indian Agriculture* (1968) and in a report prepared for the U.N. Research Institute for Social Development in Geneva[5] I have dealt at length with land reforms and rural institutions (community development, co-operatives, local councils) through many field observations. Several problems have remained basically the same since then, which is why I have added in this study only a few direct observations on villages and districts. It was, however, necessary to summarize these problems in the second part of this book, while underlining the most recent changes in rural institutions and the improvements in agricultural policy such as a greater effort in research and seeds multiplication, the growing emphasis on irrigation, improvement in the supply of inputs, acceleration of rural electrification and of village roads.

Beyond the Indian Case

In discussions on Third World rural development the Indian case comes up frequently because of the size of the country, the amount of information available on it[6] and the number of studies conducted over three decades. This gives one an opportunity to review, in the light of India's example, the main issues that are being widely debated presently: the attack on poverty, self-reliance and the selec-

[5]Chapter on Asia in United Research Institute for Social Development, *Co-operation and Other Institutions in Rural Development* (Geneva, 1969).

[6]Unlike several other developing countries, India enjoys a great deal of freedom in discussions and studies on development and national problems, no matter whether foreigners or Indians are involved.

tion of technologies. Beyond the specificity of each country, one can perceive some basic principles which are valid at least for Asia, where about two-thirds of the developing world lives.

Diversity of Approaches

It is beyond the scope of this book to present a long, detailed field study followed by more theoretical conclusions, or a full review of the literature on the subject. However some reference has to be made, at this stage, to scholars and administrators who deal with similar problems. Then, in the final chapter we discuss the most disturbing question: the wide discrepancy between fieldwork and the dogma and rhetoric so much in vogue nowadays.

The first thing to look at is the time dimension. Rural life does not change rapidly and words like 'green revolution' or 'miracle rice' are grossly misleading. As will be seen, the rapid changes which occurred in north-western India were made easy by several decades of substantial change and technical innovation *before* the advent of the new seeds of wheat. Secondly the introduction of new seeds and their success vary a great deal, and hence cannot be assessed over the short period of a few years. Some scholars were prompt to underline the failure of new rice varieties in the early years. (This was true, but is less so now.) Others reached negative conclusions about wheat when yields levelled off in 1973 and 1974. Yet, wheat expansion has picked up again in the last five years. Nor is it possible to comprehend the evolution of wages and employment in just a few years.

To sum up, several studies on the so-called green revolution were either premature or should have reached only tentative conclusions. Typical in this regard is Francine Frankel's book *India's Green Revolution* (1971) which gives an account of a survey conducted in 1969 only two years after the beginning of the real expansion of the new seeds in India.[7] More striking is Lester Brown's book, *Seeds of Change* (1970): 'The word "revolution" has been greatly abused but no other term adequately describes the effects of the new seeds on the poor countries.' Further, while referring to India, Pakistan, and Indonesia, he adds: 'The incidence of hunger is beginning to decline as food consumption rises.' It is interesting to remember that, five years earlier, the same author had been forecasting the growing dangers of famine in the Third World.[8] Even the father of the new

[7]Other references to F. Frankel's book will follow in Chapter 16.
[8]L. Brown, *Increasing World Output* (Washington, 1965).

seeds, N. E. Borlaug, talks in 1969 of 'spectacular progress' in Asia.[9]

We must also examine publications of a different kind, such as village studies. The time dimension appears prominently in Scarlet Epstein's *South India, Yesterday, Today and Tomorrow* (1973) where the author resurveys two villages in Karnataka, first studied in 1954–6. She very ably combines economic and social variables. Another work which will be referred to later, is the extraordinarily complete and detailed study of a village in Madhya Pradesh conducted by the French anthropologist Jean-Luc Chambard over a period of twenty years, from 1957 to 1977.

Among district studies let us cite Joan Menchler's *Agriculture and Social Structure in Tamil Nadu* (1978) devoted to Chingleput district, an interesting study of production, income and other changes occurring in villages. The French geographer Jean Racine gives a detailed account of Thanjavur district and of another area nearer the interior of Tamil Nadu (*Deux Etudes Rurales en Pays Tamoul*, 1976). More comprehensive in scope is the collective research directed by B. H. Farmer, *Green Revolution* (1977), in north Arcot district. Tamil Nadu and Hambantota, Sri Lanka. These areas have been surveyed only once, but a team of researchers covered practically all the aspects of what we call the global process of rural development. In her last book, *In Defense of the Irrational Peasant* (1979), Kusum Nair emphasizes the differences in behaviour between Punjabi and Bihari farmers. In a lively manner she confirms what I have been trying to show in some districts of the Ganges basin.

While it is not possible to quote all the general studies on Indian agriculture, I would like to mention at least some of them. B. Sen in his *Green Revolution in India* (1974), and C. H. Hanumantha Rao in *Technological Change and Distribution of Gains in Indian Agriculture* (1975), work at the all-India level. With great clarity and balance, they bring out the main trends in agriculture, giving due consideration to social factors, an approach which I have followed to some extent in the second part of this book. *Agricultural Development in India—Policy and Problems* (1979), edited by C. H. Shah and C. N. Vakil, contains a wealth of information on practically all aspects of the subject. Most of the best Indian specialists have contributed a chapter and there are also some foreign contributors. Such a review has made my task easier in my concluding chapter. Special mention

[9]N. E. Borlaug *et al.*, 'A Green Revolution Yields a Golden Harvest', *Columbia Journal of World Business* (September–October 1969).

must also be made of G. S. B. Bhalla and Y. K. Alagh's *Performance of Indian Agriculture* (1979). They study districtwise agricultural growth trends for the period 1962-5, i.e. before the introduction of the new seeds, to 1970-3. Although data are bound to be approximate, they show the right trends and the enormous differences of growth, which confirm our own findings.

There is a large quantity of literature on agrarian reforms, rural institutions and administration, some of which will be quoted in my last chapters: publications by the U. N. Research Institute for Social Development in Geneva, by the Overseas Development Institute, London,[10] reports and books by Indian scholars and administrators such as A. Beteille, M. L. Dantwala, Ashok Mitra, Raj Krishna, B. B. Vohra—all men of very sound judgement and experience. In many ways these studies help us get a clearer picture of what is happening in rural India.

To sum up, the research methodology followed in this book aims at combining several approaches, while emphasizing fieldwork and close contact with villagers. The advantage is that this produces a broad picture: macro and micro planning, economic and social factors, basic policy options, all spread over a ten-to-fifteen year period.

No doubt there are some risks involved in this kind of approach. My reservations on massive data computation may not be palatable to scholars or experts who believe in sophisticated mathematical models. Some may regret that the number of case studies is relatively limited. On this latter point I would like to seek the support of V. Pareto who wrote: 'The importance of facts matters more than their number.'[11] Needless to say, there can be no one single research methodology for such a wide and complex topic. Mine is only one among several approaches.

[10] Let us mention this particularly shrewd observer of India, Guy Hunter and, among several publications, *Policy and Practice in Rural Development* (1976) edited by G. Hunter, A. H. Hunting, A. Bottrall.

[11] V. Pareto, *Traite de sociologie generale* (Geneva, 1968), p. 285.

CHAPTER 2

An Early Start

Robert Currie, Settlement Officer, Mirpur, wrote in his report dated 1 March 1862, 'This [Mirpur] is an average sized village of ordinary appearance: to the south the lands are good and temporary wells can be sunk.... To the north and east, however, the soil is rather light and sandy and quite unirrigated'.[1]

When I visited Mirpur in 1963 I found it much as Currie had described it a century earlier. Like many villages in the Bulandshahr district of western U.P., Mirpur is situated in the middle of fields which, broken occasionally by clumps of trees, stretch for miles in unrelieved flatness. Yet appearances are deceptive. Although physically unchanged, Mirpur, in the last century, has undergone profound social and economic change.

The first change has been in the population. In 1961 Mirpur had 1,227 inhabitants (with a density of 444 per square kilometre) as compared with 451 in 1861. While the total area of the village (276 hectares) has remained the same, by the time of the second settlement in 1889, all area available for cultivation had been cleared. From that date onwards the only way to expand was to increase yields per hectare. By 1961 the irrigated area had trebled to cover 192 of a total of 255–60 cultivated hectares. The quality of irrigation had also improved, all temporary wells being replaced by masonry wells. In the first decade of the twentieth century the *mot* system (leather bucket pulled by a pair of bullocks) was replaced by the more efficient Persian wheel. The first tubewell installed by the main zamindar appeared as early as 1949 and was soon followed by two more. In the mid 1950s a state tubewell was constructed, and a power line for tubewells (private or public) cut across the countryside.

The cropping pattern, too, had altered. Cotton had given way to sugarcane towards the end of the last century, and by the 1930s a

[1]First Settlement Report 1859–63.

better variety of sugarcane had replaced the local one. By 1947 the Agriculture Department had already released improved seeds of wheat. In 1954 a development block was opened in Mirpur. Farmers now began to use small doses of chemical fertilizers—mostly ammonium sulphate. Things such as farm implements, however, had not changed much. The wooden plough reinforced with an iron nail, and the seed drill attached to the plough (which had been in use for a very long time) remained the same. To cut fodder for cattle, farmers used a chaff-cutter worked by hand instead of the simple chopper used, for instance, in eastern U.P. Both the preparation of the seed beds and the tilling of the land were done with particular care. For wheat and sugarcane (the main crops) the farmers would, after each ploughing, level the soil with a heavy plank drawn by oxen. They would do eight to ten ploughings and levellings which involved very heavy work.[2] Sugarcane was then made into raw sugar (*gur*) in small, open places known as *kolu*. The gur was then sold at Unchagaon, three kilometres away, or Jahangirabad, the nearest small town, fourteen kilometres away. Unchagaon was the block headquarters and was connected to Mirpur by a very bad fair weather road. Since the late 1950s, however, Unchagaon has been connected to the outside world by a metalled road open to vehicles all year round.

Even as late as 1920–5, only a limited amount of money was in circulation at Mirpur. Forty years later a barter economy and home consumption were still important, but the use of money was spreading. There was a weekly market at Unchagaon, more wages were paid in cash and more wheat and raw sugar were being sold. Before Independence the *lambardar* (main zamindar) in Mirpur had founded a primary school. This was later expanded. In addition some secondary schools were opened in the block during the 1950s.

The last, most important change was the abolition of the zamindari system. The three zamindars retained the land—a total of 36 hectares—they were cultivating themselves. Most of the remaining land was already being cultivated by occupancy tenants (farmers who had an occupancy right mentioned in the land records and who could not be ejected unless they failed to pay rent to the zamindar). These tenants either kept the same rights as *sirdars,* i.e. they enjoyed all rights on the land except that of selling, or they acquired full ownership rights as *bhumidars.* In order to do this they were required to pay

---

[2]One ploughing of 0.25–37 hectares per day, depending on the strength of the bullock.

an amount, equivalent to ten times their former rent, to the state.

Caste patterns in Mirpur had not changed. The Jats remained the dominant caste. They owned the larger part of the land (150 hectares if the lands of the occupancy tenants were counted) and represented the largest group—386 in 1961. At the other end of the scale were the Chamars, 223 in number, many of them landless labourers who had changed their names in order to be called Jativs.[3] Then there were the Lodhas, an already rising caste group which called itself Lodha Rajput. They numbered 137. After the Lodhas came the Brahmins (71 in number) and several other castes such as the Thakurs, Vaishyas, Kumhars (potters), Dhobis (washermen), Bhangis (scavengers) and Muslims. Of these groups the Jats have always been known for their hard work and spirit of enterprise and are rightly considered one of the best agricultural castes. In addition the Brahmins, Vaishyas and Lodha Rajputs in particular, are also said to be good farmers.

What were the results of all these changes in terms of production? Around 1963 wheat was yielding an average of 1,200–1,300 kilograms per hectare. This was partly due to irrigation (though this was often inadequate) and partly to improved seeds and the use of small doses of chemical fertilizer. Maize yields were about the same. However, both cereals were above the yields recorded in eastern U.P. where they would often amount to 700–900 kilograms per hectare. This was also true of sugarcane yield: while in eastern U.P. the average yield would be about 3,000 kilograms per hectare, here it was nearer 6,000 in terms of raw sugar for the first crop and 3,600 for the *ratoon* or second crop.

These data thus show how unreasonable it is to talk in general and sweeping terms of a static agriculture and conservative farming. Two sets of factors are worth mentioning here. Although Mirpur lies in the most isolated part of Bulandshahr district (in an area that was not greatly affected[4] by the network of irrigation canals constructed by the British in the latter part of the nineteenth century), it has nevertheless felt the impact of these canals. This led to a substantial regional process of growth which manifested itself in the building up of an infrastructure, an agriculture, the expansion of market places

[3]These changes of name are typical of the process by which various castes seek a higher social status.

[4]Only a small part of the fields is reached by the tail end of a tertiary canal and most of the irrigation relies on wells.

and of small towns typical to western U.P. districts. Added to this was what we might call the human factor—a set of excellent agricultural castes. Most of the medium-sized farmers were still illiterate or barely literate in 1963. This, however, did not prevent them from adjusting to changes and innovations and improving their crops in a perfectly rational way.

Standards of Living in the Early 1960s

'Are your conditions of living any better now than they were ten or fifteen years ago?' This was the question we asked of everyone during our first stay in Mirpur. Thirty-five of the fifty-four landowners interviewed answered in the affirmative. The majority of these owned at least two hectares of land—which could be taken as the minimum economic size of holdings in those days. With two hectares a family could cover its basic needs out of the farm produce whether it was self-consumed or sold. Raw sugar was the main source of cash. This was followed by wheat. Maize was hardly sold and jowar and bajra were used as fodder for cattle as well as eaten by the farmers and their families. Farmers with medium and large sized holdings kept bullocks and generally had one or more buffaloes supplying milk which was consumed at home.

The few rich farmers—this included the three zamindars, two with 13 hectares each, one with 10 hectares and some others with 6–8 hectares—lived in brick houses. They ate well—often they would have fruit and vegetables in addition to their basic diet of cereals, milk and pulses. Occasionally they even drank tea. And several of them also owned bicycles. In contrast, most of the medium sized farmers (those who owned 2–6 hectares) led a very frugal life. Things such as fruit, vegetables and tea were luxuries for them. Their houses were generally made of mud. By working hard, however, they managed to save some money and most of their children—largely the boys and sometimes the girls—went to school. Small farmers (with around 1 hectare) faced even more difficult conditions. At best they just managed to make both ends meet.

At the end of the scale were the tiny landowners and landless labourers who somehow managed to eke out a living. There was a glaring contrast in the appearance of the 'medium' Jat or Brahmin farmers who looked fairly lively, and the Jativs who looked depressed and miserable. When I questioned the Jativs on the progress made during the last ten or fifteen years, I was often given the same sad, rather bitter answer *kuchh nahin* (nothing). Most of them were also severely in debt to the local moneylender who extracted from them an interest of 3 per cent per month (36 per cent per year). Unlike medium and upper farmers, the poorer people had hardly any access to the primary co-operative society opened in Mirpur.

Many Jativs complained that there was insufficient employment This seemed strange, particularly when landowners sometimes found it difficult to engage extra labour. When I questioned them about this the Jativs explained that it was not always worthwhile to work for as little as Re 1 a day. This was the standard rate in villages in that area. They would do this sort of work only when there was no other way out. We also noticed among them a kind of inertia, due, we supposed to their poverty. This, however, was not the case with all scheduled castes. One Bhangi, for instance, was doing fairly well. He had different sources of income—he worked some months on a kolu, he had a small buffalo and was also raising pigs which he sold to a military farm. In addition one of his sons worked in Delhi from where he sent home Rs 30 every month.

By the time we had concluded our survey we wrote: 'Thus, in this village, in a comparatively rich and advanced district, between 35 and 40 per cent of the families manage to attain a fairly satisfactory standard of existence... at the price of unremitting labour. Nearly a third of the village lives a poor existence, and the rest fall somewhere in between.'

A last important point should be noted. In villages less remote than Mirpur, where overall development has been faster, the wages of landless labourers were higher and often moneylenders' rates of interest lower. Even at Unchagaon it was impossible to find a casual labourer for less than Rs 1.50 or 1.75. And in villages near the main roads the rate of interest often fell to 24 per cent.

The Future as Seen in 1963–4

It was already obvious that the acceleration in population increase was then only just beginning. Hence the people of Mirpur were obliged to increase production, encourage its diversification, and find jobs outside the village. In those days, out of 200 families, 45 men were working outside (in the army, police, in clerical and administrative jobs and in teaching). Many of them belonged to the upper castes. Family planning was practically non-existent. However, married women were very conscious of the problem. Many of them were surprised to see that my wife (in those days) had only two children. They would ask all manner of questions. When, from time to time, we went to Delhi, some of the village women would come and see us before we left to ask my wife to bring them back some *dawai* (medicine) from Delhi 'so that we can stop having so many children'. In addition to a high birth rate, the infant mortality rate and the still births were very high and involved useless pregnancies and much pain. Whenever I raised this question with the men, the response was rather poor. Clearly, they did not feel unduly concerned.

Since population was bound to increase faster, at least for a certain period of time, what was the outlook for the economy? Although Mirpur was already fairly advanced, a large potential for growth still remained untapped. The main problem was that of irrigation. There were still 60–70 hectares of land which were only rain-fed, and the irrigated plots were often poorly supplied, especially in the command area of the state tubewell.[5] Chemical fertilizers were still used in a very limited way and, as far as new seeds were concerned, in those days one still spoke only of improved seeds, as opposed to the newer high yield varieties. In the field of administration, too, there were many defects. There were delays and malpractices in the operations of credit co-operative societies, and the calibre of the block personnel was rather low. The infrastructure was insufficient — village roads were poor, power was available only for tubewells, trade was confined to only a few tiny shops in Mirpur and the bazaar of Unchagaon was still very small. And, as far as new outlets for jobs outside the village was concerned, expectations could not be too bright in view of the overall situation of unemployment already prevailing throughout the country.

---

[5]A common feature of state tubewells in U.P. was that the command area was too large to allow for good irrigation. In addition, the maintenance and operation of state tubewells was not satisfactory.

CHAPTER 3

The New Growth Process

Until the mid-1960s, the growth process had relied on very few modern techniques and it was not far from reaching its upper limits. Because of the increasing population pressure, new means of production had to step in.

Consolidation of Holdings

During our first stay at Mirpur, the consolidation of holdings was under way. This tedious and complex task can involve all sorts of malpractices, though in Mirpur itself the operations went smoothly, thanks to a good consolidation officer. They did, however, pave the way to agricultural expansion as in Punjab and Haryana in the early 1960s. In addition, the consolidation process ensured that land records were checked and rewritten. This was fortunate for us, as it meant that we could get a clear and more reliable picture of our area.

If we compare the situation in 1965 — the end of the consolidation — with that in 1979, we get the following data:

	Number of Households	Cultivated Area (in hectares)
1965		
0–1.50 hectares	70	50
1.50—2.00 hectares	11	20
2 hectares and above	52	180
	133	250
1979		
0—1.25 hectares	62	49.06
1.25—2.00 hectares	25	38.50
2 hectares and above	47	161.40
	134	248.96[1]

No striking changes are noticeable. There has been some increase in holdings of below 2 hectares but this is because these holdings

[1]This does not include a few hectares belonging to people living in other villages.

19

were, after the deaths of the fathers, divided between the sons. Nor does there seem to have been any major change when we look at land-ownership castewise. The lands of the Jats have come down from 150 hectares to 138, those of the Brahmins from 16.25 to 13, those of the Jativs from 20.50 to 19 and those of the Lodha Rajputs have risen from 28.50 to 35.25.[2] The other castes record very small changes upwards or downwards. Sharecropping still plays a very minor role in Mirpur. Only 10.55 hectares of land are cropped by people other than the owners and only one relatively large farmer, a Thakur, who owns 4.30 hectares, uses Khatik sharecroppers. The other non-cultivating owners — for example widows or old men who cannot attend to the fields — have between 1.30 to 1.40 hectares each.

The Expansion of Tubewells

In the field of irrigation, however, certain changes are visible. By 1963-4 it was evident to farmers in the Mirpur area that existing irrigation needed improvement and that the hitherto rain-fed plots could be irrigated. Thus it was that the consolidation of holdings had barely been completed when six new private tubewells were installed. After 1967, when the new high-yield varieties (HYV) of wheat were introduced, the movement went further and today all the cultivated area is irrigated, and much more adequately so than in the early 1960s. All the tubewells are privately owned, and the Persian wheels as well as the state tubewell have fallen out of use. Several land-owners have managed to get loans from the District Co-operative Bank for the construction of tubewells. It is worth emphasizing that, out of the 48 tubewells, 10 belong to owners of less than 2 hectares of land. (The total investment cost is Rs 7,800 — 1978-9 — and mainte-nance and operations per year are Rs 2,000). Of the crops that are grown in the Mirpur area the new seeds of wheat require 5-6 water-ings as against 3-4 for the old varieties. Sugarcane requires regular irrigation all the year round except during the few months of the rainy season.[3] From a strictly economic point of view there is some over-investment in tubewells and one wonders whether it would not

[2] However these figures cannot be accepted without qualification, for they do not indicate the value of the land. The Jats got some better plots—which explains the fall in area—and some of the farmers, especially Lodha Rajputs, selected unirrigated plots at that time, hence getting more land.

[3] Average rainfall in western U.P. is rather low: 840 mm, the bulk of it during the monsoon. The winter rains, which are very small but which nonetheless play a decisive role for unirrigated wheat, are very irregular.

have been better to have fewer tubewells but larger and deeper ones. It has sometimes happened, especially after poor rains, that the water table has gone down by a few metres. It would also be useful to have joint tubewells; however, in a society like Mirpur's this is hardly conceivable, except perhaps amongst the Lodha Rajputs who are a more cohesive caste than the others.Elsewhere I have talked of the quarrels, suspicions and rivalries within castes, often even within one family, which prevents such co-operation. Farmers who have too much water sell some to their neighbours who have no tubewell.

New Seeds and Chemical Fertilizers

In 1966 block officials in Mirpur supplied seeds of hybrid maize for the kharif season. The results of these were poor and even today maize yields remain mediocre. Farmers also pay less attention to maize than to the main crops, i.e. sugarcane and wheat.[4] New seeds of Mexican wheat were introduced in the rabi of 1966–7.[5] At the instance of the village level worker from the block some farmers experimented with these. Altogether 10 hectares of land were sown. The amounts of fertilizer used were substantially below the recommended dose but one of the farmers, Karanlal, a Vaishya, managed to secure 2,000 kilograms per hectare instead of the 1,200 or so he had had the year before. Others were quick to learn and in the next season they introduced Mexican wheat seeds. These high-yield varieties need to be renewed every four or five years.[6] The farmers in Mirpur were quick to learn this too.

Gradually the consumption of chemical fertilizers also increased. In 1963 many farmers spoke of the 'white' (nitrogen) or the 'black' (phosphate) fertilizers. Today they are able to distinguish between urea, ammonium sulphate, super phosphate, di-ammonium phosphate. All these names have become part of their day-to-day discussions. As a result of the expansion of irrigation and the introduction

[4]The problem should deserve more attention because it is widespread in north-west India. Even in Punjab average maize yields rose slowly as compared with wheat.

[5]Local and even improved seeds tend to lodge with rather high doses of chemical fertilizers which prevents high yields. Thus in Mirpur, in 1963, very good farmers enjoying adequate irrigation, improved seeds of wheat and chemical fertilizers, could not get yields above 2,500 kilograms per hectare. The high yield varieties of wheat or rice are dwarf or shorter than traditional ones, which reduces the risk of lodging; genetically, also, they react well to higher doses of fertilizer. They may also have a shorter duration than local seeds.

[6]Hybrid seeds (maize, jowar, bajra) must be renewed every year.

of new seeds and fertilizers, crop yields have doubled. This can be seen from the figures below:

Average Yields of Wheat
(kilograms per hectare)

Year	Quantity
1961–4	1,200–1,300
1975–6	2,000
1977–8	2,500

Several farmers with medium (2–3 hectares) and larger (4 hectares and above) sized holdings managed to secure as much as 3,000–4,000 kilograms per hectare by applying the recommended doses of chemical fertilizers. We found that practically all small farmers were using the high-yield varieties of seeds but many of them could not afford the recommended doses of fertilizers. However, despite this, there were no farmers who were not applying at least some dose of chemical fertilizers both for wheat and sugarcane. For this reason their yields were between 2,000–2,500 kilograms per hectare. The lowest yields we recorded in our interviews were 1,900 kilograms per hectare.

Other cereals such as bajra and jowar are cultivated during the kharif and often harvested 'green' to be used as fodder for cattle. The grain yields for these cannot be specified, but they have probably not increased much. Sugarcane remains an important cash crop. However, although sugarcane yields have improved because of better irrigation and more chemical fertilizers, its progress cannot be compared with that of wheat. In the early 1960s farmers got an average of 5,000 kilograms per hectare of raw sugar (the ratio of cane : raw sugar is about 10 : 1). In 1977–8, because of exceptionally good climatic conditions farmers recorded yields of 12,000 kilograms of raw sugar, but in more normal years — as in 1978–9 — the average has been around 6,000 kilograms.

Secondary crops such as pulses and peas do not indicate changes in yields. No new varieties have been released so far and their acreage seems to have decreased in favour of wheat. Mustard, often intercultivated with wheat, has perhaps declined in area and no new variety has been introduced here either. Mango orchards are old and badly maintained. They continue to play a minor role in the village economy and only a few mangoes enter the market. Some years ago farmers began growing broadcast paddy in the kharif and they are still experimenting with this. Yields, thus, are rather low.

As to vegetables, there were very few in the 1960s although it would have been possible to grow them on the tiny patches of land around people's houses. This lack of vegetables is a common feature in many parts of India, Pakistan and Afghanistan, where vegetables do not form part of the normal diet, except among the richer people. This situation remains much the same today. Farmers are either too busy or not interested enough to grow vegetables for home consumption. As for growing vegetables to sell, they face several constraints which we shall speak of later. Some farmers have, however, just begun to grow potatoes on small plots of land.

Bulandshahr district has always been well known for its milch cattle. In the 1960s sales of milk and ghee were not very high. They have subsequently improved and milk and ghee are now being marketed in Unchagaon where several milk collecting firms have been opened to supply milk to the fast expanding Delhi market. A buffalo[7] gives 4–7 litres (sometimes 8–10) of milk a day. This sells in Unchagaon for Rs 1.50 per litre and there are several small farmers and landless labourers who are now trading in milk. The main sources of fodder for cattle remain the tops of sugarcane stalks, the stacks and leaves of jowar, bajra and maize as well as some weeds and grass. Some farmers have started devoting small plots to lucerne and alfalfa.

Small-scale Industries and Machinery

Tractors are no longer an uncommon sight in Bulandshahr district but they still play only a minor role in Mirpur. Here, the main zamindar has one. Karanlal, a farmer we spoke of earlier, has the second — and only other — one in the village. He uses it for his own fields and hires it out from time to time.[8] Farmers still get up in the early hours to plough their lands.[9] The plough, the seed drill, and the levelling plank have not changed. On the other hand, the number of small electric threshers is increasing.[10] These are made in small district towns or in Haryana and are used for threshing wheat or maize. They cost Rs 1,200 and can thresh 120 kilograms of wheat in an hour. All the kolus for cane crushing are by now also using electrical

---

[7]The price would be roughly Rs 1,500–2,000.

[8]At Rs 10–12 for two disc ploughings for 0.06 ha.

[9]The period October–November is extremely busy because it is also the beginning of cane harvesting and crushing.

[10]Electricity was introduced in the village in 1965.

engines. The juice, however, is still boiled in the traditional way. Eight flour mills have been opened in Mirpur and the women no longer have to do the painstaking work of making wheat or maize flour on their mill stones. Now that bullocks are no longer used for the Persian wheels, they are used to set the chaff-cutter in motion for fodder.

Trade

In addition to the trade which revolves around milling or threshing wheat, a number of people have their grain threshed and milled by paying a fee to the owners of the machines. This fee is often paid in kind — the owner of the machine keeps 2.50 kilograms of grain for every 40 kilograms threshed. Mirpur now has some half a dozen small shops selling groceries, cloth, vegetables (mostly potatoes and onions), batteries, matches, cigarettes. A young Muslim, formerly a fitter in Punjab, has returned to Mirpur and has equipped a small workshop to repair pumps, motors and crushers. He bought a lathe for Rs 8,000 and sold his piece of land to buy more material. He has also managed to get a loan from the Punjab National Bank to set up his business, and he now has an apprentice working for him.

Electricity

Electricity first came to Mirpur in 1965. Today, power plays an increasing role in the development of the village. For several reasons it is more profitable for farmers to use electric engines rather than oil engines for their tubewells. Electricity has also opened the way to some of the small enterprises mentioned above, several of which are run by farmers in addition to their agricultural work. Small industries have also appeared gradually and the installation of a mechanical and electrical workshop is no less striking.

While all these factors show the importance of rural electrification, there is a big snag. In order to make a real impact power supply must be reliable. This is far from being the case. There has been, for many years, an overall shortage of electricity in most parts of India. In addition to the lack of power because of deficiencies in planning and delays in the construction of power stations, other problems arise because of poor maintenance facilities. But in all fairness one must admit that it is not an easy task to create countless electric lines in the countryside, to connect tubewells, to provide electricity to small workshops and houses. Now, however, practically all the villages around Mirpur are electrified.

The electricity board faces several types of difficulties. Pilferage of power is quite common, meters are tampered with and record very low bills. It was to counter this that the U.P. Government introduced a flat rate system. Electricity lines and transmitters are not properly maintained, and lines are frequently overstretched. And then there are the vagaries of the monsoon on which hydro-electric power relies. When we visited Mirpur in the late 1960s and the early 1970s several farmers complained to us about the unreliability of electricity. During our stay in the village in September 1978 power breakdowns were very common and could often last a full day. Fortunately, in that year the monsoon was strong and there was ample water for the sugarcane crop. But, in general, such a situation is extremely troublesome and damaging. In one year there was hardly any power supply during the months of April to June — the hottest months in the year — with the result that much sugarcane was ruined for lack of irrigation. Other troubles occur at threshing time when machines remain idle in the absence of electricity.

The only other source of energy is biogas. Karanlal, the farmer we met before, is the only farmer in Mirpur who has set up a gobar gas plant. Biogas is still an expensive source. Karanlal's plant has a pit 18 feet long by 6 feet wide, built of bricks and cement at a cost of Rs 2,000. It has a heavy lid of pig iron which cost Rs 1,800, and is fitted with an iron gutter and a pipe. It supplies the house with cooking gas and electricity. In order to set up this plant Karanlal secured a subsidy of Rs 800 as well as a loan of Rs 4,000 (at 10 per cent interest) from the block. The loan has to be paid back in five years. As an additional source of supply for the pit, Karanlal has built a w.c.[11] (at a cost of Rs 1,000) that is directly connected to it. In spite of this, he still has to spend roughly Rs 1,000 per year to buy the extra manure needed for his plant.[12] Apart from being expensive the gobar gas plant is not always reliable and can stop working in winter

[11]This is the only w.c. in Mirpur, in addition to the one I had ordered near the house where I was living. Villagers follow the old custom of going to the field.

[12] We shall see that cheaper devices are being introduced. Even so, only the medium or larger farmers can afford them. A solution that envisages collective units is not really feasible because of the social reasons mentioned above in connection with tubewells.

because fermentation does not take place easily.[13] In addition, it is not possible to use gobar gas plants to energize tubewells because this would mean that the plants would have to be built in the fields and the transportation of manure would become difficult.

Trade and Transportation

Trade and transportation have improved considerably in the Mirpur area in the last fifteen years. The network of district and sub-district roads has increased. The road from Jahangirabad to Unchagaon is now asphalted and a bus service has been opened. However, there is still an area of about 10 kilometres where Mirpur lies, between the tail end of good roads, and Mirpur is dependent on a very bad fair weather road which is often cut off in the monsoon and becomes unusable when the winter rains are heavy. Several farmers have altered their transportation systems. The wheels on their old carts have been replaced by tyres and the new cart tyres are called 'buggies'. Buggies are drawn by one buffalo rather than two bullocks as carts were. The Mirpur-Unchagaon road, which is only three kilometres long, is so bad that even under normal climatic conditions a buggy can carry only eight quintals instead of the sixteen that it manages on a good road.

In spite of these constraints, the overall expansion, as we have seen in Unchagaon (6,000 inhabitants), is remarkable. Today the main street has doubled in size. There are 141 shops and workshops — from milk, flour, cloth, stationery shops to blacksmiths, sawmills, bicycle repairers, radio repairers, motor workshops and even a photographer. The Punjab National Bank has opened a branch in Unchagaon and there are eight doctors. From Unchagaon trucks bring vegetables and milk to Bulandshahr and Delhi. These changes seem all the more remarkable when we consider that they have taken place in one of the most isolated parts of the district,[14] and that the expansion elsewhere must be greater.

The Growing Role of Prices

In keeping with all these changes and developments, farmers in our area have gradually become more price-conscious and today prices

[13]From December to the end of January night temperatures are only 5–10 degrees centigrade above zero and sometimes it touches freezing point.

[14]Even in Jahangirabad (20,000 inhabitants) supplies were poor and one had to go to Bulandshahr in the 1960.

play an increasingly complex role in their lives. The farmers have to take into account both the prices of inputs such as electricity and fertilizers, and of the outputs. In the 1960s, for example, the rather high prices of wheat helped the promotion of the high yield varieties. Later, when I visited Mirpur in 1975, the farmers complained bitterly about the prices of chemical fertilizers. Similarly in 1978–9 they were concerned about two things. The previous year had seen a bumper harvest in sugarcane and there was a glut of sugar in the market with the result that prices of sugar had fallen sharply. Farmers thought in terms of reducing the acreage devoted to sugarcane but the question was—what could they grow instead? At the same time the price of wheat was also considered rather low in relation to the cost of inputs and labour, although the prices of fertilizers had been reduced. Some farmers had begun to grow potatoes but here too prices were falling.

How far is Mirpur representative of other such villages? In order to determine this, I visited several villages around the Mirpur area in the 1960s and found that what we had observed in Mirpur was not exceptional. Certain data which we collected at the village level also confirmed this. Bulandshahr district is one such example.

In 1979 Bulandshahr district (estimated population 2.23 million, density 522, area 4,265 square kilometres)[15] had 11 large and medium scale industries (above a one million rupee investment) and 663 small-scale units. This includes 27 agro-based factories—such as flour mills, cold storage for potatoes, workshops, 149 engineering units for foundries, electric pumps, chaff-cutters and agricultural implements—but does not include very small village units as in Mirpur or Unchagaon.

The net cultivated area (334,300 hectares) has not changed, but irrigation and double cropping have expanded. In the 1960s there were very few private tubewells. In 1971–2 there were as many as 11,700, and by 1977–8 this number had gone up to 24,200. In addition there are 564 state tubewells (22 state tubewells were closed between 1975–9) which are larger than the private ones. Seed multiplication and renewal is doing fairly well. Foundation seeds for wheat and rice come from Pantnagar Agricultural University, or from Kanpur, and Bulandshahr now has three seed multiplication farms. During the kharif maize (18,000 to 100,000 hectares) has tended to fall in favour of paddy, the acreage of which has increased above

[15]The district was split up in 1971, losing two blocks which joined Ghaziabad district. The figures omit these two blocks.

10,000 hectares. In the last few years wheat has remained fairly constant at around 190,000–200,000 hectares. Its area has roughly doubled since the early 1960s, thanks to more double cropping and a fall in the area of sugarcane, barley and peas. Sugarcane covers around 45,000 to 50,000 hectares.

The use of chemical fertilizers proceeded very slowly before the advent of new wheat seeds. Consumption was 765 tons in 1955–6, 890 in 1960–1. It jumped to 12,300 in 1968–9 and 18,000 in 1974–5. At this point it fell slightly because of supply difficulties and the price increase. Later, prices came down and supply conditions improved and consumption went up: 28,000 tons in 1966–7, 30,700 in 1977–8, 32,600 in 1978–9 (in terms of nutrients).

This break-up of the consumption of fertilizers confirms two tendencies that are widespread in India as well as in other Asian countries. Consumption data show a definite imbalance in favour of nitrogen fertilizers which can damage the soils. Attempts are now being made to reduce this imbalance in favour of phosphatic fertilizers and to some extent, potash.[16] The consumption of these fertilizers has been rising faster than that of nitrogen between 1974–5 and 1978–9.

To sum up, Mirpur's economic trends fit well into the overall district pattern, i.e. a sharp increase in wheat output, a growing diversification of agriculture and the creation of many small-scale industries.

[16]All the district data have been collected in district offices. They should not be considered precise, but the trends indicated are certainly correct.

CHAPTER 4

How They Live

Before we look at what part the people have played in the growth process in Mirpur, it is essential that we turn to population statistics and patterns in the village. The population in Mirpur increased by 17.8 per cent (1.7 per cent per year) between 1951-61. In 1961 there were 200 families of whom 70 had no land. Between 1961 and 1971, the population increased by 22 per cent, with 1,497 people in 1971. During the last decade the growth rate fell to 20.57 per cent and the number of people in 1981 was 1,805.

In spite of these trends, which imply a fall in the death rate and, possibly, some fall now in the birth rate as well, the death rate of children was very high, particularly among the poor. The following table gives some examples of the number of children, living and dead, per landless couple.

Number of Children in the 1960s (per couple)

Caste of the couple	Living	Dead
Kumhar	5	4
Bhangi	3	6
Dhobi	4	2
Muslim	2	7-8
Jativ	1	2-3
Jativ	4	5
Jativ	5	4
Lodha Rajput	2	4

Although the birth rate is going down, the change has been moderate. Family planning has made definite progress since 1963. Awareness of contraception is increasing and everyone, man or woman, speaks openly about it. Although there are cases of sterilization, the campaign conducted during the Emergency does not seem to have hit Mirpur unduly. Women are keener than ever to discuss the matter, often entering into in lively conversation about all aspects of their sexual lives, as my wife told me. Among the men the attitudes vary. There are some signs of inertia and carelessness. For example, land-owners with 1 to 6 hectares of land are aware that, after their deaths their lands will be divided between their sons, and that the more sons they have, the smaller each share will be. Yet this does not seem to worry them unduly. In this respect even some of the educated young couples are rather careless, and they often have several children. Others, especially young husbands who have been to town, do prac-tise family planning and understand that it is better to have fewer children. Marriages still take place early, especially among the lower castes. Girls are now married at the age of 13 or 15 and boys at 18.

Among the less poor and the more educated the age at marriage is rising. It has gone up to 18 years for girls and 22 to 25 years for men. While this confirms trends observed elsewhere, these changes are not yet significant enough to have affected the birth rate very much. We felt that a more vigorous family planning campaign could probably have produced better results, especially if more women had been contacted and given help. We felt this particularly because in all our discussions with them nobody raised any objections of a religious nature to the idea of family planning. It is true that every couple wanted at least one son, but it seemed possible that the people would, or could, be happy with two or three children. In trying to find out whether people regarded children as assets in terms of an increased source of income, we came across different sets of reactions. On the one hand there were the landless or the small landowners and, on the other, those who do not rely exclusively on their own labour force, but who have some assets, particularly land. Among the first group we found it extremely depressing to interview old and weak Harijan couples who had lost all their children at an early age. Such people were keen to have more children and, for this reason, often reluctant or unwilling to practise family planning. This, however, had a limited impact on the birth rate because of the high number of casualties. We also found, as the following data will show, that the medium and upper farmers were the ones who had more children, not the poorer ones. This is contrary to the assumption that the poorer a couple is the more children they have.

All these problems were perfectly clear in the early 1960s. Land-owners had played one part of the game well — that of increasing production. And they had barely begun to win the other part — that

Caste	Landholding (in hectares)	Number of Children per Couple (1960)	
		Living	Dead
Brahmin	3	7	3
Brahmin	3	8	2
Jat	1.50	4	none
Jat	2.50	4	3
Jat	4.00	7	2
Jat	10.00	4	1
Jat	2.00	6	2
Lodha Rajput	1.90	8	none
Lodha Rajput	1.30	6	3
Jativ	1.12	2	6

of achieving a sharp fall in the birth rate. We shall now turn to some actual cases to illustrate our points.

The People who Remain as Poor as They Were

Bhasi was a 26-year old Kumhar (potter) who was not doing his traditional work any more. He had neither land nor cattle. He was married and had one child who died, while another, a daughter, was alive. When we interviewed Bhasi he was working at a kolu and earning Rs 5 per day. Occasionally he was able to earn a little more by doing casual work in the fields. He owned only the set of clothes that he wore. His standard of living went down when his three donkeys died of some disease. He had used them for transporting bricks which enabled him to earn Rs 7–8 a day. His diet consisted mostly of bajra and maize and, when mustard was in season, some boiled mustard leaves.

Manthuri, from the same village, owned an oil press which used a bullock. He lived with his wife and his two children. Seven or eight of his children had died when they were very young. Manthuri, too, had only one set of clothes and if his standard of living was not going down, it was certainly not improving. From time to time he worked as a casual labourer. In addition he raised a small buffalo which belonged to a landowner. When the buffalo begins to give milk it is shared by the two men.

Bunder, a Jativ, was also landless. His two sons had died and his only other child, a daughter, was married and lived in another village.[1] He wore an old shirt and a ragged dhoti, his only clothes.

[1]Girls of all castes are practically always married to somebody of the same caste but in another village.

When he was not working in the fields for Rs 5 a day, he collected grass along footpaths and sold it. He complained bitterly about his lot. Another Jativ, Nan Singh, 50 years old, had lost four of his nine children. His two boys went to school and the daughters helped at home. He worked as a permanent labourer for a large landowner and earned Rs 100 a month. He had only one set of clothes and was in debt to the tune of Rs 1,000. He and his children ate chapatis, they never drank milk and hardly ever ate any meat,[2] which they could not afford.

We also held discussions with a group of Bhangis (sweepers) who were paid in kind according to the old jajmani system. Their life was hard and, to add to their troubles, their houses (which have mud walls and thatched roofs) had fallen down in 1978 when the rains had been heavy. Other accidents, not necessarily natural ones, can also happen. Ram Sarup, a Kumhar, had left one large landowner five years ago. When we met him he was working partly as a potter and partly as an agricultural labourer. His life remained as hard as before: one set of clothes and a blanket, no milk, no meat, only maize and bajra and very rarely, chapatis made of wheat flour, and the maintenance of his four children. And then one day a robber took away his few pitiful belongings.

Finally let us look at a very unusual case in Mirpur: a family that had been quite rich and is now getting poorer and poorer. Kirpal Singh was an educated, 60-year old Thakur. He lived with his wife; his only child, a daughter, was married. Thirty years ago, his father had been a fairly well-to-do farmer with 4.4 hectares of land. Like other Thakurs — the only high caste in Mirpur that is not very agriculture-oriented — Kirpal Singh did not develop his land fast enough. When his father died the land was divided between the four sons. After selling bits of his share Kirpal was now left with only 0.37 hectares. He had to borrow the bullocks of a Jat neighbour for ploughing but he still had two buffaloes. His land was not too well cultivated and he did not normally manage to secure 2,000 kilograms per hectare of wheat.

The Poor who Become Less Poor

Nandram, a Jativ, lived with his wife and four children — the two older ones attended Mirpur's primary school. Nandram was landless and worked as a field labourer. He earned Rs 5 a day plus some food

[2]Jats and other high castes are often vegetarians, unlike the lower castes.

but sometimes managed to get work as a mason which got him twice this amount as well as food. He also owned a buffalo which gave between five and six litres of milk a day. Most of this was turned into ghee and sold. This brought him Rs 90 a month. Nandram also owned three small buffaloes. He did not complain or look miserable and was always alert in tapping as many sources of income as possible. Dalchand, a Bhangi, had no land. Of his four children, two girls, and a boy who was at home, were married. Dalchand had spent six years in the army in Bombay and then returned to Mirpur. When Tez Pal Singh, the main ex-zamindar, bought a tractor, Dalchand got the salesman to teach him how to use it and he now earned Rs 150 a month as a driver. His buffalo produced 3.5 litres of milk a day of which 2 litres were sold. There were also two small buffaloes that would one day give milk. Dalchand borrowed Rs 600 from the Punjab National Bank at Unchagaon at 4 per cent interest in order to buy pigs. He bought seven for Rs 700 and sold them a year later for Rs 1,000. Yad Ram, a Kumhar, had given up working as a potter because he had trouble getting enough earth. Then, with a loan of Rs 2,500 from the Punjab National Bank he bought a *tanga* and a horse. He now earns Rs 30 a day although it costs him Rs 8 to feed his horse. He also has two buffaloes which yield four litres of milk each, per day. Some of this is sold and some consumed at home. Yad Ram, like some of the others interviewed, admitted that his life had improved. In his home both adults and children were better fed today than they had been fifteen years ago. There were, in addition, some Dhobis who worked under the jajmani system. Sirpal Singh, for instance, washed clothes for approximately twenty to twenty-five families and earned 1,000 to 1,200 kilograms of grain per year. Amar Singh, Sirpal's eldest son, had attended primary school at Mirpur and done a few more years at Unchagaon's secondary school. Smart in his short trousers and canvas shoes, he worked as headman at a kolu and was paid Rs 6–7 plus food for a day's work. Later in the year, he was employed as a casual labourer at Rs 5. He was raising two buffaloes which would soon begin to give milk.

We also had broader discussions with Jativs and others during several visits paid to the scheduled caste quarters. As we have seen above, some of them remain very poor and mentally depressed, but many of them seem to be better off today. Extreme caste barriers[3] seem to have disappeared. In the words of Bihari Lal, a 90-year old

[3]This, of course, does not imply eating together or intermarrying.

Jativ, 'there have been substantial changes' (*parivartan*). He says, 'When I was twenty years old during the First World War, we could be beaten by high caste farmers. If, by mistake, we happened to touch their clothes we would have to pay them for new clothes to replace the old ones which had become "polluted".' As late as the 1960s Jativs were not allowed to sit next to Jats and others. Today some Jativs sit on the same cot as the Jats. 'Besides', emphasizes Bihari Lal, 'more Harijan children attend schools and our diet has improved.' On the whole the Jativ men, women and children are better dressed today than they were in the 1960s. They are also more alert and articulate.

Small Farmers and the Green Revolution

Roughly speaking, a small farmer in Mirpur can be defined as one who has less than one hectare of land. This usually compels him to seek some additional work to maintain his family and himself. Tika Ram, a 50-year old Jativ, was one such small farmer. He lived with his wife. Both his adult sons were in Mirpur. One was married and had a little daughter. The other was still a bachelor. The family owned 0.4 hectares of land and had no bullocks. This meant that they had to borrow a pair for ploughing. They had a young buffalo for whom they needed to collect grass. They planned to sell all of her milk when she began to produce. Tika Ram inherited half of his father's land while the other half went to his brother. In the 1960s the land was located in the non-irrigated area of Mirpur. Today there is a tubewell nearby from which he can buy water. In the rabi he grows HYV wheat using only a certain quantity of urea. He claims he is able to get a yield of about 2,500 kilograms per hectare. This appeared rather high to me, particularly as he did not seem to be applying the recommended doses of urea. In the kharif he produced maize but got only a few quintals. Half of his land was devoted to sugarcane. He got 1,600 kilograms of raw sugar, all of which was sold. Tika earned additional money by working as a casual labourer. He had no debts and his living conditions have improved with time. Thanks to irrigation and the new wheat he was much less dependent on buying grain — he needed to buy only a few quintals a year.

Another Jativ, Chiranji, was 26 years old and had had two years of schooling. He was quick-witted and did not seem to have any complexes about belonging to a scheduled caste. He lived with his wife and three children, and owned 0.5 hectares of land on which he grew wheat in the rabi followed by maize and bajra in the kharif. Thanks to the application of urea and di-ammonium phosphate (DAP) as well as the water he bought from a nearby tubewell he managed to make the equivalent of a yield of 2,560 kilograms per hectare. He kept his wheat but sold his bajra. In August every year Chiranji bought a pair of bullocks because prices were low and he sold them later, in May, for Rs 2,000. He also made and sold cane stools. By doing all this and by using HYV seeds Chiranji has managed to improve his lot and to grow enough wheat to feed his family.

These two cases show how increasing production has, in some cases, counteracted the division of already small holdings. Tika and Chiranji today produce more grain than their fathers had managed to grow on twice the land area.[4]

Sibhur, also a Jativ, had even less land — a mere 0.12 hectares. He had to borrow bullocks from a farmer to plough his land and, in exchange, he worked a few days for him. Twenty-two years old, Sibhur had been married three or four years and had a young daughter. He grew wheat and then maize. For the former he used some urea and then bought farm manure which saved him 200 kilograms (1,300 kilograms per hectare). He worked twenty to twenty-five days in the month for other people and made Rs 5–6 with food every day. He had no debts and managed to save some money to buy grain and a few odd items.

Finally, there was Tez Singh, a Lodha Rajput. He was middle-aged. Two of his sons were already working, two were still small like the two daughters. His father had died quite recently and, for the time being, Tez Singh and his brother (his wife and three children as well) were continuing to live and work together. The two brothers had inherited 0.94 hectares of land and this was irrigated by another Lodha's tubewell. Half the land was devoted to wheat which, because of applications of urea (but, as in the earlier case, with no mixed or phosphate fertilizer) and farm manure, provided an equivalent of 2,500 kilograms per hectare. The wheat was followed by jowar, bajra and maize. The second half of the land bore sugarcane. Both the brothers sold most of their raw sugar. They had two bullocks and two buffaloes which yielded 2.5 litres of milk each per day. All the milk was consumed at home instead of being sold, an indication of a not-too-acute situation. However, both men needed to find addi-

---

[4]In the 1960s the rain-fed plots yielded less than 1,000 kilograms per hectare of wheat and could not bear any sugarcane.

tional sources of income because, in spite of the increase in wheat production, what they earned was not enough for a household the size of theirs. Thus they also worked as labourers.

For a long time Hulassi, also a Lodha Rajput, worked as a permanent labourer for the main zamindar. His only asset was a buffalo. After the abolition of the zamindari system Hulassi managed to buy 0.3 hectares of land. He devoted the whole of his land to sugarcane which, especially in the 1950s, brought in more money than cereals. He also took on, on a share-cropping basis, 0.5 hectares of a field and 0.4 hectares of a mango orchard, from a Jat. When we met Hulassi in 1963 his standard of living was already improving because of his hard work and intelligence. By that time he had also bought a second buffalo whose milk he would convert into ghee and sell for Rs 60 a month.

Hulassi is now dead but we met his son, Iqbal Singh. Iqbal Singh lived with his mother, his wife and their young son, and his two brothers one of whom had three children. The youngest brother was a student at a college in Bulandshahr. Iqbal and his brothers now owned 0.88 hectares of land.[5] They grew wheat on 0.56 hectares. They used low doses of urea and di-ammonium phosphate and were only able to produce 1,200–1,400 kilograms (2,100–2,300 kilograms per hectare), which was just enough to cover their requirements. They grew sugarcane and got 2,500 kilograms of raw sugar which they sold. After the death of their father the brothers bought a buggy for Rs 2,000 which they borrowed from a moneylender at 36 per cent interest.[6] Every month they ran a transport service for two to four days and earned Rs 15 per day. They had one bullock which was used, along with the buffalo, for ploughing. Their buffalo gave 3 litres of milk a day. one of the men took the milk to Unchagaon on a bicycle and sold it for Rs 4–5. With the help of some farmers the brothers managed to construct a jointly owned tubewell for Rs 7,000. After some time they had trouble with their partners and bought up their share for Rs 3,500. Today they sell water to different people and make Rs 200 a month. Iqbal Singh is still fairly young but he manages to do very well.

Medium and Upper Farmers

As we have seen in the previous chapter, before the advent of the

---

[5] They still take, on a share-cropping basis, 1.25 hectares in a nearby village. They pay half of the inputs and get half the crop.

[6] By now only Rs 500 remains to be repaid.

HYV the minimum economic holding was roughly 2 hectares and sometimes 1.75. The progress of irrigation and the improvement in wheat yields have brought this figure down to around 1.25 hectares. This means that a number of the small and medium farmers are now somewhat better off and, if their lands have become small through division, they have not been hit too hard.

Girraj Singh, a 50-year old Khatik, lived with his wife and son who, unfortunately, could not speak. His two daughters were married and lived elsewhere. When we met his father Sukharam in 1963–4, the latter was a fairly big farmer with 3.75 hectares of land, but he was supporting a large household which included his three sons, their wives and children. As today, they were then devoting about half their land to wheat followed by jowar and maize in the kharif, and the other half to sugarcane. Wheat yields were 1,200 kilograms per hectare. They produced 1,500 kilograms and sold one quarter of the produce. Although his father's land was not too well irrigated, Girraj Singh was co-owner of a tubewell. His other partners were two Lodha Rajputs. On his father's death Girraj inherited 1.30 hectares to which he now applied the equivalent of 80 kilograms per hectare of urea and the same of di-ammonium phosphate. This gave him 2,100 kilograms of wheat on 0.75 hectares (2,800 kilograms per hectare). He needed half of this and sold the rest. He also sold most of his raw sugar, and whatever maize he managed to grow was all consumed at home. Jowar and bajra fed his two bullocks and two buffaloes. From the latter he got 10 litres of milk a day during the lactation period. Half of this was sold to one of the milk-collecting units at Unchagaon and from this he made Rs 7.50 a day. In the summer Girraj made Rs 100 out of the sales from his new mango trees. He was managing fairly well. He had rebuilt his house with bricks and his family enjoyed better food and clothes, but he had had to borrow Rs 2,000 at 24 per cent interest for the marriage of one of his daughters.

Kacheru was ageing when I met him during my first visit. He was one of the few Jativs living reasonably well with 1.6 hectares, all irrigated, though not always adequately, by the state tubewell. He was already using some chemical fertilizers and getting good results from his wheat and cane. He died some years ago and now his only son, Rohtas, lives on the land with his mother, his wife and six children some of whom are in their teens. Rohtas's eldest son was married and worked as a labourer in Mirpur. Rohtas had neither bullocks nor buffaloes so he rented a pair of bullocks at Rs 5 for one ploughing-cum-levelling, and bought water from a private tubewell to irrigate his land. On one hectare he sowed HYV wheat with 160 kilograms per hectare of urea and the same of di-ammonium phosphate. He also added some calcium and managed to get between 2,500 and 3,250 kilograms per hectare. In the kharif 0.5 hectares were sown with maize — this gave 650 kilograms — the rest with bajra and jowar, partly sold as fodder, partly used to feed his buffalo. On the rest of the land he grew sugarcane. Rohtas also made some additional money by using his buggy for transportation. His diet was based mostly on cereals and pulses but he managed to buy milk from time to time. He lived in a brick-walled house. However he, too, had debts amounting to Rs 4,000, which he had borrowed at 36 per cent interest for his son's marriage.

As we have already mentioned, the Lodha Rajputs represent one of the economically and socially rising castes. They have not yet reached the stage where they can share the same *hukka* as the Jats but they may do so. However they do meet and mix freely with other castes and economically several families are doing well. Nawat Singh, an illiterate Lodha Rajput, was both wise and clever. When Nawat lived in a joint family with his father and his two brothers they (23 persons in all) owned 6.9 hectares of land, part of which lay in the rain-fed area. Already in those days Nawat and his brothers were improving their crops by applying some chemical fertilizers on irrigated wheat and sugarcane. They had two buffaloes, four oxen, two camels. But they could sell only a very small amount of wheat as sugarcane was their main source of cash. All the milk they produced was consumed at home. At the time of the consolidation of holdings, the Lodha Rajputs chose to have land in the unirrigated parts so that they would be entitled to a larger area in exchange for their irrigated plots. They installed two tubewells and were quick in adopting HYV wheat and increasing their use of chemical fertilizers. Nawat's joint family broke up some years ago but the brothers managed to keep their thresher and tubewells together (the father is still alive). When we met him, Nawat had 1.55 hectares. Under his roof were his wife, his three unmarried daughters, two of his unmarried sons who helped him, two who were at school. The eldest son lived in Kanpur where he worked as a mechanic in a factory. Nawat produced 4,000 kilograms per hectare of wheat — thanks to proper doses of urea and DAP and some farm manure. They changed their seeds periodically and were thus able to sell 12 quintals which fetched around Rs 1,300. In 1977 their sales of raw sugar amounted to Rs 5,000. In 1978 this came down to Rs 3,750. This was when prices fell from Rs 100 a quintal to Rs 75. After wheat Nawat grew maize, jowar, bajra and he had two bullocks and buffaloes each of which yielded between 6 and 7 litres of milk per day. He now feels more comfortable because he has his own home[7] with brick walls and a *chaupal* where he can sit and smoke his hukka. However, Nawat is well aware that he cannot push his yields of wheat much further and is thinking of devoting some of his land to chillies, a crop which, on a mere 0.25 hectares, can give a return of Rs 4,000.

Let us now look at some Brahmin families. Khanchand was in his late forties when we first met him. He had four girls and four boys, all very shrewd and hard-working. Part of his 3 hectares of land were rain-fed and gave a poor yield of wheat followed by bajra in the monsoon. Other parts of the land were irrigated by a Persian wheel. Khanchand's main source of a cash income was from the sale of raw sugar. Today Khanchand's family has progressed beyond this state. They have rebuilt their home with bricks and have enlarged their chaupal. Their home has electricity and they have a table fan in summer. They have a radio, some bicycles, the men wear watches, the women wear better saris, tea is no longer a luxury. How did they manage?

Unlike the Lodha Rajputs, Khanchand had, for a long time, played a political role within Mirpur. He was close to the block officials and had taken loans from the co-operative society. But this was not the main reason. He had also worked hard, ploughing and harvesting with his own hands, until recently. He set up a tubewell, used HYV wheat, and fertilizers; his eldest son worked in a secondary school in Mirpur and also did some work outside. Another son was a teacher in Unchagaon and helped to tend the fields. The third son was a clerk and the last one was studying for his B.A. Except for the youngest son, all Khanchand's children were married. His daughters lived in other villages — he had managed to get them married without incurring too many debts. He can now afford to have a permanent labourer to work for him.

Diwan was one of Khanchand's relatives and was about the same age with roughly the same amount of land. His story was also rather similar. His three eldest daughters were married and only one, who was born in 1963, was still at home. The three boys were married and

---

[7]This is one of the frequent reasons given for the breakdown of joint families.

had children. Two of them taught in a nearby village, the third was a policeman in Delhi. Diwan's family now lives in better conditions than they did earlier and this is due to the same factors — increased production, more sales, and employment outside the farmland.

It is now time to take a look at the Jats, the dominant caste. Here we will look only at the medium and upper farmers.[8]

Ram Singh provided a very good example of the Jat spirit. He had only attended a few years of primary school but this did not prevent him from understanding and implementing improved techniques on his 3.12 hectares of land. His six children were either at school or very small when we met him in 1963–64. He had, at that time, had some difficulty with bureaucratic red tape in getting a loan for the construction of his tubewell. But in April 1968, when we saw him again, he was the proud owner of a tubewell, standing by and watching a superb crop of wheat being harvested. Two of his sons are now working in Delhi, one of them as an engineer. The third one is working in Jaipur as a sanitary inspector. One daughter is married and the two younger children are at school.

Ram Singh, now about sixty years old, still worked hard. Both his home and the clothing of his wife and children had improved, although one still found him in his fields barefoot, wearing an old dhoti. Ram Singh had much more wheat to sell (average yield 3,200 kilograms per hectare) and with all his adult sons away, he tended to sell his sugarcane as well. Like other people he was aware of the need for technical innovation and had experimented with paddy. Similarly, Bhola Singh, another Jat, had also managed quite well. In 1963 he owned, along with his brother, 4.75 hectares of land. Their crops were already improving and they had already started irrigating a rain-fed plot which, until then, had yielded only 700 kilograms per hectare and that too when the winter rains did not fall. With irrigation and some mixed fertilizers he managed to get double this quantity. Both brothers usually sold more than half of their wheat and most of their raw sugar. Maize and bajra were consumed by the household and the cattle — two pairs of bullocks, one cow, two buffaloes. His main sales would provide Rs 6,000–7,000. At that time his eldest son was beginning his B.A. in one of the district colleges.

Today Bhola lives separately from his brother but he manages quite well on his 2.5 hectares. In 1968 he installed his own tubewell on

[8]Although we have taken only the cases of medium and upper farmers there are some poorer people as well.

a cash payment of Rs 11,000. His wheat yields have risen to 3,200–3,800 kilograms per hectare. Of this he keeps 1,200 kilograms and sells 1,400, as well as his raw sugar. Grain grown during the kharif is kept at home. Maize is for the household, jowar and bajra are used as fodder for his pair of bullocks and the two buffaloes. Apart from building a new house in 1972 Bhola bought a threshing machine and he now also sells water from his tubewell. His eldest son works with the Seeds Corporation outside Mirpur. The other son is expecting to get an administrative job. The three eldest daughters are married and the two younger ones are at home. Because his sons were no longer there Bhola had to use more labourers than before. Like other farmers who are considering new crops, he also wonders whether, in the face of the sharp fall in the price of sugar, it would not be worthwhile to start growing potatoes and vegetables.

A Jat who started at a lower rung, Girraj Singh, had only 1.5 hectares when he inherited another 0.5 hectares from a relative. He could not afford a tubewell and had to buy water from others. Gradually, because of the application of higher doses of urea and DAP, Girraj improved his yields and he now sells between 20 and 24 quintals of wheat per year. His sugarcane yields were not high because he lacked the money to use enough fertilizer. He had two bullocks and one buffalo whose milk was consumed at home. His eldest son worked as a bus driver in Jahangirabad and earned Rs 600 a month on which he maintained his family in Mirpur. Another son was away, studying, and the last one was attending a local school. The daughter was married. Girraj had improved his lot although he was clearly not doing as well as some of the others. Many Jat farmers presented rather similar stories: rapid growth from a relatively advantageous starting point as in the cases of Ram Singh and Bhola Singh; less spectacular progress, but still substantial improvements in crops, production, and living conditions as in the case of Girraj.

Finally, let us pay a visit to Tez Pal Singh, formerly the main zamindar. Tez Pal Singh enjoyed respect and consideration and was from time to time asked to give his advice on local affairs. But he did not take an active part in village politics. He had always been a good farmer managing his 13 hectares wisely. He had been the first to start a tubewell, nearly thirty years ago. He made full use of new inputs: seeds, fertilizers and, more recently, a tractor. He now gets 2,500–3,000 kilograms per hectare of wheat as compared with 1,600–1,800 in 1963 and sells a hundred quintals instead of the 13 he was selling then, because, in addition to increased yield he now devotes more of his land to wheat. On one part of his land he grew sugarcane. The rest of the land was, in the rabi, devoted to pulses, peas and some barley, and on one hectare he grew mangoes. Tez Pal Singh was growing old but he was still alert. He had five permanent labourers, one of his sons helped in farm work and he himself supervised his crops. There was no luxury in his house but he maintained a good standard of living. He had not joined the co-operative because he did not need it. He had spent a lot of money on educating his children and his son, who used to ride a bicycle, now has a motorcycle.

Summing Up

The many individual cases reviewed above confirm the overall trends of the economy analysed in the previous chapter. Extreme poverty has been substantially reduced thanks to a growing diversification of the economy and more contact with the world outside Mirpur. The wages paid to field labourers have increased in real terms — from Re 1 in 1963 to Rs 5 or 6 in 1978-9. Forty kilograms of wheat, which in 1963-4 would sell for Rs 17-22 were priced, in 1978, at Rs 44. The national index of consumer prices for food and other basic needs roughly trebled in this period. During the wheat harvest labourers now received 10 kilograms of grain per day as against 5 kilograms before. Apart from this, employment opportunities in agriculture have risen, as also in transport, construction work, trade and milk supply. If today some people still remain very poor, there are also many who are less poor, and whose new-found sense of confidence is helping to make them more conscious of their rights. Small farmers who own around 0.59 hectares of land have not been left out of the green revolution. All of them are using new seeds of wheat and some doses of chemical fertilizer. In all cases yields have increased. Medium and upper farmers, many of them being illiterate, have done remarkably well by showing a quick response to practical innovations. They are better off today because they have worked hard. Yet many of them still lead a very frugal life. They are also well aware of the need to diversify their crops.

The Role of Rural Institutions

In the 1960s Panchayati Raj seemed to be rather dormant. The village Panchayat hardly functioned because there was a great deal of rivalry and factionalism. The block Samiti was equally inactive. Now there seems to be a little more activity and discussion at the village level. The development block personnel remain moderately active in extension work and the supply of inputs. On this last front there has been some improvement. Chemical fertilizers are in plentiful supply and can be bought from co-operatives and private dealers. The supply of wheat seeds also seems adequate. On the whole, people did not complain about the lack of supply. In fact, because supplies are now more than adequate, all sorts of malpractices and corruption which were common fifteen years ago have now ceased. On the other hand, the shortage and rationing of cement has led to the same abuses which were rampant under the similar scarcity conditions in the 1960s. Farmers do complain, however, about the weakest link in the economy — electricity. There are frequent power cuts and the voltage is low. They are also bitter about the poor road that leads to Unchagaon. As far as credit is concerned many medium and upper farmers remain influential in the co-operative society, in district co-operative banks and other banks. Nevertheless one does come across small farmers who are getting some help as in the case of Yad Ram, a Kumhar, who was given a loan at only 4 per cent interest,[9] by the Punjab National Bank at Unchagaon. Under the new scheme of Antyodaya, five of the poorest people[10] in Mirpur have been selected for a special loan with a subsidy to enable them to buy a buggy, a mule and some buffaloes. The selection was made fairly and the only complaint that the applicants had was that the procedure was slow.

The Future

So far landowners have managed well, often earning more on smaller holdings than their fathers or grandfathers did on larger ones. This is partly due to the latest innovations. Yet many of the farmers realize that they cannot go much further in wheat and they will have to find other and richer crops. Some of them have started growing paddy in the kharif, and already, further west in Haryana and Punjab, paddy is playing an increasing role. It can be better adapted to the climate than maize and is certainly more rewarding than jowar and millet. Apart from this, a new short duration variety of pulses has been released in Delhi. It can be squeezed in between the wheat harvest in April and the sowing of kharif crops in July. However farmers in Mirpur say that for the time being at least, they do not want to use

[9]50 per cent subsidy, 50 per cent to repay and 4 per cent interest.
[10]At least four of them were really poor.

this as there are too many power cuts in these months and the threshing of wheat is either delayed or has to be done by traditional means, which does not leave them enough time for a third crop. Some farmers feel that higher wheat yields can be combined with a reduction in some areas in favour of other crops such as potatoes or vegetables. And last of all, we have seen that the number of people who have been able to get jobs outside Mirpur has more than doubled. There is, of course, no guarantee that this will continue unless small industries and trade expand still further in big villages and small towns.

The people of Mirpur have been very clever but they cannot afford to relax now. On the contrary, they need to sustain their efforts. So far it has been the older generation which has been running the show. How will their children, most of whom have been to school, handle things? Will they have the energy their fathers had and will they work as hard as them? These are the questions which remain to be answered.

Post script: In April 1981 we received the following information on the latest trends in the village. As far as crops are concerned, the average wheat yield per hectare is now around 3,000 kilograms, which means that there has been a further increase. The cultivation of potatoes is expanding with yields of 12-15 tons per hectare. Progress in paddy cultivation is not striking. There are no problems regarding the supply of new seeds and chemical fertilizers, but the supply of electricity remains very poor and severely hinders farm operations. Finally, the road between Unchagaon and Mirpur is being metalled at last.

CHAPTER 5

The Cost of a Late Start

In 1964 when I told my friends in Mirpur that, from their village, I intended to go on to eastern U.P., they said, '*arre sahib, purbi log dhile hain*' ('oh sir, the eastern are easygoing and relaxed'). Was this really true and if so, could this be the sole explanation for the great poverty for which the fifteen eastern districts of U.P. were, unfortunely, so well known? Such questions are perplexing when we consider that for many centuries these areas had a richer agriculture than the western districts such as Bulandshahr. This problem becomes even more acute when we proceed further east to Bihar, now a very poor region but once the cradle of Indian civilization which, even in Mughal days, had supplied grain and other agricultural commodities to the upper Ganges basin because the latter was unable to feed large cities like Agra and Delhi. The answers, perhaps, lay in closely examining the area.

Nilkanth in 1964

The villages around Nilkanth are scattered in hamlets; the landscape around them is flat, broken occasionally by trees and small tanks. The hamlets contain large farmhouses of puddled clay covered with rounded tiles surrounding an inner courtyard. This decentralization of built-up areas is typical of eastern U.P. and the plain of Bihar, which has been less affected than most by the various invasions from the north-west.

Nilkanth has a total area of 418 hectares, including 362 hectares of arable land. It lies on a fair weather road, four kilometres away from the Pindra block headquarters at Mangari which is connected to Varanasi by a metalled, and then asphalted, road. The population has increased gradually as in Mirpur — in 1961 there were 2,500 inhabitants. This gave the area a density of 600 per square kilometre; in Mirpur the density was 444. Each of the four largest landowners in

Nilkanth owned 12 hectares or a little more. Then followed several smaller holdings of between 2 and 6 hectares, 2 hectares, and many (a larger number than in Mirpur) tiny landholdings, becoming smaller with the population increase. The dominant upper castes were Thakurs and Brahmins, Kayasths and some Bhumihars. The Kurmis formed an important group of middle farmers. Chamars[1] as well as other Harijans made up the bulk of the landless labourers.

Has there been any development in Nilkanth in the past century? The population increase has led people to reclaim all available land. But neither the cropping pattern, nor farming techniques, show changes comparable to what has been observed in Mirpur, although, by the middle of the last century, production must have been higher and the population larger. Because of better rainfall (1,117 mm in 50 days as against 840 in 40 days in western U.P.), paddy became the main crop covering 206 hectares. The crop was rain-fed, with the occasional help of wells. It was cultivated in different ways, most often transplanted though sometimes also broadcast, using short or medium duration seeds. In the kharif 36 hectares were devoted to pulses, maize, jowar and bajra. Sugarcane, a one-year crop, covered 54 hectares, while 200 were devoted to rabi crops. About 65 hectares of wheat, sometimes mixed with barley, 38 of barley, 51 of peas and 14 of potatoes were irrigated. In addition there were also 32 hectares of pulses which depended mainly on the brief winter rains.

In 1964, irrigation was much less efficient than in western U.P. Two state tubewells had begun to operate in 1963. These were meant to cover about 100 hectares[2] but they often delivered only a limited amount of water as in Mirpur. There was not a single private tubewell. Irrigation relied largely on wells that used the *mot* system, a less efficient method than the Persian wheel.[3] Thus water management in the kharif was far from satisfactory. Wells could not supply sufficient water for the paddy and, when rains were poor, the crop would suffer. On the other hand, during heavy or even normal rains some of the lowlands would be flooded because the drainage was poor and there were no protective bunds. Some plots of land would not be cultivated at all. Sugarcane was of a local, old variety, very thin. It had never

[1] Unlike the Chamars of western U.P., the Chamars of eastern U.P. have not changed their name.

[2] They were also irrigating other village lands.

[3] It is not quite clear why the farmers have not shifted to this. Carelessness or the depth of the water table—either of these could prevent the use of a Persian wheel.

been replaced by a better strain as in western U.P. Besides, commercialization of locally produced raw sugar was not as advanced as in Mirpur. There were also fewer sugar mills in the area and therefore less encouragement and incentive for cane growers. As to wheat, farmers were not using the improved varieties introduced some thirty years earlier in north-western India. In addition, another important factor was what our friends in Mirpur had testified to. The dominant castes in Nilkanth were not traditional agricultural castes like the Jats. So much so that Thakurs, Brahmins, Kayasths, Bhumihars, big or small, would all observe the taboo on ploughing. And on the whole, they would not do much manual work either. They were less concerned about their fields than most farmers in Mirpur. The main exception to this were the Kurmis, a rising middle caste and class. But they owned only a limited part of the land.

While talking to high caste landowners we discovered more about their general attitude. For instance I asked a Brahmin landowner (who owned 10 hectares of land) why he had no double cropping in spite of the fact that his wells irrigated half his land. His only response was 'I know, this is our weakness...' To take another example, there was a joint family of 25 Kayasths living on 4 hectares of land. The family had plenty of able-bodied men capable of working in the fields. Yet they preferred to hire one permanent labourer (who was paid Rs 30 a year and had free use of 0.6 hectares of land for his services) and several casual labourers. The landowners were thus losing land and money for work they could have done themselves and possibly done better than the hired labourers.

All these factors[4] account for the low yields of the area which had scarcely changed over decades. The average wheat yield was around 900 kilograms per hectare, less when rain-fed and a little more when irrigation was not too bad. Paddy would yield 1,000–1,200 kilograms per hectare (700–800 in terms of clean rice), raw sugar 2,000–3,000.[5] Only a few farmers had begun to use chemical fertilizers which, when they had irrigation, would enable them to get 1,500–2,000 kilograms per hectare of wheat or paddy. Animal husbandry was also less developed — there were fewer buffaloes and therefore less milk. There were comparatively more orchards but, even here, the trees were too old to bear fruit. Thus, while the population became heavier

[4] Ground water potential is by no means less favourable in Nilkanth than in Mirpur.
[5] Mirpur: for wheat 1,200–1,300 kilograms per hectare is the average and for raw sugar 5,000.

(districtwise it went up from 1.3 million in 1921 to 2.4 in 1961), production did not follow suit and landholdings became smaller without a substantial increase in yields.

Nilkanth is just one of many such cases in the Varanasi district (or elsewhere) in eastern U.P. and it is certainly not one of the worst, since there are villages with less irrigation. It reflects the conditions of areas which, unlike the western districts, have moved very slowly during the last hundred years. There has been less growth in agriculture, less urbanization, less trade, fewer means of communication. To explain these differences is beyond the scope of this work for it would involve much historical and socio-economic research. But two facts are clear: unlike the north-west of India, the middle and lower Ganges basin did not enjoy the large canal irrigation networks constructed by the British. Added to this, the caste patterns were not conducive to a dynamic agriculture.

'Poverty Does Not Leave the Poor'

Dewan, a landless Chamar, lived in a household consisting of his wife, three children and a married son with his wife. He was attached as labourer to a Thakur who granted him the use of 0.25 hectares of land. Since he had no bullocks, the landowner lent him a pair and, in return, he took the straw from the crops — wheat followed by maize. In addition Dewan received Rs 4 per month and one meal a day. His wife, who worked about one day in the week for the same man, was paid 50 paise a day with one meal. Dewan owned a cow and the half litre or so of milk it gave every day went towards feeding the small children. It was not uncommon for the whole family to eat only one meal a day.

Bulli, another Chamar, was a small landless labourer. When he had a job he received Re 1 per day and his wife got half that amount when she worked. He did not know how many days he worked on an average. Bulli was a tragic figure, weighed down with poverty, just managing to survive. There were a number of other landless people who lived under similar conditions. Small farmers were marginally better off but with half or even one hectare, they secured a much smaller yield than similar landowners in Mirpur. Then, to make things worse, there were several instances of semi-feudal relations between upper landowners and the poor — something which one hardly saw in Mirpur. It is not easy to draw a strict line between free and bonded labour but we did notice cases of exploitation due to the sheer power of the landowners. Fights, tensions, class relations therefore looked more tense than in Mirpur. And apart from this there were also acute inter-caste rivalries between the dominant Thakurs and the rising Kurmi middle farmers.[6]

When I left Nilkanth I was beginning to see the truth of the observation of a Chamar who had commented that 'poverty does not leave the poor'. In Nilkanth farming techniques were poor, many landowners were not very active with the exception of a few progressive Thakurs and Kurmis. The administration could not cope with the difficult situation. Worse still, there was tension and bitterness and no community spirit whatever. Was the future, then, hopeless?

Where Things Get Even Worse

In 1967 we selected Muzaffarpur district in north Bihar, one of the poorest districts, to work on. Interestingly, the *Gazetteer of Dharbhanga*, a district next to Muzaffarpur, and not very different from it, gave the following account of the situation towards the end of the last century. Speaking of Dharbanga, the *Gazetteer* said: 'The innumerable rivers and rivulets of the district, the alluvial soil and the usual monsoon rains make the tract one of the most important production centres of Bihar and the area has rightly been described as the granary of India... The climate is responsible for the characteristic ease loving complacent attitude...of the people. Naturally, therefore, the philosophical discussions and erotic poems found a fertile soil in the district where people are allergic to hard work.'[7]

Conditions were, however, not always so easy. When the rains failed tragic famines could occur, as in 1874. In those days a young man called H. Kisch, who was with the Indian Civil Service, organized relief works in the area. He often came across Brahmin families who had suffered greatly because of the famine. But as Kisch said, 'if you ask one of these men what work he is able and willing to do, he answers that he can pray.... The Brahmin would die without a murmur sooner than work on a tank or a road with common coolies'[8] Gradually, people from Muzaffarpur and Dharbanga got caught in the demographic trap without reacting fast enough.

From the town of Muzaffarpur we moved on to Kalpi which lies

---

[6]There were some members of the Communist Party who were moderately active in the village—something never seen in Mirpur.

[7]P. C. Chaudhury, *Darbhanga, Bihar District Gazetteers* (Patna, 1964), p. 24.

[8]P. Woodruff, *The Men Who Ruled India* Vol. II,(London, 1963), p. 105.

on an asphalted road 20 kilometres away. Kalpi has a total area of 470 hectares of which 370 are cropped, and 26 have mango orchards. In 1961 the population was 2,471 with a density of 525 per square kilometre. The land and caste pattern here is similar to that of Nilkanth. Most of the landlords are Bhumihars and there are also some important Vaishya landowners. Here again we find rising middle castes and classes such as the Kurmis and Yadavs. At the bottom of the social ladder are the various scheduled castes such as Chamars and Dusads. Very often they are landless as well. This district is unusual in that it has some very large landlords who own between 100 and 200 hectares of land. This is rare in India. These landlords use their influence to exploit the smaller farmers; for instance they often get most of the water they need for their fields and do not hesitate to send their men with *lathis* (sticks) to quieten those who complain. The poverty of agriculture here is striking in many respects. In the past, except under abnormal conditions, farmers would have reasonably good crops in the monsoon (mostly paddy) and some limited crops in the rabi (wheat and pulses). Rainfall is a little higher than in Varanasi and, until 1967, there was practically no irrigation — neither private wells nor tubewells, nor irrigation canals. Only one state tubewell had been installed some years before and this covered some of the fields in Kalpi.[9] However, the Burhi Gandak flowing near the village made for abundant water resources.

High caste landowners, both big and small, strictly respected the taboo on ploughing. As we have noted before, even the smallest Brahmins or Bhumihars would hire labourers and waste precious money. Thus the fields were badly tended and sometimes flooded. It is striking that here even the women from the poor scheduled castes would not work in the fields. In early August when we were in Kalpi we found that the rains had not yet come and paddy transplantation had been delayed. It was necessary to do the work of transplanting quickly in order not to miss the rains. Yet there was not a single woman at work because, as they said, 'It is not done'. And those of the men who did work, did so slowly and lethargically. Needless to add, the consumption of chemical fertilizers was negligible. All these factors explain why there were such low yields. The big landlords had managers to look after their crops and paid them for doing so. One Bhumihar had 4 hectares of land. He used some chemical fertilizers

[9]This did not work satisfactorily. One cemented channel remained broken and unrepaired and this prevented the irrigation of 6 hectares.

but, nevertheless, could not get more than 1,300 kilograms per hectare of paddy. He grew some maize as well, and, after the rain, some tobacco, chillies and potatoes. He also had some wheat. Rich and middle farmers did not live badly but production was so stagnant that their incomes barely increased. Small high caste farmers were also badly hit. For instance, Ram Chandra Misra, a Bhumihar, only managed to make ends meet because his two brothers had jobs outside — in the police and the railways. Together they sent home Rs 500 a month. This went towards feeding their families who were living with Ram Chandra. Ram Chandra himself looked after his fields, although he hired a permanent labourer and some casual workers. He had a much poorer standard of living than our Jats or Brahmins in Mirpur whose plots were of similar size.

With Chamars, Dusads and other low caste landless people things were worse. Not unnaturally, some of them were very bitter. They felt that they had nothing while the Bhumihars kept everything for themselves. Paswan, a Dusad, had only 0.25 hectares of land on which he grew maize in the monsoon. He had no bullocks of his own and thus had to borrow a pair. He barely managed to eat twice a day: maize, some rice with a few pickles, no milk, no meat. When I asked him whether his life had improved in the last ten or fifteen years, he replied, 'Far from it, it has got worse... and what can the block or the co-operative do for poor people like me?' To survive Paswan worked as a labourer and earned Rs 2 a day.

In spite of all this there had been some changes, however small. The dramatic drought of 1965 and 1966, when Bihar had narrowly escaped a terrible famine, had at last made people irrigation-conscious. They were now clamouring for tubewells and canals. In Kalpi, a few farmers had started, with the help of the block, to grow HYV paddy and maize and one could see the beginnings of an understanding of the need for change and the need to expand agriculture. Such hints of change, though welcome, were late in arriving, esepcially when the population pressure was already very heavy. Thus the whole process of growth was being initiated under much more difficult conditions than in the more dynamic areas where it had already begun. What would be the results of these new trends?

Kalpi was not a particularly poor village. Since it was located on a good road, its standard of living could have been higher than the overall rural conditions in several districts of Bihar which were even lower than in Varanasi district. From a comparative study of Bihar and Punjab we get the following data (relating to the early 1970s):

Year 1971	Bihar	Punjab
Surfaced roads per 100 sq. km.	14	24 km.
Unsurfaced roads per 100 sq. km.	48	152 km.
No. of buses per 1,000 sq. km.	23	50 units
No. of good vehicles	83	150 units
Consumption of electricity in agriculture	1.13	22.6 million kw/h
Consolidation of holdings	2	100 per cent of cultivated area

It is important to remember that these figures do not take into account the fact that Bihar has a much larger population than the Punjab, and that its per capita irrigated area is one-seventh that of the Punjab.[10] Non-agricultural rural activities such as trade and small industry were also lagging behind those in the Punjab. Although districts like Bulandshahr were, and remain, less advanced than the most prosperous Punjab districts, the gap was also wide between the overall development reached in western U.P. and in north Bihar.

---

[10] *Bihar and Punjab: A Study on Regional Disparity* (New Delhi, 1973); quoted in *Overseas Hindustan Times,* 26 December 1974.

CHAPTER 6
The Beginnings of Change

In 1975, and then again in 1978, we revisited Nilkanth. We found that the situation had started changing in several directions. Even in Kalpi, to which we returned in 1978, we discerned some measure of change, particularly in agriculture. In Nilkanth the consolidation of holdings had just been completed. This was no mean achievement in a village where both the division and fragmentation of holdings was acute — more so than in Mirpur. Population increase had, however, remained comparatively slow — the plus 18.3 per cent rise between 1961–71 was mainly due to a higher death rate than in Mirpur. On the other hand, irrigation was improving. Most wells employing the *mot* system had fallen into disuse and there were at that time 23 private (6 diesel and 17 electric) tubewells, in addition to the existing state tubewell. New seeds of wheat and chemical fertilizers were on the increase. There were farmers who secured as much as 2,500–3,000 kilograms per hectare of wheat, although there were others who could not manage to get more than 1,500. The average yields were 1,400–1,500 kilograms per hectare as compared with the early 1960s, when the average yields were around 900 kilograms per hectare. Along with the rise in yields the acreage devoted to wheat had gone up as well — though at the cost of barley.

However, the situation was not the same for all crops. Sugarcane, for instance, had remained more or less stagnant, production still being close to what it had been in 1964: 3,000–3,500 kilograms per hectare in terms of raw sugar. Paddy, by far the main foodgrain, had also moved slowly, except on the higher lands which were irrigated by tubewells. Here, several medium and upper farmers, having taken to new seeds and chemical fertilizers, were able to secure 3,200 kilograms per hectare of paddy (2,000 of clean rice). Fields on the lower lands were often subject to flooding and their production was normally about 1,300 kilograms per hectare of paddy (800 of clean rice).

53

Potato farming had already begun in the 1960s and was rising moderately.[1] Vegetable growing was confined to small plots.

On the whole, agricultural techniques had not changed much. No one owned a tractor and the bigger landowners often had to rent one. Electricity was still confined to tubewells and power cuts created problems. There were signs of change in other areas — Lohars (blacksmiths) in the village were making iron implements for farming, there was a small sari shop; one of the landowners had set up a gobar gas plant. Some farmers were using a diesel mechanical thresher.

Data for Pindra block confirmed the trends observed in Nilkanth. Pindra block (population 120,000 in 1971) had a cultivated area of 18,325 hectares which remained constant. As for crops, paddy yields and the area the crop covered — 6,800–7,000 hectares — had not changed, while wheat had reached 5,700 hectares. Although there were still 1,700 masonry wells, there were now also 654 private tubewells, where there had been none before 1961. Of these, 335 were diesel and 319 electric, each tubewell with a command area of between 4 and 5 hectares. There were also 246 pumping sets installed on rivers or near tanks. The number of state tubewells, each irrigating between 100 and 120 hectares (nearly half in the rabi, the rest in the kharif) had increased from 12 in 1964–5 to 42 in 1977–8. From the early 1960s till 1977–8 the consumption of nitrogen fertilizers had gone up ten times (to reach 1,743 tons in nutrients) and that of phosphatic fertilizers five times to 270 tons.

When talking about yields it is important to note that one quarter of the Pindra area is alkaline. This brings down the yields of paddy and prevents the cultivation of wheat. Where the soils get adequate rainfall paddy can yield up to 1,500 kilograms per hectare (1,000 of clean rice) and as much as 2,500–3,000 kilograms per hectare when some doses of chemical fertilizer are added to HYV seeds. When we take the average for the block, paddy yields have grown from 730 kilograms per hectare of clean rice in 1960–1 to 800 in 1977–8 — not even a 10 per cent increase — and wheat yields from 900–1,000 kilograms per hectare to 1,300–1,400. As far as the district is concerned similar trends appear in the progress of irrigation and chemical fertilizers, as the chart below demonstrates:

[1]A cold storage house has been opened in Mangari.

Area	Year (1963–4)	Year (1976–7)
Net cultivated area	330,000 hectares	328,660 hectares
Gross cultivated area	443,000 hectares	457,398 hectares
Net irrigated area	147,000 hectares	175,630 hectares
Gross irrigated area	not available	221,000 hectares

Consumption of chemical fertilizers

1963–4	negligible, a few thousand tons
1971–2	19,323 tons in terms of nutrients
1977–8	30,500 tons in terms of nutrients

Incomes and Living Conditions

In Nilkanth the process of the growth and diversification of the economy had been weak when compared with the Bulandshahr district. Employment opportunities had, therefore, grown only moderately. In 1964 landless labourers earned roughly Re 1 a day plus some food, as in Mirpur. This had gone up to about Rs 2.50–3.00, an increase that, in the face of the rise in prices, did not mean anything. Harvest-time wages — which were paid in kind — varied between 3 kilograms to 8 kilograms of wheat or paddy now. (Wages in Mirpur: Rs 5.00, sometimes 6.00, plus some food; at harvest time 10 kilograms of wheat.)

In order to ascertain how this affected the people of Nilkanth, and to look at their living conditions, we employed our usual technique of interviewing a cross-section of farmers. We began with the worst cases. The Musahars belong to a migrant scheduled caste that goes from place to place in search of work. They build temporary straw huts to live in. Their children were malnourished and the caste generated an air of acute misery. Ram Dula, a Musahar, told me he earned only one rupee and some food a day. There was no need to ask him about his living conditions. Hira, a Chamar, was little better off Fifty years old, he lived with his wife and his five children. His only assets, in addition to his hut, were three chickens. Hira worked 15 to 20 days a month earning Rs 4 per day, plus food. This was an unusually high salary but was barely adequate for him. At harvest time he got only 2 to 2.50 kilograms of wheat or paddy. Kuli Lal, another Chamar, worked as a permanent labourer for a landowner who paid him Rs 50 (Rs 100 in Mirpur) a month and fed him as well. Kuli had to make do for his wife and his five children with this salary. He was a lively person but complained bitterly of the pressure (*dabao*) the high caste landowners exerted on the poorer, low caste people. His lot had not improved in the last ten to fifteen years. A third Chamar owned 0.4 hectares of land on which he grew wheat in the rabi and, with the help of some urea, managed to get a yield equivalent to 1,600 kilograms per hectare. In the kharif he could not grow paddy because the rain water ran into the nearby tank. In addition he grew some pulses and worked as a casual labourer to supplement his income, earrning Rs 3 a day. Chindra, also a Chamar, had even less land — 0.1 hectare. He used small doses of urea for his wheat and paddy and worked for Rs 3 a day as a casual labourer. Chindra was quite for smart and he admitted that life had 'improved a bit' in the last few years. In another hamlet of Chamars we noticed that the well had fallen into disrepair and if the Chamars took water from the nearby tubewell, they had to pay the Thakur, to whom the tubewell belonged, by working for him at the measly wage of Re 1 a day.

Although many landless labourers lead the same hard life as before there were some who had improved their living conditions and others who had begun to go to school. One such young man, Chida, managed to find a job as a clerk in Mangari and bought himself a bicycle. Chida was particularly outspoken about the abuses committed by the high caste farmers. Similarly Bhagan Ram was also a young Chamar who had had a few years of schooling and was married some years ago. Bhagan Ram cultivated 0.25 hectares of land on a share-cropping basis. He paid for all the inputs and kept half the produce. He got about 200 kilograms of wheat and 160 of paddy and did fairly well by doing some odd jobs as well. He had managed to buy himself a bicycle.

Let us now move to the hamlet inhabited by the Kurmis. Clever and ready to do any manual work the Kurmis were already improving their lot in 1964. Barsati Ram, owned one hectare of land and lived with his wife and four children. One of his sons was a matriculate but had been unable to find a job. Barsati Ram managed his land shrewdly. He bought water (at Rs 18 for 6 hours to irrigate 0.25 hectares) from another Kurmi's tubewell, applied urea to his wheat and got a yield equivalent to 2,400 kilograms per hectare. He also grew some paddy, pulses and sugarcane. He was able to grow enough for his family where earlier he had had to buy food from outside. He had two bullocks, a small cow and two goats which supplied milk. One of Barsati Ram's sons had started making carpets which were sold in Varanasi. He earned Rs 60 a month. Barsati Ram himself occasionally worked as a field labourer to supplement the family income.

Thanks to all this he had been able to buy a bicycle. Interestingly, he had also realized that it was time to stop having more children and he and his wife practised birth control.

Rama Dechave, a Brahmin, and his two brothers, owned 2.4 hectares of land. Theirs was a different story. They had a large family comprising six couples and ten children. For more than ten years now the men had ploughed the land themselves because they could not afford to hire ploughmen. Their wheat was not doing well — 1,200 kilograms per hectare in 1977 — and the paddy had been particularly poor — 750 kilograms per hectare — because of the lack of water. They had practically no grain to sell; what little milk their two cows yielded was used up at home, and their only sources of cash were some sunn hemp (hard fibre) which they sold and their two bullocks which they rented out from time to time. They found it increasingly difficult to manage.

In contrast to Rama Dechave, Saka Narain Singh, a Thakur, head of a large family of twenty-four adults and children, was doing somewhat better. Three of the married sons had left their wives and children in Nilkanth and worked in Varanasi doing clerical work. Saka looked after 3.75 hectares of land, had four bullocks, one cow and one buffalo — between them they yielded 6 litres of milk a day. Two-thirds of his land bore wheat which was followed by paddy. He used new seeds and urea and bought water from a nearby tubewell, and managed to get 3,000 kilograms per hectare of wheat and the same of paddy. He was lucky in that his land was high enough not to be exposed to floods. He also grew sugarcane and sunn hemp which he sold. Because of his large family Saka had only very little grain left over to sell. He was doing much better than before although much of this was due to the earnings his sons sent him.

Kamala Prasad Singh, one of the main Thakur landowners, owned 15 hectares of land. Already in 1964 Kamala was one of the progressive farmers and when we met him again, he had two tubewells, was using HYV seeds, urea and di-ammonium phosphate in the right doses so that he was harvesting 3,000 kilograms per hectare of wheat and the same of paddy (except in the low areas where the yield fell to 1,000 kilograms). Kamala Prasad looked after his family as well as those of his two brothers who worked in Varanasi, one as a lawyer and the other as a factory manager. Another brother had taught agricultural economics at Agra University and has now gone to the United States.

Achievements and Constraints

Nilkanth has broken out of the semi-static cycle of its economy which had lasted for many decades. However, the movement is not yet wide-ranging enough to have made a real impact on the living conditions of the poor. The standards of the latter do not seem to have deteriorated in the last fifteen years; some of the poor are even slightly better off. Several of the medium (2 hectares) and upper (4–10 hectares) farmers produce more now but for many production is still comparatively low. We must also bear in mind that because population densities here are higher than in Mirpur, the process of raising wages and increasing employment is more difficult. In terms of employment, therefore, links with the outside world have not grown fast enough. Fewer people than in Mirpur have found jobs in cities. Although the bazaar at Mangari has expanded there are still not many workshops and small industries. Production and the sale of milk have hardly grown. On the outskirts of Varanasi, vegetable sales have expanded considerably — vegetables are sent from here as far as Calcutta. But vegetable growing has not yet percolated down to Nilkanth.

At the village level three main constraints are becoming increasingly serious. Better roads are needed. In Mangari the roads are so bad that camels still form one of the chief modes of transportation. As far as electricity is concerned, there are frequent power breakdowns and voltage fluctuation is high — the situation is, in fact, no better than in western U.P. This is why many farmers prefer to install a diesel pumping set or tubewell. This is more expensive than the electrical one but, at the time of our last visit, it was considered more reliable. This is no more the case now because of the shortage of diesel. State tubewells break down frequently and the lack of power in the village prevents the growth of workshops and small industries. The performance of the block co-operative has remained fairly average — there are not many complaints about the supply of inputs such as seeds and fertilizers. Although the number of tubewells has gone up, irrigation can still be expanded and drainage is certainly very poor. Too many low-lying fields get flooded even under normal rain conditions and this prevents the use of dwarf varieties (HYV) of paddy and the application of chemical fertilizers. Thus it is important to improve irrigation as well as to have drainage work; this can be done now that the consolidation of holdings is over.

Socially, too, there does not seem to have been much change. The village Panchayat hardly works. The block Samiti (council) and the Zila Parishad (district council) are perhaps a little more active but their impact on development remains limited. Tensions run high between high castes and Harijans. Fortunately there have been no severe clashes in the recent past and the Harijans do seem to have become more conscious of their rights. Conflicts between medium rising castes like the Kurmis and the Thakurs remain very live.

An Area of Slow Growth

Let us move now to Kalpi in north Bihar. Here also, population pressure has been heavy and the number of inhabitants has risen from 2,471 in 1961 to 2,928 in 1971 — an 18.5 per cent rise — and the density per square kilometre has increased from 525 to 610. Not much change is visible in the cropping pattern, paddy remaining the dominant crop, followed by wheat which is on the increase. Maize is grown in the kharif and there are a few cash crops such as chillies and tobacco. The total net cultivated area is the same as before — 370 hectares. Irrigation, which was confined to the command area of the state tubewell (80-100 hectares) is said to have reached 182 hectares, a figure which seems doubtful since only seven private diesel tubewells have been installed. With a command area of about 5 hectares each, these should add up to about 35 hectares. Thus it is more likely that the actual figure is between 120 and 140 hectares. There are three landowners who have bought a tractor each and there are a fair number of buggies on tyres. Early new seeds of paddy (Taichung N1) did not adapt well to local conditions, but IR 8 and other more recent varieties have borne good results when given adequate water. On high lands where there are tubewells this is often the case and one meets farmers who, with the help of chemical fertilizers, harvest as much as 2,300 kilograms per hectare of paddy and sometimes even 3,000. This is not an extraordinary achievement[2] but it does show a substantial increase, compared with the 1,000–1,500 per hectare in the 1960s. Rain-fed paddy can reach 1,500 kilograms per hectare when it is on medium high soils and the monsoon has been adequate. Many of the fields lie in the lowland area and are often flooded or suffer from an excess of water. On these, yields remain as low as ever — 1,000 kilograms per hectare[3], or at best 1,500. Because of proper

[2] In coastal Andhra and Thanjavur district we will meet farmers who get as much as 4,000 to 5,000 kilograms per hectare.

[3] Paddy cannot be transplanted. It is sown broadcast and is of a floating variety, i.e., the stem grows with the rising water level and can attain a maximum of 10 feet.

irrigation and new varieties of chemical fertilizers wheat acreage has increased. Some good farmers get 2,000–2,500 kilograms per hectare while others do not go beyond 1,200. Here again, compared with the 500 kilograms per hectare of unirrigated wheat in the 1960s, there has been some progress. But the area covered is not so wide. Mazie has not shown much increase.

It is necessary to emphasize that existing irrigation needs substantial improvement. The maintenance and operation of the state tubewell suffers from the usual defects. During our second visit we found that the state tubewell was out of order because someone had cut and taken away 30 metres of the connecting wire! There were also complaints that the operator gave water to non-influential farmers only against a *bakshish* (tip). The repair and maintenance of private tubewells meet with different difficulties and delays, because there are not enough workshops around. Trade within Kalpi and outside has also remained fairly static. One does not find many small industries or workshops even in the large town of Muzaffarpur where the bazaar has expanded considerably.

The trends noticed in Kalpi are representative of the Muraul block and of the district. The block (population 100,000 in 1971, total area 174 square kilometres, density 574) had practically the same net cultivated area as before — 13,400 hectares of which 6,300 were double cropped. In 1967, 2,000 hectares enjoyed assured irrigation, mostly through state tubewells and only six private tubewells. Eleven years later the irrigated area was: gross 5,700 hectares and net 5,000 hectares. Some more state tubewells, and many private ones, had been added.

Similar trends are apparent at the district level. Here too, there are problems related to the maintenance of the tubewells. The total command area was often not fully utilized because field channels have not been completed or repaired[4]. Power shortages and voltage fluctuations create other problems. In fact the shortage of electricity is such that farmers are now advised to install only diesel tubewells. The total irrigated area is as follows:

Year	District Data No. of State Tubewells	No. of Private Tubewells
1966	96	201
1974–5	144	9,560
1978–9	215	14,200

[4] It sometimes happens that field channels break down because the contractor keeps part of the allotted cement for his personal use!

Canals, tanks	6,485 hectares
State tubewells	26,328 hectares
Private tubewells	33,408 hectares

Total: 66,221 hectares

The total net cultivated area amounts to 235,500 hectares (gross 350,400). Consumption of chemical fertilizers is also on the increase, as the figures below illustrate:

Year	Muraul Block	Muzaffarpur District
1973–4	not available	4,070 (tons in terms of nutrients)
1974–5	426 tons	6,000 tons
1977–8	982 tons	13,322 tons

In a way these trends can be said to be encouraging but they lag behind what we have seen in Varanasi and Bulandshahr districts. Then there is also the lack of drainage, the waterlogging which affects wide tracts of land in north Bihar. In Muzaffarpur and Dharbanga 56,000 hectares are affected in the rabi, 70,000 in the kharif and 9,900 all the year round.[5]

Administration connected with development has not seen much change or improvement. The Collector, as in U.P., is not directly involved in development operations. He has too many tasks to attend to and does not manage to do more here than some overall co-ordination and supervision. Poor farmers complain that the block development officers or the village level workers meet only the rich villagers. Co-operative credit cannot overcome the well-known shortcomings which have been around for decades—defaults in repayment, etc. And no one ever speaks of Panchayati Raj.

Poverty and Bitterness

Such a late developmental process cannot but have had a limited impact on the conditions of a population which has been growing for at least a century, and especially so over the last twenty to thirty years. In 1967 daily wages stood at Rs 1.50 plus food. Today's wages amount mostly to Rs 2.50 and some food. In some cases they go up to Rs 3. Wages in kind can go up to 2.50 kilograms and at harvest times can be higher, up to 5 or 10 kilograms of paddy. Cash wages at Rs 2.50 imply a decline in real terms, because between 1967 and 1978 the food and general indexes of consumer prices have increased from 220 to 400 (round figures). The taboo on ploughing remains widespread

[5] *A Report on the Gandak Command Area* (Muzaffarpur, 1976).

among high caste landowners and there are different types of arrangements between the latter and the labourers. This can be seen more clearly from the case studies below.

The first of our men was Ismael Mia, a Muslim whom we had met before. In his mid-forties Ismael Mia had five daughters who helped their mother with the housework. He had two goats which gave milk. He was not working as a permanent labourer any more but he worked on a casual basis for roughly Rs 3 a day. His life went on — not really deteriorating, but certainly not improving either. In a hamlet of scheduled castes was Lakshman, a Dusad, who lived with his wife and four daughters. Lakshman's family's only assets were their four goats which provided some milk for the children. None of the children went to school because there was no money. Lakshman possessed only the set of clothes that he wore, in his hut there was a *charpai* (a string bed) and his homestead belonged to his *malik* (owner). His wife, like most other low caste women, did not work in the fields. She collected grass and sold it. Clearly, Lakshman's standard of living was not progressing. The Chamars who lived next to him were no better off. One family looked after the cow of a Bhumihar. They fed her, and when she gave milk one half of it would go to the owner and the other half would come to them. The plot on which their hut stood was one that had been appropriated by the government and allotted to them. This gave them some measure of security. They could not be exploited as they would have been had they been living on someone else's land like Lakshman. The family had very few assets, but managed to eat twice a day, mostly grain.

Leaving the landless let us look at some very small farmers. We first encountered a group of Sahas. Kapleswas, a young man, married and with one child, owned 0.25 hectares of land. He wisely grew tobacco on one-fifth of his land, which brought him a net return of Rs 300. On his other plots he had different types of pulses which, though low-yielding, also fetched a good price. He sold most of the milk from his buffalo and was very smart and outspoken: 'It is the landlords who eat and we who work', he said. He earned Rs 2.50 or 3 plus food. Six months earlier Kapleswas had had to borrow Rs 500 at 5 per cent interest per month, which he hoped to pay back after the sales of his tobacco.

Mushahar Ray was a Yadav and his family consisted of his wife and nine children. Their plot of land was 0.18 hectares. Mushahar Ray took on another 0.18 hectares on a share-cropping basis — he got half the crop but bore all the production costs. Fortunately he had one cow and two bullocks. He used the latter to plough both his own fields and those of a Bhumihar. He also worked as a labourer and did some petty trade. All in all, he managed to get through, but his life, too, was not improving.

Another Yadav, Mahindar Ray, had just got married. He lived with his wife, his father and his two young brothers. Between them they had 0.5 hectares of land, part of it upland where maize was followed by wheat, irrigated by the state tubewell; and part with paddy in low-lying land. For wheat he applied small doses of urea which gave him 300 kilograms, the equivalent of 1,500 kilograms per hectare. The urea was of no use to the paddy because of excess water in the paddy fields. Mahindar Ray's paddy yield was 250 kilograms of paddy, equivalent to 1,000 kilograms per hectare (666 for clean rice). The family had to hire bullocks because they did not have any. Their cow gave less than a litre of milk. They had taken a buffalo on rent from a large landowner which was expected to start giving milk soon. Several other Yadavs were in circumstances similar to those of these two families. They had from 0.1 to 0.5 hectares of land, in addition quite often to a pair of bullocks. This put them in a slightly stronger position than the totally landless. They were thus less susceptible to exploitation or pressures from the high castes. Apart from this the Yadavs are one of the rising middle castes and can stand their ground with the Harijans, the Thakurs or the Bhumihars.

Among the middle farmers some were improving their crops, while others had not yet overcome several constraints. Siri Kisan Chand was a Vaishya. His married son, his wife and his younger daughter were with him. Out of his 2 hectares some tracts were very poor, sandy on the river side, often flooded. He had 0.6 hectares upland where he grew IR 8 paddy, getting water from the state tubewell and securing a yield of around 2,000 kilograms per hectare. Then he sowed wheat and here too he got a good yield of 2,300–3,000 kilograms per hectare. If the water from the state tubewell was not enough, Kisan Chand bought water from a private tubewell. On 0.4 hectares he grew chillies, and got a net return of Rs 1,000; elsewhere he grew some tobacco. All in all he was obliged to buy only a small amount of grain, he had no debts and, because of higher production, his living conditions had improved.

Kalika Prasad Singh, a Bhumihar, had 6 hectares of land, part of which were near the river. His paddy gave him only 1,000–1,500 kilograms per hectare but the wheat was better at 2,000. Ram Singh, a Thakur, did rather well on his 2.8 hectares. He could irrigate one hectare on which he got one crop of paddy followed by one of wheat, both with HYV seeds, some urea and phosphatic fertilizers. For each crop he got 2,300 kilograms per hectare of grain. The lower lands, however, were less fortunate. In 1978 there was heavy rain and Ram Singh lost his entire paddy crop. In normal times he got 1,000–1,500 kilograms per hectare from this plot of land. He also grew some chillies, sweet potatoes and bananas. It was obvious that his standard of living was rising.

How were the landlords doing? The old Bhumihar we met in 1967 was still alive but neither he nor his sons took an interest in increasing production on their 40 hectares. One of his sons complained that all sorts of difficulties kept them from increasing their yields; for example, they said they lacked the money to properly level their paddy fields. They were also afraid of land reforms and the jajmani system was not working satisfactorily any more for them. The biggest Bhumihar landlord, with 50 hectares here and 80 in another village, now lived in town. He had hired a manager in Kalpi to attend to his land. With the help of the block officials he was using HYV and fertilizers on part of his land. A Vaishya, who had enlarged his concrete house, worked as a farmer (20 hectares) and as a contractor. He was clearly progressing, and had constructed two tubewells while pushing new seeds of paddy and wheat along with fertilizers.

Summing Up

It is clear that, if the population increase is taken into account, the economic growth process has not been strong and diversified enough to bring about a definite improvement in the living conditions of landless labourers, small and often even medium farmers. Irrigation, the use of new seeds and fertilizers are clearly falling behind what we have observed in Nilkanth. Some landlords are doing well. Others lack the spirit of enterprise. The conditions under which people are working are even more acute than those we have seen in Nilkanth. Irrigation is unreliable, large areas are flooded, highland rain-fed areas are at the mercy of the rains. If a greater diversification of agriculture were to be introduced, small farmers in particular would welcome it, for they could grow high return cash crops such as vegetables and tobacco and transportation would be no problem as Kalpi lies on a good road. As things stand, in Kalpi, as in much of

Bihar, the poorer castes are still very oppressed and there are often clashes between high and low castes. In Kalpi there are three major types of rivalries: between the rising middle castes and classes such as the Kurmis and Yadavs, the Bhumihars and Thakurs; between the latter and Harijans, and between Harijans and Kurmis and Yadavs.

CHAPTER 7
Slow Growth Again

In this chapter we will look at two slow growth areas in Assam and Orissa. My visit to Assam was too brief to enable me to meet and interview a sufficient number of villagers. Thus the analysis of the Assam area is largely confined to water management problems and crop yields, mainly paddy. In Puri district, however, we will look at both aspects—the standard of living and water management and irrigation.

A Large Untapped Source

Unlike the Ganges basin, the plains of the Brahmaputra were, until a century ago, fairly thinly populated. Man had not controlled the enormous flow of the Brahmaputra. Gradually the population increased until finally the region became quite populated, though less so than in Bihar or U.P. Now, densities of 300 per square kilometre are quite common in the plains, which are inhabited by 97 per cent of the population, and produce 95 per cent of the foodgrains. As many as 57 per cent of the holdings (18 per cent of the cultivated area) are below one hectare. In this area the soils are, on the whole, good and rainfall is above 2,000 millimetres a year in several districts. Although rain here is better distributed (it is spread over seven months) than in most other parts of India, rain-fed agriculture is increasingly unable to produce enough grain to match the rise in population. Irrigation has thus become a top priority in order to compensate for delayed rains and to ensure good crops during the rabi or dry season. In 1976 only 8 per cent of the net cropped area was irrigated, a very low percentage, in view of the enormous potential, both from surface and ground water. There is also a need for large drainage and flood control works.

Let us take Nowgong district as an example. Paddy fields here are not too well kept—more weeding is needed and line transplanting is rare in the lowlands. Farmers are rightly afraid to apply chemical

66

fertilizers because they fear the floods. Elsewhere paddy may suffer because of the lack of water due to late rains. Occasionally one comes across a farmer who has allowed himself to be guided by extension workers. If his land is not vulnerable to floods and if he has applied the proper doses of chemical fertilizers and HYV, he can harvest, for his monsoon crop, as much as 3,000 or even 4,500 kilograms per hectare of paddy. But such cases are not common. Farmers are happy with a yield of 1,800–2,000 kilograms per hectare. Others get only 1,000–1,500 kilograms.[1] Tubewells are the main source of irrigation and, under a World Bank supported project, a scheme to install 12,500 shallow tubewells and 2,500 small low lift points has been initiated. In Nowgong district (Juria block) 42 tubewells have been installed by individual farmers and 112 have been arranged on a community basis by groups of farmers. So far, a total of 92 tubewells have been energized; the others are waiting for connecting lines. Other signs of progress are also discernible. More and better double cropping is practised; some farmers use urea and superphosphate and get fairly high yields.

Schemes to install new tubewells and introduce new seeds face certain constraints in such areas. The first such difficulty is that of credit. After several attempts with co-operatives all over Assam, a new system was created here in order to revitalize co-operation. According to this system the state was divided into 664 *gaon* Panchayats, each with a Samabai Samiti to provide credit (short, medium and long-term) to supply inputs and other commodities and to market agricultural products. Several banks, including the Assam Co-operative Appex Bank, have adopted this scheme and support it financially. In spite of this the new system does not look too promising and the shortcomings of the old system are reappearing in this one. The poor are still often not catered for. The chairman of the Juria Samabai Samiti, for example, owns 8 hectares of land, and several members have 3 hectares or more.

In the implementation of schemes that are carried through by the Irrigation Department there are other difficulties. In Juria block the first phase of the scheme to sink and energize 92 tubewells was completed in the latter part of 1978, almost a year and a half behind

---

[1] Labourers' wages amount to Rs 5 without food. They were Rs 2–2.50 ten to fifteen years ago. They may be higher than in Bihar because the population pressure here is lighter. On the other hand, the overall level of development is scarcely higher, even if poverty is less acute.

schedule.[2] Procedural delays also occur. In October 1978, as many as 378 new applications for tubewells were collected and only 30 were forwarded to the Bank. At this time there was already a backlog of 867 pending applications of which 728 were incompletely documented. In other parts of Nowgong district there were some surface water schemes such as the one at Hatimura where water is pumped from the Brahmaputra in order to irrigate 8,400 hectares of land. Construction work on this was supposed to start in 1971–2 but, because of some delays in land acquisition, work began only in 1975–6. Yet another scheme was intended to lift water (two 40 HP electrical pumps) from Samaguri lake to cover an area of 280 hectares. Work on this began in 1975–6 but, at the time of our visit in 1978, the pumps had not yet been brought into operation. The pumps had been installed, the main canal (765 m) and its two branches (1,950 and 850 m) were lined and complete with outlets but the field channels were still lacking. Originally the idea was that they should have been dug by the farmers but, as seen in many places, this was not done.[3] Finally the government decided to do this and it was expected that it would be completed soon. A similar scheme near Chaparmukh (560 hectares) went a little further. But even here the works started only in 1975–6 and the scheme was scheduled to come into operation only towards the end of 1978.

Efforts were also made to install bamboo tubewells in Nowgong district. However all hundred units quickly got damaged because the local clay soils were not suitable for that kind of intermediate technology.[4] Though limited, these examples show two things—a large potential for growth (at least doubling the yields of paddy in the first phase) and more double cropping, sometimes even treble cropping. It is not possible for me to assess the economic levels of Assamese farmers and their main landowner castes. Are they more accustomed to careful techniques than several castes observed in Bihar? All one can assert is that they fall far behind the farmers whom we will visit in coastal Andhra. It is clear, however, that a much stronger and clearer planning policy and more stringent

[2] Each tubewell enjoys a subsidy of 50 per cent under the Small Farmers' Development Agency (SFDA) and 50 per cent as a loan for 5 years (investment cost Rs 7,125 at the 1977 price), and has a 3 HP electrical motor. In addition, each well is a hundred feet deep with a command area of 3.3 hectares throughout the year.

[3] One of the many problems is that of land requisition.

[4] In some parts of north Bihar bamboo tubewells have been successful. In others they have proved inconvenient.

implementation are required of the Assam Government in order to improve irrigation and drainage.

Physical Constraints and Poverty Near the Sea Coast in Orissa

In Puri district we selected two areas—a very poor, isolated area, and a more developed, though not rich, one. These areas were selected to assess the impact of economic growth and economic diversification, if any, on incomes.

Leaving the holy city of Puri we proceeded eastwards on a good asphalted road towards Brahmagiri, the block headquarters. After twenty kilometres we turned towards the sea on a sandy track which is often flooded in the monsoon. Five kilometres from here lie a few hamlets surrounded by paddy fields. The thatched roofs are scattered in the shadow of graceful coconut trees, wide banana trees and bamboos. It would be hard to find a more attractive landscape with such luxuriant vegetation. In the background are forests of casurinas obscuring the beach from view. Yet appearances are deceptive. This is no paradise. The whole area here has been at a practical standstill for several decades. Communications are poor, there is no electricity, the soils are sandy and almost at sea level, with the result that, because of the total lack of any sort of drainage, there is excess water even in a normal monsoon. Paddy cannot be transplanted—which could have increased yields and saved seeds—because it would be submerged in water. It has thus to be sown broadcast. Yields are extremely low— 500 kilograms per hectare (330 of clean rice). On less sandy and slightly higher soils yields can be 1,000–1,250 kilograms per hectare of paddy (660–800 of rice). Farmers usually grow a single crop in a year, unless they have some pulses in the rabi. There are no shops or workshops in the village.

In order to interview people we made our first stop at a settlement of seven families of Dumas (scheduled caste). Govin Mallik and his wife lived with their two sons—they had had one daughter whom they had lost—one of whom was married. They worked as field labourers in the paddy fields for Rs 3–3.50 a day without food. They also made bamboo baskets which brought them Rs 2–3 a day. The whole household needed 720 kilograms of rice in a year, and rice was between Rs 1.75 to 2 per kilogram in 1978. They ate twice a day, one warm meal of rice with some leafy vegetables in the evening and some cold rice in the morning. They very rarely ate fruit but managed to have fish once a week because they could catch it in the river. The men had only the *dhoti* and the *gamcha* (a kind of towel, carried on the shoulders) that they wore[5] and their huts were quite bare. Fifteen years ago these people had had a pair of bullocks which they had used for ploughing the lands of other farmers. Both the bullocks had died. Thus the living conditions of the Dumas were not getting any better.

In another hamlet lived a household of fourteen Dhobis. Bona Sethi and his wife shared their hut with their son and his wife. Their other children had died. As washermen they got, from different high caste farmers, 170 kilograms of rice in a year. They owned one small bullock and 0.4 hectares of land on which they harvested 200 kilograms of paddy (135 kilograms of rice). Since all four members ate 2 kilograms of rice per day, they had to earn enough to buy 430 kilograms, which in 1978 cost Rs 860 or 750 assuming they bought the cheapest quality. They also worked as labourers and caught some fish, mostly for food. They sometimes got Rs 3.50 by thatching the roofs of farmers' houses and putting in fences around their homes. Like the Dumas, they ate mostly rice with some vegetables and fish. They could not afford pulses. They were Rs 300 in debt, on which they were paying 60 per cent interest each year. Although they did not feel that the high caste farmers were oppressing or exploiting them, they did feel that their living conditions were deteriorating. They were also subject to a certain amount of caste discrimination—they could not use the pond of the local dominant caste, the Khandayats, for bathing or washing clothes in but could drink water from it. They were also allowed to enter temples although they did not go. In their houses there were obvious signs of acute poverty—the children were malnourished, the men had only one dhoti and the women only one sari. Of all the children only two went to school. Tuition was free but the parents did not have the money to pay for slates, books, pencils and a clean shirt. Some of the older children collected wood, which was either used in the house[6] or sold. They also collected certain leaves which were boiled and eaten. They would have liked to have done more fishing in the rivers and the sea but could not afford the boats and the equipment. Another Dhobi was slightly better off than the others. He owned two rather weak bullocks and used them to cultivate 0.8 hectares of land on a share-cropping basis. This brought

[5] Unlike north India the temperature here is warm all the year round.
[6] Two children, by working for as many as 10–15 days, can collect enough wood to fetch Rs 5.

him 100–130 kilograms of rice. He also ploughed fields for others and earned Rs 5–8 a day. Unfortunately this sort of work did not come to him often.

Links with the outside world were maintained by going to Brahmagiri to sell wood and fish. Some people had been to Puri as well but no one had been to Bhubaneshwar. These people, though very poor, did not seem to have been victimized by the landlords because there were hardly any landlords there. They also seemed to be slightly better off than similar landless people in Bihar.

Kanduri Swain, a Khandayat, had had four years of schooling. He worked for a few years in a factory in Calcutta but was retrenched and returned home. Here he lived with his wife, two sons (the elder of whom was going to school), his mother and his two married brothers. They owned 0.8 hectares of land which brought in 400 kilograms of paddy (260 kilograms of rice). Since he had a pair of bullocks he took on another 0.8 hectares on a share-cropping basis. This brought him an extra 130 kilograms of rice. Kanduri also owned a cart which he occasionally used to transport people and goods (when he got the opportunity to do so) and earned Rs 10 a day. Around his house were some cashewnut trees; he sold 15 kilograms of full nuts for Rs 100.[7] The three brothers also worked as labourers sometimes, earning Rs 3.50 a day. This enabled them to buy the 10 quintals of rice they needed in addition to their harvest. Their diet was a little more varied and richer than that of the Dhobis. They obtained some vegetables from their kitchen garden, fish twice a week, some mangoes or guavas and occasionally some dal on festive days. Each man had three dhotis, one gamcha and a light shirt. The Khandayats were not miserable but they did complain that things had become very expensive. To make things worse, in 1968 there were heavy floods which destroyed their crop and badly damaged their houses. To set themselves up again they managed to get a loan from the Land Development Bank at 12 per cent interest. When we visited them they had managed to pay back Rs 500 of the principal with interest.

Another hamlet was inhabited by forty Muslim households. One of them, Sheikh Zamal ud Din, 38 years old, was the head of a large family of thirty which included his three brothers. One brother worked in family planning, another was a teacher, the third a co-operative officer. They had 3.2 hectares of reasonably good land and 1.6 hectares of sandy land near the river which was often flooded.

[7]The fruit is 25–33 per cent of the full nut.

The latter did not give more than 500 kilograms per hectare, and the conditions were not conducive to the application of chemical fertilizers. Zamal's family had rice for five months in the year. They also had a mango orchard and some cashewnut and coconut trees which gave them a good return, and they owned four bullocks and a cow. Zamal did not find it profitable to push paddy under the present constraints, and wanted to instal a small rice mill.

His neighbour, Sheikh Sahabad Kadim had a smaller household consisting of his wife and five children. Their 2 hectares of paddy land brought them enough rice for six months only, though their yields were not bad as compared with those of the others (1,200 kilograms per hectare of paddy). On 1.2 hectares they had cashewnut trees, casurina, some coconut and some mango trees. Their yields were rather low but they brought in some cash income. However, this was not enough to maintain the family, and Sheikh Sahabad worked from time to time as a labourer for Rs 3.50 or caught fish for Rs 3 to Rs 10 a day.

Clearly, unless water management (drainage and irrigation) is not considerably improved, paddy yields cannot rise very much. And even in the best circumstances, the problems raised by a hydraulic infrastructure cannot be solved solely through the initiative of the local people. These problems can only be dealt with by putting in substantial work, time and funds. Thus it becomes necessary, in the short run, to find other ways out. The horticultural unit of Brahmagiri block has started a sound and well conducted scheme to plant coconut trees. The area is suited to such trees and there is much scope for new plantations. The trees begin to bear nuts in their sixth year and can last up to 80 years. (One hectare takes 175 trees, with 50 kilograms of nuts per tree per year at an average price of Re 0.75 per nut.) The Dumars and some landless Khandayats have been given plots of land to start such plantations. They are also technically helped by the Horticulture Department.

Brahmagiri block has a population of 71,502 (1971 census) and a total area of 312 kilometres. The low density (230) is misleading since most of the land is barely productive. There are sand beaches and lowlands; 20,000 hectares are cultivated, 19,000 of these being devoted to paddy. Low-lying lands account for 8,400 hectares, and the remaining parts are medium or high. Excess water or waterlogging affects 80 per cent of the area because there is no drainage.

A Less Isolated Area[8]

Pipli block is located on and around the main road connecting Bhubaneshwar and Puri. In the 1950s, when we first came to Puri, there was still very little traffic and the road was not asphalted. Today the main road, and others, have improved. The holy city attracts ever greater crowds of pilgrims who come by rail and bus. Thus the town of Puri has become a growing market and the villages on the roadside have benefited from this. There are also several small rice mills. One in Taizipur, for instance, was started ten years ago with equipment worth Rs 2,000, and Rs 700 a month for the maintenance and operation of the mill as well as the salaries of two workers. Here 2,000 kilograms of paddy can be husked in eight hours for a charge of Rs 1.50 per 100 kilograms of paddy.[9]

Agriculture in Pipli does not present such a dynamic picture. Of the 19,257 hectares of cultivated land, 16,590 are devoted to paddy.[10] Only 9,000 hectares are irrigated in the kharif and 5,600 in the rabi, mostly by canals. While the bulk of the paddy was grown during the monsoon, irrigation made it possible to grow 4,000 hectares of paddy and 2,044 hectares of vegetables in the dry season in 1977–8. Non-irrigated local paddy gives an average yield of 1,200 kilograms per hectare and irrigated paddy gives 1,750. High yield varieties, with small doses of chemical fertilizers and irrigation, make it possible to reach 2,500 kilograms per hectare in the rabi.[11] But, apart from isolated pockets of irrigated paddy, it is clear that agriculture has remained rather dormant for several decades, though the population has been rising. Pipli block had 83,646 inhabitants in 1971 with a density of 404. Small industries and repair workshops are hardly to be seen in the bigger villages. There is still very little machinery and equipment in the countryside.

In the 1950s, when the Hirakud dam was built on the river near Sambalpur, a large irrigation scheme was started in order to improve agriculture in the Mahanadi delta. Pipli block was reached by the first main canals and branches in 1967, but it was only in 1972–3 that full use of the water could be made because there had been delays in

[8] As in Brahmagiri, instead of concentrating on one village, we visited several of them at a distance of about thirty kilometres from Puri, off the main road.

[9] The owner, a former government clerk, extracts oil from rape seeds, coconuts and groundnuts as well.

[10] One third of it is low land and is particularly vulnerable to flooding.

[11] Such differences are common in India, monsoon paddy being more exposed to pests than paddy grown in the dry season.

the acquisition of the land necessary to construct distributaries. Even so, the system has not been working properly. According to the Irrigation Act of Orissa, field channels to bring water to the fields from the distributaries[12] were supposed to be built by the farmers concerned. This, as we have seen in Assam in a similar situation, was not done for various reasons; and because of this the farmers practise field to field irrigation which is less efficient. Finally the Orissa Government decided to take on the job so that some field channels could be completed in 1977. When we visited Pipli the beneficiaries had not had much time to enjoy access to the water because the canals had had to be closed in the dry season of 1978-9 in order to complete the canals being built downstream.

The other drawback here is that the flow of water decreases in the dry season so that the command area there is only 10 per cent of what it is during the monsoon. In certain cases where tubewells could have been installed, this has not been done. In addition there are drainage problems. Rains may fail or be delayed—which makes irrigation increasingly important—but they can also be very heavy. When the major canals were designed and constructed in the 1950s and 1960s, it was thought that there would be enough natural drainage through the old drainage canals, although, even in those days, waterlogging had already become a problem. No new drains were dug and the problem remains as serious as ever today. It is only now, after many delays, that a programme for drainage has started.

The data collected at the district level do not alter the picture gathered in our two blocks. The main paddy crop (*sarad*) covers 356,000 hectares. In 1976-7, because of the drought, the output was 255,000 kilograms of clean rice. The following year, thanks to an excellent monsoon, production jumped to 375,000. The winter paddy—*dalua*—covered 21,400 hectares in 1976-7 and 30,000 in 1977-8. Winter paddy is mostly irrigated and relies on HYV and some small doses of chemical fertilizers. Yields average 2,200 kilograms per hectare of paddy. The pre-monsoon crop (*biali*), which is sown in May and harvested in August or September, covers 17,000 hectares. In 1976-7 there was a particularly low yield of 700 kilograms per hectare; the next year it was 1,430. Often pulses follow paddy in winter as a cash crop; the 160,000 hectares sown with pulses yield 300-400 kilograms per hectare. The total net cultivated area

---

[12] From them there is one outlet for 40 hectares. As a rule 80 hectares require 1 kilometre of field channels, partly lined. The total cost is Rs 150 for 0.4 hectares.

covers 450,000 hectares, 670,000 hectares gross. Of these 12,000 are irrigated in the kharif and 50–60,000 in the rabi. The main sources of irrigation are the canals.

It is true that bad or inadequate water management plays a major role in this near stagnation of production but this is not the whole story. One wonders whether the farmers do all they can to improve their yields or whether they are simply not interested enough.

Paddy and Subsidiary Sources of Income

The same attractive landscape as in Brahmagiri block welcomed us in villages on both sides of the road thirty kilometres from Puri. In the midst of wide paddy fields, coconut trees, bamboo groves and banana trees were leaning over the houses. Here, Shikar Behara, a 45-year old Bhoi (scheduled caste) lived with his wife and two daughters, the only children still living. He owned no land and even their homestead belonged to the malik for whom Shikar worked as a permanent labourer. They did not own any cattle but looked after the calf and cow that belonged to the malik. In three years' time they would sell the calf and would be entitled to keep half the money— about Rs 300. Shikar got 2 kilograms of paddy a day all through the year, as well as one meal. His malik advanced him paddy when he needed it and also paid for Shikar when the latter had some eye trouble. His wife worked outside on a casual basis and earned Rs 3 a day. When Shikar harvested coconuts for his malik he was allowed to keep 4 nuts out of every 80. These he sold, making about Rs 10 a day. Shikar was fairly content. As a permanent labourer he had a sort of work security and he had been able to cure his eye. He owned two dhotis and one gamcha.

Arjun Behera, another Bhoi, was 60 years old. His wife was dead, his two daughters were married and his sons worked with him. He had no land and had worked as a permanent labourer, earning 4 kilograms of paddy per day for six months and Rs 60 for the rest of the year. Some years ago he stopped working and one of his sons took over. The son got Rs 300 per year provided he worked half the time for the malik. The rest of the time he worked as a casual labourer and earned about Rs 4 a day. The family raised about 10 to 15 chickens a year and sold them at Rs 5–6 each. They also made coir ropes and put together dried palm leaves for houses. The other son worked as a casual labourer; so did the two wives who earned Rs 3 a day per head without food. The whole family managed reasonably and their living conditions had improved somewhat because there were now four wage earners.

Kumar Behera, also a Bhoi, had spent some time in school. Young and alert, he lived with his wife, his little son and his old father. Kumar cultivated 0.4 hectares on a share-cropping basis and borrowed his malik's bullocks free of charge. He applied no chemical fertilizers on his low-lying plot which gave him only 300 kilograms per hectare of paddy out of which he kept half. In the rabi he got some pulses and he also grew potatoes and other vegetables. Last year he lost his rabi crop because of bad irrigation. In normal years he managed to get about Rs 500 from sales. He also raised chickens which brought him about 60 to 80 rupees a year. He worked every alternate day for his malik and got Rs 400 a year. The rest of the time he did some casual work and earned a little extra money.

Another hamlet that we visited, was a Dhobi settlement. Here Hari Sethi, 45 years old, married and with three sons and two daughters (three other children had died), was the owner of 0.4 hectares of land. He took on another 0.4 hectares on a share-cropping basis. Yields were equivalent to 750–1,000 kilograms per hectare of paddy. Apart from this, as washerman and working for forty households Hari received another 300 kilograms of paddy every year. He and his eldest son added to the family income by working as casual labourers. They worked 180 days in the year and earned Rs 4 each per day. Hari complained of rising prices and felt that his standard of living was falling for this reason. Yet he did not look miserable.

Jaya Rout, a Khandayat from another village, lived with his wife and two small children. He owned 0.54 hectares of land to which he added another 0.4 on a share-cropping basis. His fields were partly irrigated and, by using HYV seeds and small doses of chemical fertilizers, he managed to get the equivalent of 2,400 kilograms per hectare of paddy in the kharif. This was followed in the rabi by pulses and vegetables (brinjals, pumpkins, cucumbers) which he sold and which earned him another Rs 1,000–1,200. He managed to save 150 kilograms of paddy, after providing for his home, to sell. In addition there were thirty coconut trees around his house. These bore approximately 300 nuts which he sold for Rs 125. He also had some mango, jackfruit and papaya trees. Jaya Rout's case illustrates how irrigation can make a difference not only in economic but also in social terms. Since he was able to irrigate part of his fields his income had increased substantially, and he added to this by ploughing his land himself and by occasionally doing other work.

Rabindranath Patra, another Khandayat, had a similar story. He managed quite well with his 1.2 hectares of irrigated land on which he grew paddy (1,875 kilograms per hectare) and vegetables, and 0.8 hectares of unirrigated land on which he grew pulses. He also had a hundred coconut trees which brought him Rs 300–375 a year, as well as some banana trees from which he earned Rs 300. Rabindranath was young, quick-witted and hard working. He took no account of the taboos on ploughing. He did, however, worry about his four younger sisters whose marriages would prove expensive for him.[13]

Finally we came to a big Brahmin landowner, a lively 80-year old man who was afraid of possible land reforms and had split up his 16 hectares of land between his nine grandsons. Of his two sons, one worked in the Secretariat in Bhubaneshwar and lived with his father. The other worked as a clerk in Pipli and had his home there. HYV seeds of paddy were used on 2 hectares of irrigated land but they did not bring in good yields because they were used without chemical fertilizers. Coconut trees and fruit were grown on another 2 hectares which gave an income of Rs 3,000 a year. Twelve hectares remained unirrigated with a yield of 1,100–1,150 kilograms per hectare of paddy and, in the rabi, some plots were sown with pulses. Such mediocre yields did not seem to concern our Brahmin very much. Basically, his life remained comfortable and, being an influential man, he was not worried about the money required for the marriages of his daughters. If he needed any he could always borrow from the co-operative society.

Summing Up

Water management problems are delaying the beginnings of crop improvement in Pipli block. It will be a fairly long time before the network of irrigation canals (including the field channels) and the drainage system are completed and put into operation. However the block has been able to develop slightly because of the growth of Puri as a centre of pilgrimage. This has led to the growth of markets in Puri—for fruit, vegetables, chicken—and several earning opportunities such as transport, loading carts, etc. Because of this the poor are now clearly less poor than in the isolated hamlets of Brahmagiri.

[13]Among other things Rabindranath's in-laws had given him a bicycle worth Rs 350 and he still expected a radio set. Needless to say, most of the cost of a marriage is borne by the girl's family.

Wages here are a little higher—usually Rs 4 a day as compared with Rs 3.50, and there are various subsidiary activities of a non-agricultural nature. Yet we must also consider wages and food prices, indicated in the wage chart below:

Wage Chart for 1954–78[14]

Year	Daily wages	Price of 1 kilogram of paddy
1954–5	Re 0.85–1.00	Re 0.18
1965	Rs 1.75–2.00	Re 0.40
1978	Rs 3.50–4.00	Rs 1.16

Clearly the wage trend seems to be declining although it has been somewhat compensated for by the activities we have looked at above. In spite of the fact that the poor have not become poorer, their standard of living has not risen much and the whole area still lacks the impulse to move more dynamically.

[14]*Gazetteer of India*, Puri (Bhubaneshwar, 1976), and field observations for 1978.

CHAPTER 8

Back to More Dynamic Areas

From the poorer areas as in Bihar and Orissa, we now move to Thanjavur and Guntur districts, two more dynamic districts in the deltas of the Cauvery and the Krishna. We first surveyed Thanjavur in 1964 and then in 1978. Guntur district was first looked at in 1967 and then in 1978.

Thanjavur (Tanjore), for many centuries one of the cradles of Hindu civilization, was known for its political power, its economic activity, its arts and letters. The oldest irrigation works built in the Cauvery delta around Thanjavur go as far back as the first century A.D. These were later considerably improved by the Chola kings. During British rule Thanjavur went through a period of agricultural expansion when irrigation was improved, roads developed and an efficient system of administration set up.[1] Some signs of this early prosperity still remain today. At the beginning of this century, of the 619,000 hectares cultivated, 380,000 were irrigated mainly by government canals. Paddy covered 77 per cent of the cropped land and Thanjavur had, as today, a surplus of rice.[2] However, such prosperity was found primarily in the well-known Brahmin villages of the old delta. The new delta has different caste patterns and social relations and it was for this reason that I chose to work on it.

Unlike the old delta, the western part, being outside the command area of the canal system, remained unirrigated for centuries. It was thus unable to support a large population and many of the inhabitants emigrated. According to the last land revenue settlement (1924) the village of Kila Ulur had a total area of 558 hectares, of which 141 were *inam* land which belonged to a temple and were distinct from the other fields; 370 cultivated hectares belonged to the farmers. In those

---

[1] The level and impact of British administration were far from even and the results of the differences can still be felt today.

[2] *The Imperial Gazetteer, Tanjore District* (Oxford, 1908).

days there were only 103 hectares of paddy, 160 of groundnuts and about 100 hectares sown with the low-grade millet common to the south (*cholam, cumbu, ragi*) and cultivated during the monsoon. This picture began to change after the completion of the Cauvery Mettur Project (C.M.P.) in 1935 and the construction of canals in the new delta. In 1964, the data for Kila Ulur, without the temple land, were as follows:

Area irrigated by the C.M.P.	232.4 hectares
Area irrigated by private temporary wells	83.8 hectares
Unirrigated area	36.2 hectares
Homesteads, tanks and casurina woods	3.5 hectares

Paddy fields—300 hectares—had practically eliminated millet. Groundnut, ragi and small coconut plantations had about 4 hectares each. When turning to paddy, farmers adopted crop patterns that are typical of Tamil Nadu—two crops of short duration (105 days) following each other on the same plot, *kuruvai*, from the end of June to September, and *thaladi*, from the end of October to February.[3] The third crop, *samba,* covered three-quarters of the paddy land and lasted 180 days from August to January.

Towards the end of February the C.M.P. sluices would be closed for lack of water in the reservoir and would remain closed until the next monsoon. However, with local or improved seeds (not the HYV) and very small doses of chemical fertilizers, average yields in the early 1960s amounted to 2,000 kilograms per hectare of paddy (1,350 kilograms of clean rice). Some farmers even managed to get 2,700 kilograms per hectare of paddy and a few large landowners sometimes secured 4,000 kilograms per hectare. Figures for the whole district were as follows:

Kuruvai	1,700 kilograms per hectare of rice
Samba	1,640 kilograms per hectare of rice
Thaladi	1,375 kilograms per hectare of rice

Similarly, once the canals were closed ragi and groundnut were intensively cultivated on small plots of land irrigated by temporary

---

[3] This calendar is connected with the rainfall pattern. September is a month of transition between the south-west monsoon (July-August) and the north-east monsoon in October and November. See J. Racine's *Deux Etudes Rurales en Pays Tamoul* (Bordeaux, 1976), p. 18. As the author emphasizes, this distinction is questionable because there is, in fact, a substantial irregularity in rainfall.

wells, and these plots yielded roughly 400 kilograms per hectare of ragi[4] and 575 of shelled groundnuts.

Although these past achievements seem brighter and better than those in eastern India, there were shortcomings which were fairly striking. The maintenance and operation of the canals by the Public Works Department (which was responsible for irrigation) were open to criticism. The canals were not lined and water losses by percolation were heavy. In addition, they were not properly desilted. There was also the fact—one, however, that could not be helped—that the canals were not perennial and land was unused from February to late June except the small patches irrigated by temporary wells.

The village of Kila Ulur lies some distance away from the district road coming from Thanjavur to Orathanad. It is surrounded by paddy fields, coconut trees and bamboos. When we visited it the only way of getting to the village was to walk a distance of one and a half kilometres, or to make a detour around the road and take a very bad, non-metalled road which led to Kila Ulur. In the village there were a few tiny shops and tea stalls as well as some handicraft shops. The people sold paddy, coconuts, and fish which they managed to catch in the hot season just as the tanks were going dry. Electricity was just reaching the village. The population in Kila Ulur increased very slowly between 1901 and 1951 (from 1,310 inhabitants to 1,444). By the 1961 census there was a moderate acceleration of 9 per cent above 1951 which brought the number up to 1,574 and the density to 352 (*inam* land and casurina not included).[5] The complexity of land records in Madras and the fact that they are not up to date made it difficult for me to make a precise analysis. According to information gathered in the village, the break-up of holdings was as follows:

Less than 0.4 hectares	70 holdings
0.4 to 2 hectares	100 holdings
2 to 4 hectares	35 holdings
4 to 6 hectares	15 holdings
Total	220 holdings

[4] Yields of ragi, when not irrigated, could not have been much above 400 kilograms per hectare.

[5] The average decennial rate for the state is + 11.8 per cent. The reasons for this low rate, as compared with most states, are not clear. It cannot be due to immigration alone.

There was little share-cropping as most farmers were owner-cultivators.[6] Interestingly, Kila Ulur had no high castes, the dominant one, the Kallars, belonging to the Shudra category. The Kallars were followed by the Ambalakarars, a caste that is somewhat inferior in social and economic status. The bulk of the Harijans, often landless, were Paraiyars.[7] The Panchayat of Kila Ulur was more active than the ones we had seen so far. Under the chairmanship of a Kallar it had improved some access roads, sunk two drinking water wells, constructed a library and a new school hall and planted a hundred coconut trees on common land.

What was the standard of living in the village like? The Paraiyars lived in a separate hamlet some distance away from the Kallars. Their houses were poor but the poverty did not seem acute. They were better off than the Chamars in Nilkanth or Kalpi, and their daily wages were somewhat higher. The women kept quite busy in the fields, transplanting, weeding and harvesting paddy. For this they were paid Re 1 a day. In the slack season people made mats from fibre that they dyed and wove. By doing this a family could earn Rs 50-100 a year. In the month of May the Paraiyars remained busy catching fish from the emptying tanks, for which they were paid Rs 1.50 a day plus some fish. Some people also worked on road repair and the construction of canals.

When asked about their life, several Paraiyars said that though their material conditions had scarcely improved in the last fifteen years their social status had risen. Caste barriers had, of course, not disappeared. For example the Kallars did not eat with the Harijans and there was no intermarriage between the two. But some of the worst abuses had been done away with. The Harijans were allowed to bathe and wash in the Kallars' tank and the Kallar temple was now open to all. They had also been given some land to cultivate and whereas in the past they were not allowed to stop in the Kallars' hamlet and had to go barefoot through it, they now had access even to the tea shop there. There had also been some progress in the field of education. Several Paraiyar children were now attending school, and a young girl had even gone to high school.

Small farmers, with below one hectare of land, managed fairly well because of the relatively good yields. Swaminathan Malusuthi, a 50 year old Kallar, lived with his wife and two children, 20 and 17 years

[6] There is more share-cropping and other types of tenancy in the old delta where Brahmins own land but do not do manual work.

[7] The term pariah comes from this word.

old respectively. Half of their 0.8 hectares was double croped and the other half was devoted to samba. They had a surplus of 560 kilograms of paddy a year for sales. They also sold eggs from their chickens and the wife earned some money by working as a labourer. Swaminathan had learnt, through the co-operative society, to apply ammonium sulphate to his crops. Several other Kallars owned only 0.2–0.4 hectares of land and were compelled to seek work along with their wives. They augmented the family income by selling coconuts from their trees, selling chickens and fishing. Their standard of living was not high but again they seemed to be able to manage by eating rice and some ragi, fish or meat once a month.

Pichaya Thewar was one of the big Kallar landowners. He owned 4 hectares of irrigated land, 1.2 hectares of which were double-cropped and 2.8 of which were in samba. He also owned 0.12 hectares of coconut, banana and mango trees. In addition he had bullocks, cows and chickens. Pichaya's standard of living was rising and like other Kallars, he was working with his own hands, using outside labour only when necessary. He produced 11,000 kilograms of paddy of which 6,700 were sold. Thus this area was well on the road towards further growth and this trend was not confined to only a few large farmers. The landless here were no doubt poor, but their conditions were more acceptable than what we had seen so far.

Another Case in Guntur District

'The Circar (Guntur district) instead of having improved during the long period it has been subject to the peaceful sway of the British government is actually in a worse state now than it was when it was ceded by the Nizam upwards of fifty years ago', wrote the Commissioner in 1845 when he was sent from Madras to investigate conditions in Guntur district. There were several factors which explained this state of affairs. As the Commissioner put it, 'The canals of the Cholas had long been choked or forgotten in the delta of the Krishna'. The good alluvial soils were poorly cultivated, and irrigation was confined to a few wells and tanks. Paddy occupied only a small area and millet and pulses of low yields were dominant. Under the impact of natural calamities such as cyclones or drought, things became worse. In the 1833 famine, for example, more than half the population was wiped out. The administration, too, was in a fairly miserable condition.[8]

[8] See R. E. Frykenberg's fine analysis in *Guntur District 1788–1848* (Oxford, 1965), pp. 2–8.

By the middle of the nineteenth century the situation had begun to change. The government introduced drastic administrative reforms in order to increase efficiency, and weeded out corruption and other malpractices. In an attempt to resume the great Chola tradition of canal irrigation, Sir Arthur Cotton built the Anikut barrage at the head of the Krishna delta and criss-crossed the land with canals.[9] Between 1860-70 the resumption of irrigation in the delta enabled paddy to entirely replace millet. Nurseries were started towards the end of June so that transplanting could take place by the end of July and the crop be harvested in the third week of November. Tobacco was introduced in the fringes of the delta and this brought in a fair amount of money to the villages, which in turn led to labour expansion through the construction of several factories. Guntur was also connected to various villages and towns by a wide network of roads. This classical process of growth was helped by the presence of several excellent agricultural castes—the Kammas, Reddis, Kapus—who can be likened to the Jats in their spirit of enterprise and their hard work.

As we left Guntur and moved towards the sea, we crossed, after a few kilometres, the Buckingham canal, a wide waterway from where the irrigation canals begin. A short distance away, not far from the road, lay the settlements of Manchala village. Manchala had a population of 1,462 in 1961; the total area of the village was 313.2 hectares, of which 266 were cultivated. The Kapus were the dominant caste, there were twenty Brahmin families and the bulk of the landless labourers belonged to the Yanadis, a scheduled tribe. The two biggest landowners each had 12 hectares of land. Next in line were 9 holdings of 4-8 hectares, 23 of 1.6 hectares, and 140 others with less than 1.6 hectares. Water was released at the end of June and by January the canals were closed for lack of water. The practice in Manchala was to grow only one paddy crop during the monsoon. In the dry season farmers sowed pulses which yielded a few quintals per hectare. They also grew sunn hemp.

In the last ten to fifteen years there have been several changes. Paddy seeds (not to be confused with HYV) have improved and moderate doses of chemical fertilizers have been introduced along with some pesticides so that yields have increased by about 50 per cent to 2,800-3,500 kilograms of paddy per hectare (two-thirds in

[9] Sir Arthur did the same work in the Godavari delta. He also improved the Cauvery system in Thanjavur.

terms of clean rice). In 1967 we found that the village had acquired a few small shops. Many poor people seemed to be managing because of secondary activities[10] in addition to their work in the paddy fields. The Yanadis were particularly clever and their women worked in the fields like the men.

In the summer of 1967 we went directly from Guntur to Muzaffarpur. The contrast between paddy transplantation in both areas was remarkable. In Manchala the paddy fields were well tended, properly levelled, well irrigated. We saw teams of strong and lively Yanadis pulling the shoots from the nurseries, women transplanting in lines of fifteen or twenty, wearing bright, gay colours and singing. In Kalpi the picture was different—badly levelled fields, inadequate water management, poor Chamars at work and no women in the fields. In Manchala paddy yields were two or three times higher than in Kalpi and the wages paid to workers amounted to Rs 3.00, sometimes 4.00, compared with Rs 1.50 in Kalpi. Going through the paddy fields, interviewing Yanadis in their hamlets, I did not come across any case of what could be called abject poverty. Touring the west and east Godavari districts a year before me, Daniel Thorner had come to similar conclusions: 'There even the families of agricultural labourers, who were utterly landless, earned enough to eat three rice meals per day, supplemented by vegetables, spices, chillies and occasionally dried fish and tea.' Referring to the houses of labourers, Thorner added, 'They were worlds apart from the wretched shanties I had entered in north Bihar.'[11] Under such overall conditions it does not seem strange that small farmers were doing fairly well.

Venkataswarulu, a Kapu, 35 years old, lived with his wife and his five children. With 0.6 hectares of land he had enough paddy to feed his family and was even able to sell a few quintals. At the end of the dry season he earned Rs 150–300 from the sales of pulses. Venkataswarulu had a pair of bullocks and two buffaloes who yielded two litres of milk each per day. In addition to using his bullocks for ploughing his own fields he would rent them out and earn some more money. He made sure that he kept his family and himself well-fed and clothed.

[10]One of the men collected hair which he made up into chignons to sell in towns. Others caught rats or fish. We will come back to these subsidiary activities in the next chapter.
[11]D. Thorner, 'Coastal Andhra: Towards an Affluent Society', *Economic and Political Weekly* (annual number, February 1967).

His neighbours, five brothers and their families, had 0.4 hectares of land each. They had to work extra in order to get enough rice to feed themselves. Some of the extra money they earned was used to buy fertilizer for their crop. They worked hard and looked after their crop—they even rented a sprayer from the Panchayat for their rice—and managed to increase their yields from the equivalent of 2,250–2,500 kilograms per hectare of paddy to 3,750. In the dry season they would cultivate and sell pulses.

The medium and upper farmers had similar stories to tell, the only difference being that several of them were fairly well off. The Brahmin landowners were also increasing their yields by carefully supervising their permanent and casual labourers. Ramakrishna, one of the largest landowners, had seen his fields increase from 2,500 kilograms per hectare in 1952 to 3,750 fifteen years later, in 1967. Each of his permanent labourers was getting Rs 150 a year with 500 kilograms of rice and some clothes.

Similar trends were observed in many other villages in the delta. They show the different phases which the area has gone through in one century. Until the early 1950s there was an expansion within the traditional framework of techniques combined with increasing sales of paddy. Then Manchala entered a second phase with the appearance, in a limited way, of new inputs—fertilizers, pesticides, improved seeds. All these boosted yields further and also made for a diversification of the economy and brought in more subsidiary activities.

CHAPTER 9

The Next Steps

As we visited these villages and districts again we found that there were signs of change all along. New inputs seemed to become more common as we proceeded. However, this did not imply any drastic change in techniques and patterns of work. Wages improved in real terms and the economy began to diversify more and more into subsidiary activities. In Kila Ulur new seeds of paddy appeared in 1964. The first to appear was a semi-dwarf variety (ADT 27)[1] bred in India. This was followed by others, also from India (ADT 31) and the Philippines (IR 20), and some of them were cross-bred. Although the three crop patterns did not change substantially, yields rose because of the new seeds and because there was more pest control[2] as well as greater usage of chemical fertilizers. Techniques such as ploughing, transplanting, weeding and harvesting remained the same. Average yields of paddy in kilograms per hectare in Kila Ulur, over an approximately ten-year period, are shown in the chart below.

	Year (mid-1960s)	Year (late 1970s)
Kuruvai	2,400	3,600
Thaladi	1,850	2,770
Samba	2,240	3,360

As far as other crops are concerned it is possible that the groundnut yield may have increased marginally. Black and red gram (pulses) sown after paddy remained at the same level of a few quintals per hectare.

Other changes were also visible in Kila Ulur. Four farmers installed a 5HP pumpset each to supplement canal irrigation, and although no

---

[1] ADT 27, a semi-dwarf variety, was used for double crops: 80 hectares in the district on an experimental basis in 1964, 80,000 hectares in 1966.

[2] A number of farmers, even small ones, would spray their fields twice against stem borers and leaf rollers.

one owned a tractor, it was possible to hire one from outside the village. The number of shops in the village increased as did the sales of milk, which was bought in by a co-operative located in the neighbourhood. In order to help the farmers who had cows, a cattle shed where they could milk their cows had been constructed close to the newly built road which the milk truck took.

In order to assess the impact of the growth process on incomes and life-styles we looked at the various castes, their living patterns and economic conditions. We began with the Pariayars, who lived in neat and well maintained huts.[3] Kolandyan, one of them, had two wives because his first one could not bear children. His second wife had three children—a boy and two girls, one of whom was already married. The family had no land. Kolandyan worked three months a year repairing bunds and doing land levelling; he spent three months in paddy cultivation and the rest of the time he was busy with groundnut cultivation. For all this work he earned roughly Rs 5 plus one meal a day and, at harvest time, 7.2 kilograms of paddy a day. In the last three months of the year he would make mats, earning Rs 3 per piece. Kolandyan's second wife also earned a few rupees a day for transplanting and other small jobs. The family had a cow which gave one litre of milk a day and this was used for the children; there were also some chickens which permitted the family to eat eggs. In addition there were three coconut trees near the house; each bore a hundred nuts a year which were sold at Re 1 each. Neither Kolandyan nor his wife complained about their lot. Although they did not own bicycles or watches they managed to make do, each owning a few sets of clothes.

Chinaya, also a Paraiyar, had been married nine years but had no children. He owned 0.12 hectares which he mortgaged for a thousand rupees when he needed money. Chinaya spent most of his time doing coolie work; in addition he earned Rs 3 plus two meals every half day for ploughing and Rs 5 per day for pulling shoots. His life had certainly improved. Wages for pulling shoots had trebled and for harvesting he received 7.2 kilograms of paddy as compared with 4.8 ten or fifteen years ago. According to him he now lived 'in a civilized manner'.

Another Paraiyar of the same name lived with his wife, his two sons (aged twenty-two and seventeen respectively) and his daughter. One of the boys had been to school. Chinaya owned 0.4 hectares of land,

[3]Their homesteads were built on land which had been given to them by the government long ago.

half of it in kuruvai and thaladi, the other half in samba. The family produced enough paddy for their own needs and even managed to sell some quintals. They also had a pair of bullocks. The SFDA gave them a loan to buy a buffalo which yielded five litres of milk a day, two of these being sold at Rs 1.50 per litre to the milk society at Mela Ulur a few kilometres away. From his four coconut trees Chinaya sold fifty nuts and ate the others. In addition to this the father and sons also worked as labourers, transplanting and harvesting paddy. The family's earnings enabled them to buy chemical fertilizers and seeds which boosted their yields. Consequently they were better off than they had been before, when we met them.

Purulai, a Paraiyar, was the same age as Chinaya. His eldest son worked with him. Another son, who was educated up to high school, was a truck driver and was about to leave for Kuwait. The youngest boy and the girl were at home. The father owned 0.8 hectares, half of it double cropped, half in samba. The double cropped fields yielded the equivalent of 4,000 kilograms per hectare while samba gave only 2,150 kilograms per hectare because the soils were rather alkaline. Purulai's family had to hire bullocks for ploughing. Purulai himself was ageing and did not work much—most of the work was handled by his sons. The family was living better now than it had done fifteen years ago. Some of this was due to the fact that the father had taken certain risks. He borrowed Rs 20,000 in order to educate his truck driver son (and it is expected that the son's savings from Kuwait will come back to the family), and he took another loan of Rs 3,000 from the Land Development Bank to build a house.[4]

We spent several hours on different days in the Paraiyar quarters, talking to them. On the whole they seemed to be a lively, cheerful set of people. Although they were still poor their conditions had improved. Male wages had ranged between Re 1 and Rs 2 plus some food. Now they often come up to Rs 5 with one meal. This means an increase in real terms. At harvesting time, they usually receive 6 measures of paddy now instead of 4 (without food) per day (one measure is equal to 1.2 kilograms). In 1964 farmers were selling one bag of paddy (one bag equalled 57 kilograms) for a price ranging from Rs 20 to Rs 26. In 1978, off-season prices in June to August would be around Rs 60-65 and at harvest time Rs 50.

Apart for the Paraiyars there are also many Kallars and

[4]This is a typical example of how loans which should have been given only for productive purposes have been used differently.

Amballakarars who have very little land. Kalyamurti was one such who had to maintain his family on 0.6 hectares of land, one third of which was doubled cropped and 0.4 hectares in samba. On the samba land he also grew groundnuts. Natarajan, who was 42 years old, had 0.36 hectares. He lived with his wife and his only son; three of his children had died in the seventeen years of his married life. All his paddy was double cropped with HYV, fertilizers and pesticide sprays. He managed to get 4,200 kilograms of paddy altogether. He had a pair of bullocks and did not need to do any extra work since he sold his entire first crop for Rs 1,350. His son, on the other hand, did some work in order to supplement the family income.

Tholappa Thevar was already increasing his crops and income when I met him in 1964. In those days he had 1.6 hectares of irrigated land which gave him good yields. In 1974 he bought 0.4 hectares from two very small farmers. He now had three instead of two pairs of bullocks, one being used to pull his cart. His yields of paddy continued to increase and he harvested a total of 6,200 kilograms out of which 2,800 were sold, the balance being consumed or used to pay harvesters. When the canals were closed Tholappa dug three temporary wells to irrigate 1.2 hectares of groundnuts sown at the end of December, after samba, and harvested at the end of April. He sold most of it for Rs 4,000.

Large Kallar landowners had not been slow in increasing their crops. Thus Thirugnanam was, with 6 hectares, one of the richest men. He harvested over 4,000 kilograms per hectare in kuruvai, 2,850 in thaladi and 3,800–4,300 in samba. He had another 2.4 hectares devoted to groundnuts. Nadesan, a Kallar, was no less clever. He inherited one hectare from his father. He managed to go to school for two years. When his first wife died, he married again and he now has four children. He became a specialist in spraying twenty years ago and bought a hand sprayer for Rs 1,090. When we met him in 1978, for half the year he was spending twenty days a month spraying and making a fair amount of money. However, he only worked 4–5 hours a day because there is a health hazard in spraying; in addition he repaired cycles and earned a few extra rupees. Nadesan lived quite well but did not fit into the classical Weberian ideal. He was a jolly fellow. At the end of our discussion he admitted he was obliged to sell his land because when prohibition was abolished[5] some years ago, he began gambling and drinking.

[5] It has been re-introduced since.

Growth Trends in Thanjavur District[6]

There has been a fair amount of growth in Thanjavur. Paddy remains the dominant crop, covering 600,000 hectares (gross) out of the 650,000 devoted to food crops including maize, millet and pulses. Then there are 4,000 hectares of sugarcane and the same area of vegetables and fruit. Under the impact of new seeds the area devoted to samba has fallen (from 360,000 hectares to 320,000) while kuruvai and thaladi have expanded by 50,000 to 100,000 hectares. In spite of irrigation the district remains vulnerable to drought as was the case in 1976–7 when, because of poor rains, the canals did not supply enough water. The next year the district was hit by a devastating cyclone. For each of these two years the combined average yield for the three crops fell to 2,600 kilograms per hectare. If we compare two good years we get the following data:

Paddy Yields (in Kilograms per hectare)	1964-5	1975-6
Kuruvai	2,640	3,640
Thaladi	2,260	2,715
Samba	2,700	3,040
Combined	2,645	3,225

Practically all paddy yields are covered with new seeds. While growth has been substantial it is less spectacular than what we have seen for wheat in the north-west. This is mainly because of the constraints it has to face. Irrigation, for example, poses one of the major problems. Unlike the Ganges and other northern rivers, which are fed both by melting snow and rains, rivers in the Deccan rely only on the second source, namely rain, which is not always reliable. Thus it is necessary to complement existing irrigation facilities by bringing in groundwater sources as well. In the early 1960s a programme to do this was started under the initiative of the Collector. In 1964–5, 248 filter points and 57 borewells were installed. A little over ten years later, in 1976, this number had gone up to 18,800. More than two-thirds of these wells and points have been constructed in the old delta where soils are less porous than in the new delta and water has to be lifted from a lower depth.[7] With roughly 60 to 70,000 tubewells it should be

[6]The data given here come from IADP, Thanjavur, *Progress Report* (1978).

[7]Filter points or shallow tubewells, usually 5 HP irrigating 2 hectares; borewells, deeper tubewells 7–10 HP, irrigating 3–8 hectares. The power supply here is much better than in the north. This is due, among other factors, to better administration. Investment cost in the old delta was Rs 6,000 to Rs 10,000, the yearly operation cost was Rs 375 to Rs 500 per hectare for electric tubewells and Rs 600 to Rs 1,250 for diesel.

possible to irrigate at least 140,000 hectares.[8] Such an expansion should not only favour paddy but should also enable farmers to raise a second or third crop during the closure of the canals, or to raise richer crops than unirrigated pulses. However, there is one slight drawback in this. Such tubewells are less of a benefit here than in the villages of the Bulandshahr district because the main supply of water still comes at a very cheap rate. Thus, medium farmers particularly, may face a cost benefit ratio that is less attractive, though certainly interesting, than in areas where tubewells are replacing wells with bullocks or are introduced in rain-fed areas.

Drainage measures are still badly needed in the lower part of the Thanjavur delta to help prevent floods and fight salinity. The maintenance of canals also requires improvement; some need to be reconstructed and others lined to reduce seepage. While the coverage under seeds is very large there is still room for improvement. Most seeds being used at the moment are gradually being replaced. Consumption of chemical fertilizers has increased from 17,050 tons (in terms of nutrients) in 1964–5, to 68,045 tons in 1977–8. In addition the balance between fertilizers is much better here than in many areas where phosphate applications are too low compared to nitrogen. Over the years the use per hectare of nitrogen has reached 66 to 85 kilograms and the use of phosphoric acid 25 kilograms, as opposed to 11.3 and 9.8 in 1964–5. It seems to me that there is some imbalance between the increase of paddy yields which should have risen more and the increase in fertilizer use. This could be due to water management, insufficient pest control or seed defects. Plant protection has become quite popular.

The consolidation of land holdings here will be a much more complex process than in the wheat and sugarcane areas because the fields are criss-crossed with canals and tributaries so that a whole realignment of canals will be necessary.

The expansion of crops in the dry season does not depend only on irrigation but on other complex factors. Immediately after the last harvest in January and February, the soils of the old delta are too sticky to be ploughed and it becomes necessary to wait for twenty-five days, a delay which has been cut down to ten days in the new delta where soils are lighter. Green and black gram have been cultivated for centuries. Now, better varieties (of 65 days' duration) are being

[8] Within twenty kilometres from the coast the ground water is saline. About 10 per cent of the cropped land is affected by salinity.

released. They need two light ploughings, small doses of chemical fertilizers and pest control, and can yield 1,000 kilograms per hectare, about double or three times the yield of traditional pulses. Cotton can also be introduced on 60,000 hectares of the old delta; this could lead to ginning and textile factories. The cultivation of vegetables during the monsoon is hindered by too much water. There are roughly 3,000 tractor units (usually 36 HP) in the district and only 100 power tillers because these are rather expensive.

So far, small industries have not expanded as much as they have done in western U.P. or in Punjab and Haryana, although they are certainly more advanced than in Bihar and Orissa. There is, however, hope for development because of the high level of rural electrification.[9] Other activities, such as the cultivation of mulberry trees for silk, are also beginning. The Collector, who, in Tamil Nadu, plays a much more direct role in developmental activities than in northern India, has started prawn breeding schemes in river estuaries and through artificial ponds of sea water as is being done in Kerala. They can catch 1,000 kilograms per hectare which are sold for export at a price of U.S. $ 6.50–7 per kilogram.

The cost benefit ratio of paddy cultivation has been falling in recent years. At the time of our visit the selling price of paddy was around Rs 75 per quintal which was Rs 10 below the procurement price for coarse varieties,[10] a situation which may have changed at the end of 1979. At an all-India level the production of paddy had decreased due to drought in several states and the procurement price had been raised to Rs 95.

It is important here to mention one last significant growth factor. The general level of district administration in Tamil Nadu is high in comparison with the northern states. In addition, Thanjavur being one of the main surplus districts and also a difficult area because of social tensions, Collectors are always selected with particular care. In 1964, as in 1978, I was struck by the competence and efficiency of the district head. Thanjavur was also one of the first districts under the Integrated Rural Development Programme (IRDP) in 1961. It has had good agricultural district officers and a better overall staff pattern than in many other districts.

[9] Most villages of Tamil Nadu are now electrified.

[10] At the end of 1978, a conference of several political parties, including the CPI and the Indira Congress, threatened to abandon kuruvai cultivation and to stop applying chemical fertilizers if the procurement price was not raised. *Sunday Standard,* 31 March 1979.

Has the Green Revolution Turned Red?

Thanjavur is quoted as a case of the green revolution turning red. From 1967 to 1969 there were violent clashes between landowners and labourers, or among the labourers themselves when local people, who refused to work unless their wages were increased, prevented workers from other districts from coming to work in Thanjavur. The worst fights occurred in the village of Kilvenmani where 43 Harijans, mostly old people, women and children, were burnt alive.

The question, in fact, is not simply one of the green revolution turning red. It is a much more complex one. First of all a distinction must be made between the new delta which received irrigation late and where population densities are lighter and the number of landless labourers fewer, and the old delta. In the old delta many landowners are Brahmins who do not till the land themselves.[11] This does not mean that there have been no conflicts and tensions in the new delta; relations between the Kallars and Paraiyars are not always smooth. Apart from this, the old delta has known, since 1943, an active communist party, well rooted in village life—a rare phenomenon in India—so that the labourers here are better organized than elsewhere. This has had an impact on the increase in wages through successive agreements between landowners' organizations and labour unions led by the communist party, some of them as early as the 1940s, others in the late 1960s and the early 1970s. These agreements have also led, in the last few years, to group labour contracts through collective bargaining. They enable labourers to get better wages in kind for harvesting and threshing. Teams of labourers charge around one-sixth of the paddy collected or threshed daily. Although they were not the main or sole cause of the conflict, the new seeds also had an impact on social tensions.[12]

In Guntur District

After seeing the Krishna delta during the paddy transplanting season we went back there at harvest time at the end of November 1978. We found again the same atmosphere of activity all round. 'Yes, things

[11] This does not mean that there has been no conflict in the new delta (where relations between Kallars and Paraiyars are not always smooth).

[12] See the excellent analysis by A. Beteille and his criticism of Francine Frankel's book in his *Studies in Agrarian Social Structure* (New Delhi, 1974), Chapter 9, and K. C. Alexander, *Agrarian Tension in Thanjavur* (Hyderabad, 1975) and, more recently, C. Arpathuraj, S. S. Vallinayagani, S. Kesavan Nair, *Levels of Hiring Agricultural Labour* (Madras, 1978).

have improved since you came first', said one Kapu landowner, 'but we still face various problems. And besides, last year we were badly hit by a cyclone.' Paddy yields had increased from 2,800–3,500 kilograms in 1967 to 3,750– 4,125 kilograms—a growth which, though not negligible, could have been higher. Several tracts of land were not suited to HYV because they were too alkaline or lacked adequate drainage.[13] In the past canals were closed from the end of January to the end of June or early July, thus preventing a second paddy crop. In certain years now it has been possible to release water all year round because of the Nagarjunasagar dam and its canals. Farmers have taken advantage of this but it has still not been simple to grow a second crop because paddy is transplanted at the end of January and harvested by the end of April or the beginning of May, the hottest time of the year, which is not very convenient because at this time the crop is susceptible to certain diseases. I asked the farmers if it would have been possible for them to alter the crop calendar and adopt the Thanjavur pattern or to have two paddy crops as in the Godavari delta with the first harvest in early November instead of towards the end of the month. They replied negatively because the rainfall schedule was not the same as in Thanjavur. Moreover, to have two crops as in the Godavari would have been too risky because of the heavy rains and cyclones which could have occurred in late October and early November.[14]

The first important requirement here was not to increase crop yields but to improve the network of old canals. Floods were not only caused by the lack of drainage but also by the poor maintenance of canals, particularly breaches in the dykes and bunds. Then, farmers upstream tended to take too much water at the cost of those downstream. A good drainage programme would improve yields in the low-lying areas. Villagers complained that they had been paying a

[13] While the improved variety, Akkulu, can resist temporary submersion, this is not the case with dwarf HYV. Things get worse in years of severe floods as in 1977 when many fields did not yield more than 2,000 kilograms per hectare. Another improved variety, Mashuri, requires 100 kilograms per hectare of nitrogen fertilizer, 75 of phosphate and the same of potash (in terms of nutrients). It yields an average of 3,750 to 4,125 kilograms per hectare, which is not particularly high, but typical of good non-HYV. A new HYV, MTU 4407 (dwarf variety, 140 days) was first released in 1977. This can yield up to 5,600 kilograms per hectare of kharif as well as rabi.

[14] In the Godavari delta, water is released earlier and the rains are much less heavy by the end of October and early November. This means that harvesting can be done at this time without too much risk. Then rabi paddy can start earlier. This explains the greater progress of rabi here.

drainage tax of Rs 15 per 0.4 hectares for the past ten years but nothing had been done so far. The authorities replied that they undertook works by turn. One had the impression that very little, if anything, had been done in the past ten to fifteen years to improve the canal systems and to eliminate shortcomings and defects. Although there were shallow tubewells and filter points in other villages, in Manchala there had been none so far. It seems that ground water was often brackish so that even wells for drinking water were scarce. There were only four drinking water wells and no hand pumps. When canals were closed in winter, farmers grew pulses, mostly black gram, some without ploughing the land after the harvest of paddy. Yields have not changed—in good years they get 500 kilograms per hectare, in mediocre ones 300. Most of it was sold at the fairly high price of Rs 250–300 per quintal, depending on the season. Some people also grew sunn hemp.

While the basic crop pattern has not changed in Manchala, the same cannot be said of all villages. Around Chebrol, a small town the vegetable belt is expanding—chillies, for instance, give a net return of Rs 4,400 for 0.4 hectares. A number of farmers have sold their bullocks because they find it more economical to use tractors. There are two in the village and, if necessary, villagers rent one from outside.[15] Puddling is also done with cages attached to the wheels. Petty trade and transportation are increasing. A man carries fifty kilograms on his bicycle (sometimes as much as a hundred) to Chebrol, three kilometres away, for Rs 5, and to Guntur, eleven kilometres away, for Rs 10. Until recently, farmers used to hull their paddy by hand at home or have it done in rice mills located in small towns. In 1974 a Kapu from another village built a rice mill, the only one within a radius of 1.5 kilometres, with an investment of Rs 60,000. It can mill 500 kilograms of paddy in an hour at Rs 3 per bag of 75 kilograms of paddy. The owner employs one mechanic and three coolies, the latter being paid Rs 100 or 200 a month depending on the amount of work they have to do. They also receive some rice as tips. The mill operates the whole year round.

Population growth has been very slow. Official records show a 7 per cent increase in the decade 1961-71 (i.e. 1,559 people). This is due, to a great extent, to migrations from the village to the cities, particularly among the Brahmins. Family planning seems to have made a

[15] Two ploughings for Rs 35/0.4 can be done in two or three hours. They pay Rs 20 per day for ploughing with bullocks (0.3 hectares in a day).

commendable impact. In the last few years as many as a hundred women have been sterilized. The primary health centre, which covers several villages, sends mixed teams for propaganda and the women's response is particularly good.

It was not possible to scrutinize land records which did not seem to be particularly up to date. Statements by local officers were also confusing. The land records mentioned 454 holdings, another source 360. And several of these holdings belonged to people living in neighbouring villages. The only point that emerged clearly was that Brahmins were on their way out and their lands were being bought up by Kapu farmers.

How They Live

The Yanadis, a scheduled tribe and mostly landless, had shifted their huts on to the 0.4 hectares allotted to them near the school on the other side of the road. They felt this left them free to stand on their own feet. They did not have to do any compulsory work for the Brahmins who often owned the plots on which they had their homesteads. There was, among them, a kind of self-respect which was lacking in Bihar. The landowners, too, admitted that the Yanadis were less dependent on them. They had suffered from the cyclone and many of their houses had been damaged, but all of them have since been rebuilt. Each household received Rs 150, one sari per woman and rice for one month. In most huts there were a few beds, some people had bicycles and, between the sixty families, there were three transistors. The women were very interested in family planning and five of them had been sterilized. Most Yanadis agreed that their living conditions were improving moderately. They worked for about six months in the paddy fields. They also recovered paddy stolen and stored by rats in the bunds surrounding the fields, and managed, thus, to occasionally get a few extra kilograms. Many of them, particularly children, caught rats with bamboo traps and earned 25–30 paise for each animal. For eight months in a year they fished in the canals. This brought them sales of Rs 3–4 per day, sometimes more. When it was time for the birds to migrate in the winter they put up nets and caught between three and four birds a day which were sold for a few rupees each. They also raised and sold chickens, repaired bunds in the dry season and harvested pulses.

One of the Yanadis, Jugla Pichaya, was over 50. He had four boys and two girls, one of whom was married. When asked about family planning he did not seem too keen on it, because he needed children to earn money. He had no land, and he, his wife, and his grown-up sons worked in the paddy fields. They also caught birds and fish. He had one hen and some chickens and sold some eggs, which earned him Rs 4.50 a month. He ate three meals a day in the rainy season with fish twice a week. Yet, although he did not seem to be very poor he complained that prices had gone up. He also owed Rs 150 to a Kapu for whom he worked. He had two sets of clothes and went to the movies in Chabrol four times a year.

Koteswara Rao, who was in his thirties, lived under similar conditions but he felt that if prices had gone up, wages had done so too. In 1967 wages for men were Rs 3–4 a day without food. In 1978 they had reached Rs 5–6 for transplanting, and wages for weeding had doubled from Rs 1.50 to 3. At harvest time workers often got the equivalent of Rs 5–8 in paddy. For threshing, a particularly long working day, they received ten kilograms of paddy and two meals. This was an increase of a few kilograms over the rates of 1967. For repairing bunds, wages had risen from Rs 1.50 to Rs 5. As for permanent labourers, there were the illustrative cases of Yanadis working for Brahmin land-owners. They used to receive 1,050 kilograms of paddy a year, along with Rs 200 and a set of clothes. They now got 975 kilograms, Rs 700 and some clothes. Paddy prices had gone up from Rs 46–53 a quintal to between Rs 80–93 (these are selling prices at different times of the year). The All India Consumer Price Index and the Food and General Index had risen from 213 and 228 in 1967–8 to 405 and 400 in 1978–9. In short, wages in real terms had roughly followed the increase in prices, or even overtaken them slightly.[16]

Let us shift to the Kapus, particularly the small landowners. Bolli-munta, one of them, lived with his wife and his two sons. They had 0.4 hectares of land and no bullocks, so they had to rent a pair. They cultivated their land carefully and harvested the equivalent of 3,750–4,125 kilograms per hectare—except under abnormal conditions as in 1977 when the cyclone washed away half their crops. In the dry season they sowed black gram which yielded 300 kilograms. In normal years the family got enough rice and they were able to eat 2.5 kilograms a day with pickles, leafy vegetables and mutton every fortnight. The father also worked as a labourer. Some of the work was free under mutual aid and some was paid. He was also employed

[16] Wages in cash show an increase of 66–100 per cent, if not more; wages in kind have increased further.

for the harvest and made around Rs 250. His wife did transplanting and harvesting and earned about the same amount. The youngest son went to school but he also did some work. The family had a buffalo which gave two litres of milk, one of which was sold.

Nimma Ankamma, another Kapu, was 40 years old and had a large family—his old father, his wife and five young children. He owned 0.8 hectares of land and rented 0.2 hectares from another farmer to whom he gave 6 bags of paddy (450 kilograms). He kept all the rabi crops for himself. He used his two buffaloes for ploughing, used farm manure and urea and mixed fertilizers on his fields and obtained a good yield of 3,750 kilograms per hectare of paddy. The family needed 8 kilograms of paddy a day which he kept, selling the remainder of about 400 kilograms. On 0.4 hectares he grew black gram (200–300 kilograms) which he sold for Rs 250–300 per quintal. On the rest of the land, after paddy, he grew sunn hemp which he sold, and fodder. His paddy surplus had increased. Nimma had been smart in making the best use of his land but he could have done even better if his land had not suffered from poor drainage. Apart from this, such small farmers were particularly vulnerable to accidents. In Nimma's case, for example, his paddy fields were damaged by heavy rains in 1976 and the next year the cyclone hit him hard. He had to borrow Rs 4,000 from the moneylender at 20 per cent interest to set himself up again. He also complained that he had too many children. In view of this he had got himself sterilized.

We met several Kapus each of whom had 1.2 hectares of land. They managed their crops as carefully as Nimma and got roughly the same yields of paddy which left them with a surplus for sales. Some of them made and sold ghee. One young man, Yenabotu Venkataraja Rao, managed fairly well though he had only 0.4 hectares. He rented 1.6 hectares, sold milk from his buffalo, ploughed for others with his bullocks and undertook some further jobs which enabled him to buy chemical fertilizers and proper paddy seeds. He produced enough paddy to feed his family and had a reasonable amount to sell.

Several centuries ago Manchala village was granted to some Brahmin families. In 1967 these Brahmins were big landowners with 6–7 hectares of land, who bought fertilizers and supervised field operations. These landowners are now ageing and gradually selling their land—about 40 hectares have been sold so far—to Kapus. One of them has sold three-fourths of his land because he needed some money to clear his debts. What remains to him is rented out because he can no more supervise his workers. His sons are educated and all have jobs in the cities, one of them being an engineer with Air India. Such sales of land do not seem to have produced a drastic change in the landholding profile because each buyer usually buys only a small plot. Thus one Brahmin has sold five hectares to more than twenty Kapu families. The situation of the Vaishya families is different. Many of the young men have also left for the city but the fathers have remained, looking after the land. The local Panchayat remains fairly active as before and there are paved streets. Electricity is more widely used.

At the Block and District Levels

Guntur district is a heterogeneous one and it would be wrong to consider Manchala as representative of the whole area. In the interior are vast stretches of dry land which support a poor millet. In the command area of Nagarjunasagar, cotton is on the increase. Tenali block, to which Manchala belongs, lies entirely in the delta. Paddy is by far the dominant crop with 18,800 hectares in the kharif out of a net cultivated area of 22,375 hectares. As seen in Manchala, canals do not always remain open all year, hence rabi paddy, though increasing, could do much better.[17] Black and green gram cover 12,000 hectares. Improved varieties of seeds remain predominant as in Manchala. In our discussions both at Tenali and Guntur, we got the impression that the breakthrough was yet to come. Improved varieties of seeds had reached their maximum yields. It will be interesting to watch the results of the latest HYU.

Drainage problems, which were not so acute in Manchala, were worse at the tail end of the canals. However, when the rains were slightly heavier than normal, sometimes as many as 50,000 hectares of land were submerged (total delta net cultivated area: 172,000 ha). As far as the supply of fertilizers was concerned there was no shortage. For Tenali block alone consumption had increased from 718 tons in 1966–7 (in terms of nutrients) to 5,760 in 1977–8. The same could not be said of pesticides. In fact when I was there I witnessed a demonstration by rich and poor farmers who were demanding a better supply of pesticides. Another problem here is that there are many spurious manufacturers of pesticides. Apart from this we have no overall data on the development of the delta part of the district.

[17]The rabi crop is usually better. There is no risk of flooding and less disease than during the rains.

There do not seem to be many small industries in big villages or subdistrict towns although the towns have considerably expanded and attract more vegetables and fish and milk. Many new buildings have come up, not only in Guntur, a bustling city, but also in Tenali. There are bigger bazaars, more trade, cinema houses and restaurants and more medium-sized industries. The streets are densely populated and there does not seem to be much acute poverty.

The first striking point, when we compare growth in wheat areas, is the complexity of paddy cultivation under different crop calendars and various rainfall schedules. Apart from this there are water management problems in the canal systems. Yet progress is impressive when compared with the slowly awakening villages of Bihar or Puri district. The growth process, which began very long ago, has also reached the poor in terms of better wages and more employment. It is time now for us to leave the rich alluvial basins and see how men and women struggle against physical constraints such as soils, rainfall and irrigation.

CHAPTER 10

Where Nature is Unkind

Leaving the district town of Satara we proceeded to Koregaon, the block headquarters and also a small market place. A few kilometres from Koregaon, on a good metalled road, we stopped at the village of Karwad, thirty kilometres from Satara. The landscape was typical of vast tracts of Maharashtra: plains, eroded plateaux, flat hills with black rocks, dry rivers and generally poor crops.

Between 1951 and 1961 the population in Karwad increased by 28 per cent to 1,173 inhabitants, a rate even higher than the average for the state. (This was partly due to some immigration.) At first glance the density per square kilometre seemed to be low (175) as compared with the Ganges basin or the deltas of the east coast. However, density figures are meaningless if we do not take into account the types of soils and crop yields. Out of the total area of 672 hectares in Karwad, 606 are said to be cultivated and only 92 are irrigated. Nearly half the total area has fairly good soils, although their quality is inferior to the soils of the alluvial plains. Some parts of the land (232 hectares) are mediocre and others (97 hectares) are very poor. These lie on the slopes of the plateau, furrowed by erosion and able to bear only very sparse crops. If the rains fail, 40–70 hectares of land cannot be cultivated at all and many others give a very low yield.

It is interesting to see how the people of this area adjusted to this hostile physical milieu. There were about 200 holdings which belonged mainly to the cultivating owners. To have enough to live on one's own farm, and to build up some small savings, it was necessary to have 0.8 hectares of irrigated land and roughly 3 hectares of non-irrigated land. One-fifth of the landowners, who together owned 160 hectares, were above this minimum. At the other extreme were 70–80 families who lived at a bare subsistence level and had about 100 hectares between them. Some 80–90 families had an average of a little more than 3 hectares each and the number of totally landless was around 30 (this included dependants). The Marathas, who comprised

80 per cent of the population and owned the largest amount of land were the dominant caste. Clever and tough, they had been accustomed, over centuries, to struggling with nature. Apart from this their strong martial traditions were widely known. There was only one declining Brahmin family. Most of the Harijans were land-less and belonged to the Mahar caste, also a tough and enterprising people, much more alert than the Chamars we visited in U.P. There were some Muslims, mostly landowners, and some Nandiwalas, a wandering group that had come from Andhra and settled here, but later moved on.

On non-irrigated land, farmers grew jowar and bajra, the basic foodgrains. Yields varied greatly according to the soils and the amount of rain but on the whole they were low—330–460 kilograms per hectare for jowar, rarely more than 270 for bajra. This was not enough to feed the village. Fortunately the village had some richer cash crops and this enabled the farmers to buy extra grain. In adition, groundnuts were cultivated on about 100 hectares of land and, provided the rains were not too disappointing, they gave a yield of 450–500 kilograms (shelled) per hectare. Farmers made the best possible use of their irrigated land. Apart from a few hectares that were dependent on small dams (*bandhara*) most of the 92 hectares relied on wells using the *mot* system but, instead of the leather scoop, farmers used a metal pail which, when pulled by bullocks, would empty automatically into the channel. Out of the 27 masonry wells, 10 were by then using pumpsets with an oil engine (command 1–3 hectares) as there was no electricity. Farmers first expanded the area devoted to potatoes from 5 to 31 hectares mainly because potatoes were selling profitably in Koregaon and Satara from where they were sent to Poona. Between 1952–3 and 1964–5 the area under sugarcane increased from 3 to 11 hectares and the yields grew to 6,500 kilograms per hectare in terms of raw sugar.[1] Chillies and vegetables were also being grown in larger quantities, and there were some groves of banana trees. More recently, the biggest landowner had introduced grapes for the Bombay market, as was also being done in other parts of Maharashtra. Other farmers followed with grapes, so that soon 2.5 hectares were covered with vineyards—the net profit on grapes was considerable in those days, roughly Rs 12,000 per hectare. Farm manure and chemical fertilizers were being used for all cash crops,

[1] Climatic conditions are better because it is warmer in winter than it is in north India. Plots of land are also smaller and very well-tended.

particularly since the block had been opened in 1957.

The non-irrigated area was at the mercy of the rains which had a low average and were erratic. Even the irrigated plots did not enjoy a definite supply of water because the ground water potential was limited. Until March it was possible for pumps to operate for eight or ten hours a day. After this their operating time was down to a few hours and several wells would simply stop providing water at all. It was thus easy to see how fruit, vegetables and sugarcane suffered under such conditions. I visited Eksal just before the monsoon and found several sugarcane fields turning yellow and the vegetables withering.

Living Conditions: Some Case Studies

Govin Pandurang Sawan was a Mahar who lived with his wife and four children. Of his 0.8 hectares of land a part was mediocre and rain-fed. Govin grew mainly jowar and some groundnuts during the monsoon. He also had a small plot of land irrigated by a well, where he grew wheat. Altogether, he got 400 kilograms of cereal a year. In order to feed his family he needed to buy another 800 kilograms. To make ends meet Govin worked eight months with the largest landowner and earned Rs 2 a day. He learnt how to cultivate grapes and had a vineyard on 0.1 hectare of land; he also grew chillies. The well which irrigated his land was built seven years ago with a loan from the co-operative. When we met him Govin's existence was still precarious but was showing signs of improving gradually. He already owned one bullock, a heifer, two chickens and a goat, whose milk was kept for the children. The family ate jowar as its staple food, meat once a month and occasionally an egg.

Another Mahar, Maruti Aba, was not doing as well. He did not think it worthwhile to cultivate his 0.6 hectares of rain-fed land which he let out at Rs 40 to a landowner who had 2.8 hectares of his own. Aba himself earned Rs 50 a month as a road repairer around Koregaon.

Shivaram Ramchandra Bhosle was a Maratha farmer who owned 2.4 hectares of dry land and 0.6 hectares of irrigated land. His family consisted of his wife, his four young children, a daughter-in-law and her baby. He grew mainly jowar and bajra in the monsoon, and also had a small plot on which he grew groundnuts to sell. The water supplied by his well was insufficient to irrigate crops in the rabi or to grow chillies or sugarcane. Every year he had to spend Rs 300 on buying 440 kilograms of cereals. He had no bullocks of his own and hired a pair for Rs 100. He had neither buffaloes nor cows. His own milk supply—half a litre per day—came from his two goats. Apart from this, Shivaram had borrowed Rs 1,400 (interest-free) from some neighbours for the wedding of his eldest daughter and Rs 900 from the block for digging his well. Somehow, he managed to make ends meet. Although he was unable to improve his crops, he made do because he received some money every month from his sons, one of whom worked in a spinning mill in Bombay and the other in the army.

Hanumanth Genu Bhosle, another Maratha, was a medium farmer whose living conditions were improving slightly. He and his brother owned 3.6 hectares of land and their two families consisted of thirteen people. They were lucky to have one-third of their land irrigated. On this they grew sugarcane and bananas and, more recently, grapes. They managed to more or less cover their needs in cereals, and made money on the sales of their cash crops. They also had three bullocks, two cows, one buffalo and two small buffaloes. The children, thus, had enough milk to drink.

Finally we came to the main landowner, a very shrewd and hard-working Maratha. He had started with only 0.4 hectares but by 1964 had managed to accumulate 15 hectares. Nearly one-third of this land was irrigated by three wells, each equipped with a pumpset. In addition to jowar in the kharif on his dry land, he had 1.6 hectares of sugarcane, 2 hectares of vineyards—which he had been the first to introduce into the village—and some vegetables and chillies. He had a large family; two of his married sons helped him, the other four were at school or university. He had three pairs of bullocks, a grain mill—the only one in the village—and even an old car, vintage 1939, which he used for delivering fruit and vegetables to Satara. He was the typical local boss and was Chairman of the Panchayat. One of his sons was active in the co-operative.

As in Kila Ulur, here too, the Panchayat did more than just exist on paper. It had to its credit some streets paved with bricks; a new school building which had replaced the first one built in 1924,[2] improved drinking water wells and some oil lamp posts. The block and district administration was involved in the Panchayati Raj experiment under which relatively extensive powers had been given to local councils,

[2]Primary education was more energetically encouraged in Maharashtra than in states such as U.P. or Bihar.

especially—as in the case of Maharashtra—at the district level. The achievements of the people's representatives were (not only in Karwad but all over) more substantial than in northern India, and the administrative set-up had been strengthened. While the Collector remained in command of the district, another IAS officer of the same rank was the CEO (Chief Executive Officer) of the Zila Parishad, or district council. In Satara, at the initiative of a particularly able and dynamic officer (S. Rajgopal) new development schemes were being given a boost and a large family planning programme had been started with successful sterilization camps.

Thus, in Karwad, it was possible to say that farmers had made the best use of their limited agricultural potential. There could, of course, have been more anti-erosion work than was actually done but the scope for larger yields on such soils, and with such erratic rainfall, was narrow. The farmers did their best to make as much money as possible out of irrigated cash crops but here too they faced serious obstacles. They could not greatly increase the number of wells due to the limited supply of ground water, which depended on the uncertain rains for replenishment. However, in spite of a much smaller expansion, the overall standard of living was not lower than in Mirpur. Of the 200 families here, 125 men had found a job outside, many in Bombay and Poona—cities that were growing in industry, trade and the services. Several men had also joined the army or the police.

Other villages in the neighbouring taluks were in a position similar to that of Karwad—poor rain-fed agriculture and some rich irrigated plots, many men working outside and sending a part of their savings home to their families. However there were also certain more serious cases. In Phaltan block, I visited villages whose soils were exceptionally poor, with even less irrigation potential. These were classified, even under normal conditions, as scarcity areas.

The Following Phases

We stopped in Karwad again in November 1975 when the villagers were harvesting a bumper crop because the rains had been generous. The whole village, like so many others, was awakening again after very severe drought in 1970, 1971 and 1972, when foodgrains had been ruined and cash crops had shrunk because most wells had run dry. From 1975 onwards conditions began to improve. The third time we went to Karwad was in 1979 and things were still fair to good. Yields of rain-fed jowar and bajra had remained more or less static at the 1964 level and jowar now covered 200 hectares. The rains are so uncertain that farmers cannot risk sowing HYV of hybrid jowar or bajra along with chemical fertilizers on dry land as this does not produce higher yields if the crops lack sufficient moisture. Groundnuts also occupied the same amount of land without any appreciable rise in yields. Irrigation had expanded from 92 hectares to 130 and had improved in quality. All wells were now equipped with pumpsets, 24 of these used electricity which had now reached Karwad, 15 relied on diesel oil.[3] This is probably the maximum that can be done because, as in the past, the water supply is by no means regular. In the hottest months (April to June) some wells hardly work, even if the previous monsoon has been normal and has replenished the ground water. In spite of these shortcomings, irrigation has paved the way for some progress: in 1979, 28 hectares of wheat were sown in the rabi giving 1,500 kilograms per hectare, less when the weather had been too warm.[4] Hybrid jowar covered 24 hectares. Some fields, well irrigated and with fairly good doses of chemical fertilizers, yielded 1,750–2,000 kilograms per hectare whereas others gave 750. Paddy was sown on 8 hectares with a rather mediocre yield of 1,250–1,500 kilograms per hectare.

Richer crops had expanded from 45 to 50 hectares (gross area). Sugarcane, which had practically disappeared because of successive droughts, was picking up again with 2 hectares. Grapes occupied 4.4 hectares. Papaya, which was confined to a few odd trees, was now planted on several plots with a total of 2.8 hectares. Potatoes had fallen from 31 to 4 hectares because of a disease. They had also become comparatively less productive. On the other hand, onions had 4 hectares, garlic 6, brinjals 4.4, cabbages and other vegetables 8, and chillies 10. Often farmers grew two or more crops of vegetables in a year. Net returns per 0.4 hectares of vineyards amounted to Rs 5,000–6,000 as against Rs 4,800 in 1964. This low increase was due to the general expansion of grapes in several districts of Maharashtra.

---

[3] Pumpsets fixed on open wells should not be confused with tubewells as found in U.P. or Punjab. To dig tubewells in this kind of terrain would be both difficult and expensive because of the layers of hard rock. As it is, the digging of an open well is much more expensive here than in alluvial soils where there is hardly any hard rock.

[4] Winter is less cool than in the Ganges basin.

Each crop of vegetables gave the farmer a net return of Rs 1,000–2,000 per 0.4 hectares. Papaya brought the highest net return with Rs 10,000 for 0.4 hectares.

Other changes were also discernible. Animal husbandry had not developed much but some farmers had got together and bought five crossed Jersey cows. One landholder had bought a tractor. Because the village had been electrified there were now two flour mills (in 1964 there had been only one), one oil mill and some threshing machines. In addition there were shops that sold grocery, cloth, etc. Population growth had slowed down in the decade 1961–71 to a decennial rate of 14 per cent. This was because the Nandiwalas had moved on and because family planning had improved. The family planning campaign had been started under the direct leadership of the CEO in the 1960s. It had since gathered momentum and already in 1975, of the 300 couples in Karwad, some 50 men and 32 women had been sterililzed. The campaign gathered strength during the Emergency and by the end of 1978 this number had gone up to 85 for males and 57 for females.[5] The number of men who were working outside the village had risen from 125 to 170. The primary school had expanded and it now had over 300 students. Apart from this 17 boys and girls attended secondary school in Koregaon.

Progress and Obstacles

Though the farmers could hardly have done more to increase their yields and diversify production, the overall movement of the economy within the village and around it was not strong enough to push agricultural wages up significantly. While the latter were higher in 1964 than in Mirpur (Rs 2 without food as compared to Re 1 with some food), in 1979 wages in Karwad were only Rs 4 without food as compared to Rs 5–6 with food in some parts of western U.P. When considering price trends it is possible to say that in real terms, agricultural wages had fallen somewhat. However, the number of landless people in the area was few and their income was not entirely dependent on agricultural work as they also managed to find work outside.

We had a long talk with Govin and other Mahars we had met in 1964 and 1975. Their twelve households were adjacent. Six of the men were working in factories in Bombay and Poona and they sent money

---

[5] During the Emergency there were cases of abuse and excesses in Maharashtra, but I did not hear complaints about any such cases in Karwad.

home. The father and brothers who stayed in the village were full of initiative. Govin had installed an electric pump on the well that he shared with his brother. They had taken a loan of Rs 5,000 from the Co-operative Bank, one-third of it as a subsidy for small farmers. Govin made the best use of his 0.4 hectares of irrigated land, a little more than half of which was covered with vineyards. Seeing how profitable papaya was, he planted 0.12 hectares with these trees and on the rest of the irrigated land he grew vegetables. On his dry land he gathered the same amount of jowar as before. He also worked as a field labourer, owned one bullock, one cow, one goat and some chickens. He had a brother who owned 0.4 hectares and was also a part-time tailor. Their children went to school. Although life remained hard for such people there had been some definite improvement in their living conditions and one felt that their self-respect and self-confidence had increased.

Sampat Dadu Bhosle was looking after his fields when I met him. With his 2 hectares of land he had to maintain his family and his old parents (six people in all). Ten years ago he had bought and installed an oil pumpset on his well. This had cost him Rs 4,000. He had just planted 0.10 hectares with papaya trees. In addition he grew red chillies (0.10 hectares) and, on 0.2 hectares of irrigated land had sown hybrid jowar with a low dose of chemical fertilizers. On a few other irrigated plots Sampat Dadu cultivated red gram partly to sell and partly to use at home, and some vegetables. His rain-fed land was located on poor soils and yielded only 250–500 kilograms per hectare of jowar. Nearer the hills he had some other plots which were even poorer. Here, if the rains were good, he managed to gather some grass as fodder. Dadu could just about manage to get through. He earned some money from the sales of cash crops and fruit and had to buy grain for his requirements.

Another Maratha, Shankar Gopal Bhosle, enjoyed better living conditions. Thirty-two years old, he had only one son and a daughter. His parents were still alive and he looked after his younger brother who was at school. Two other brothers were away, one in the army, the other in a textile mill at Bombay. Each of them sent home Rs 1,000 a year. The total landholding amounted to 2.8 hectares. Half of it was irrigated by a pump which Shankar took on rent for his well. He grew potatoes and beans, hybrid jowar without chemical fertilizers, and also had 0.10 hectares of paddy with a mediocre yield of 100 kilograms (1,000 per hectare) and groundnuts. On his rain-fed plots Shankar Gopal had jowar (250 kilograms per hectare) and the same yield for bajra. They had one bullock, one buffalo, 2 cows. In a good year the family produced just enough grain. If the rains failed they would buy a few quintals because they had some savings from what the brothers sent and from the sale of potatoes, beans and ground-nuts. Shankar admitted that his standard of living had improved—he had a radio in his house as well as a bicycle which he used for shopping in Koregaon. But it was surprising that he had not tried to push richer crops at all.

Sriman Bandhu Pawar, a young man, did better. He lived with his wife and mother. His well-cum-pumpset irrigated 0.6 hectares. On one-third of it he grew a soft variety of sugarcane which was sold (for chewing) in the bazaar. One third of his land had chillies which grew between the papaya trees that had just been planted. Another plot had become a vineyard. Sriman Bandhu also cultivated spices which, with proper doses of chemical fertilizers, brought in more than Rs 3,000. The non-irrigated fields (0.4 hectares) supplied a few quintals of jowar of which the family consumed six in addition to one of wheat and rice. Sriman Bandu had no bullocks and hired a pair when he needed them. He had two cows which together gave half a litre of milk a day. Sriman's family lived quite well—he had been able to buy a pump and, after four years, he had repaid the debt of Rs 7,000 that he had incurred when he got married.

Another farmer, Gulab Rao Bhosle, seemed to be a rather large landowner with his 7 hectares. Yet practically half of this land was not cultivated. Other rain-fed plots brought a poor return. His irrigated land (one hectare through two wells and one pumpset) did not enable him to do as well as Sriman Bandhu and, because the irrigation was not reliable enough to have vegetables or fruit orchards, 0.4 hectares were to hybrid jowar, followed by wheat.

The village boss, whom we had met earlier, had died and his holding had been divided among his six sons, each one getting 3.66 hectares of which half was irrigated in each case. The father had had 7 wells with pumpsets. Five of the sons lived in Karwad and the sixth was a lawyer in Satara. He had a man to look after his fields. Although the sons had inherited a fair amount of money from their father, they still had to work hard in order to keep up their standard of living. They were now experimenting with animal husbandry with the five Jersey cows bought by their father.

If overall conditions in Karwad have not deteriorated, this is due to some increase in production, mostly in cash crops, and to the fact that a growing number of men are finding jobs outside the village. What, however, does the future hold? For how long can Bombay, Poona and the smaller towns continue to provide a safety valve for the surplus labour? Today the number of landless people in Karwad is small, but the fragmentation of landholdings is increasing. How, for example, will the sons of Govin, the enterprising Mahar, do? Villagers place great hopes in the Dhom project which should finally be linked to Karwad by a canal which is expected to irrigate dozens of hectares of dry land presently outside the command area of the wells. This will certainly help but there are still villages that have barely any potential for irrigation.

At the District Level

The Zila Parishad of Satara has expanded considerably. There are big buildings where all the administrative offices are located. While elected officials usually remain more concerned with politics, patronage and influence, the district officials, the Collector and the Chief Executive Officer, both of the IAS, are of high calibre. District planning has expanded through several special schemes. There has been some growth in the irrigated areas. Out of a net sown area of about 650,000 hectares, 82,000 are now irrigated as against 71,000 net in 1960–1. More than half depend on wells. Out of 42,000 wells, 7,420 are fitted with oil engines and 4,630 with electric ones. The use of chemical fertilizers has increased but consumption remains low since it is largely confined to the richer irrigated plots, as the figures below show:

Total consumption in terms of nutrients (in tons)	1963–4	1976–7	1977–8
	900	10,980	8,258

As far as irrigation is concerned, actual irrigation often remains below the above figures, as these refer to the potentially irrigated area. Production of foodgrains traced, after the bumper crop of 1960–1 (253,000 tons), a downward trend until 1972–3. Under the influence of better weather it picked up from 1974–5, reaching 357,000 tons in 1976–7, and 384,000 tons in 1977–8. It fell by approximately 50,000 tons in the following year. In wheat, there has also been a definite expansion from 11,000 tons in 1960–1 to an average of 40,000 tons per year for the period 1976–7 and 1977–8. Rice output also roughly doubled to reach an average of 47,000 tons for the last two years. Rice and wheat increases have been helped by the progress of irrigation although most of the irrigation has been in favour of the richer cash crops.

A Look at Ahmednagar District

Most of Ahmednagar district is more vulnerable to drought than Satara. We visited several villages in 1971, which was one of the worst years. The monsoon had failed and there had been no rain till the middle of August; hence many farmers had not even sown bajra. With the few late rains that came they had tried their luck with jowar. As in Satara they had tried to make the best use of all available irrigation. There were some canals that used water from the rivers and several wells equipped with pumps. Farmers cultivated sugarcane, chillies, vegetables and had small orchards on irrigated plots. In 1971 in Chitali, of the 80 wells with pumps, 30 had completely dried up and sugarcane, like the other crops, had been ruined. The other pumps were able to supply water for only a few hours a day.

When the rains are favourable—as in 1975 or 1978—farmers obtain a few quintals of bajra (maximum 340 kilograms per hectare) or rabi jowar (480 kilograms per hectare). These yields decline by more than half when the rains fail. On the other hand, when groundwater is not in short supply, there are farmers who, with 0.5 hectares of irrigated land and 1-2 hectares of dry land, manage reasonably well because of the high returns they get from cash crops. In both districts more efforts are now being made to expand irrigation under the Drought Prone Areas Programme. The Small Farmers' Development Agency is also giving particular attention to loans-cum-subsidies which are granted to small farmers. This has led to some increase in the net irrigated area, which reaches about 12-13 per cent of the net cultivated area when the water supply is reliable.

CHAPTER 11

In Some Other Parts of the Deccan

The huge peninsular part of India is so diverse in both natural conditions and human surroundings that, in order to get a slightly larger sample, I am adding brief observations on a few more areas, some personal, some based on research done by other scholars. We will consider two areas in the north-eastern corner of the Deccan, in south Bihar which enjoys fairly high rainfall and has a sizeable amount of paddy land. From there we shall proceed to the hills of Orissa along the aborigines. Finally we shall come to the north-western part of the Deccan in an area of rather low rainfall where jowar remains the main foodgrain, followed by wheat.

In the North-east of the Peninsula

My attention was drawn to the Palamau district in the hilly areas of south Bihar by a very good study conducted by Sudipto Mundle.[1] The whole area has for long remained isolated from any process of growth. Severe famines hit the villages in this district in the nineteenth century and there was a 'large scale exodus of labour' to the tea estates of north Bengal and Assam. It was only after 1951 that the population began to expand fast: 975,176 in 1951, 1.5 million twenty years later. Over 90 per cent of the people depended on agriculture. While the net sown area barely increased between 1921 and 1951, large tracts of land were reclaimed from the forest during the next decade when the net sown area grew from 250,000 hectares to 306,000. By that time, most of the available land must have been opened to the plough, since there has been no further upward trend during the next fifteen years.

Irrigation by means of tanks, small canals, reservoirs and wells has expanded in twenty-five years, from 28,000 hectares to 74,000 hectares, but irrigation is not always reliable. The average rainfall is relatively high: about 1,000 millimetres, and in some areas up to

[1] S. Mundle, *Bonded Labour in Palamau* (New Delhi, 1978).

113

1,800 millimetres, but there are often chances of the monsoon failing.

Crop yields do not show any clear and decisive upward trend. Paddy fields, rain-fed or irrigated, are widespread in the lower parts of the valleys. The monsoon crops yield around 400 kilograms per hectare (clean rice), the irrigated winter crop about 900 kilograms. Maize varies from 500 to 800 kilograms per hectare. Potatoes, also expanding in the area, remain, in spite of some improvement, at the very mediocre level of 5–6 tons per hectare. As Mundle notes of landowners, who belong to the group with 0.8 or less than 0.8 hectares, such households are 'deficit households or near deficit households' (p. 91). Most of their land is devoted to foodgrains. Farmers have hardly any surplus to sell and, unlike our people in Satara district, they have no small irrigated plots devoted to cash crops. Job opportunities outside the villages are very limited. The urban population in the district amounted to only 4.7 per cent in 1971. There are not many other outlets in the district and the old option of employment in the tea estates has been practically closed. Besides, there are still many very isolated villages which can be reached only by travelling several hours on a bad road. Livestock, on the other hand, has increased substantially.[1]

Year	Cattle	Buffaloes	Goats	Pigs
		(in thousands)		
1951	639	111	185	31
1971	810	133	338	44

Fallow land and forests (48 per cent of the geographical area for the latter) offer possibilities for grazing, but fodder has to be reduced in the dry season and there is the danger of deforestation if the cattle population increases. The growth in sown area during the 1950s may have prevented a serious deterioration of the overall balance between population and resources, but the situation was bound to deteriorate after 1960, when such an increase practically stopped.

These factors, combined with the monetization process, which developed from the turn of the last century onwards, had a severe impact on the growing landless population, even if manpower remained relatively scarce. Bonded labour became common. As Ramdas Haldipur emphasizes in his foreword, bonded labour is 'not a remnant of the feudal past, but rather a product of the penetration of commercialism and the profit calculus in a *backward* agriculture' (italics mine). Labourers, often Harijans or scheduled tribes, fell into debt,[2] accepted permanent employment with high caste, large or fairly large landowners under more difficult conditions than free agricultural labourers.

The author of the study presents the following table (p. 171):

	Wages and Employment		
	Daily Wages in Grain	Daily Hours of Work	Annual No. of Days Employed
Free Workers	1.75 kg	9.25	182
Bonded Workers	1.45	11.22	239

Landowners do make some profit in this way, but even the rather larger ones (those with more than 10 hectares) still produce so little with that they cannot save enough to invest in irrigation, new seeds or fertilizers. On the other hand, in spite of its defects, the system offers some sort of security for the bonded labourer. As Mundle points out: 'Under the archaic and harsh circumstances of Palamau a bonded labourer's freedom ... may well mean no more than the freedom to starve' (p. 183). For this reason and many other factors related to the influence of large landowners, the implementation of the Bonded Labour System (Abolition) Act 1976[3] is far from simple. A year after the Act was supposed to have been implemented, 613 bonded labourers had been identified in Palamau district. This is likely to be an understatement of the actual number. A comprehensive programme of economic rehabilitation is needed; this is gradually being introduced in Palamau. Such specific schemes are no doubt welcome but it is equally essential to promote the overall expansion of the area—by no means an easy task, since natural conditions here are not as favourable to agriculture as in the plains.

Another Case

When proceeding by car from Patna to Orissa, we stopped for a few days in another hilly area of Bihar, about sixty-five kilometres southwest of the town of Gaya in the district of the same name. During the monsoon, the average rainfall here is 750 millimetres; this is complemented by a few scarce winter rains. Lutua village is located at a distance of four kilometres from the nearest asphalted road and market place, in a valley surrounded by hills covered with forest.

[2] Usually for relatively large loans (Rs 100 or above) on occasions such as marriages (p. 174); in such cases no interest is charged (p. 177).
[3] The question of bonded labour came up in public discussions in 1974 and 1975.

Because of the Bhoodan movement in the 1950s Harijans here were allotted pieces of land. The main crops are grown during the rains, paddy in the lowlands, and maize, pulses and jute elsewhere. In the rabi there is wheat, other pulses and some plots of potatoes. Here and there are patches of sugarcane. In 1970, a team belonging to a voluntary agency (Brothers of all Men) from France[4] began to take part in extension work: training of young men in agriculture, levelling of fields, irrigation through wells usually fitted with a Persian wheel. Irrigation was a top priority because the rains were not at all reliable. They could be insufficient or fail totally, as during the acute drought of 1966.

Although there have been definite improvements in this area, several shortcomings and defects remain, Many families have settled recently in Lutua and other villages. Before this they had lived on forest produce, cutting and selling wood, collecting wild fruit, raising cattle. They are gradually learning to become careful farmers. In the meanwhile the old shortcomings—poor levelling of the fields, insufficient tillage of the land, late sowing, lack of farm manure, still exist. In addition the soils are not of a high quality and erosion is severe even on mild slopes. Last, but not least, the population pressure is beginning to be felt. A number of holdings distributed twenty years ago are now divided. The amount of rain is barely sufficient for paddy, except in very good years, and consequently yields are around 900 kilograms per hectare for local varieties, without chemical fertilizers. On irrigated demonstration plots HYV with a moderate dose of chemical fertilizers can yield 3,300 kilograms per hectare.[5] Local maize performs better with 1,750 kilograms per hectare. As to wheat, it is around 1,000–1,300 kilograms per hectare, except on a few properly irrigated plots where HYV crops are sown with some fertilizers. Farmers there can get 2,250 kilograms per hectare. Yields of raw sugar do not exceed the low level of 3,300 kilograms per hectare.

In the course of our interviews with farmers we came across people whose standards of living were significantly higher than in Palamau. Some young men had been educated: Bigan, who was one of them, had even worked in Calcutta and Dhanbad. His father owned 1.5

---

[4] The following data are taken from J. P. Dardaud, *Promotion des Petits Paysans dans la zone de Lutua* (Paris, 1977).

[5] Farmers complain of the damage caused by rats. As in other places, there are farmers and labourers who dig out the paddy stored by rats.

hectares, most of it having been granted to him by the Bhoodan movement. The three eldest sons worked with him. They had a well with a Persian wheel. Unlike many other farmers, they levelled their irrigated plots properly to bear potatoes, some vegetables and sugarcane. The family also had four buffaloes and two cows. They had begun a few years earlier to apply small doses of fertilizers, which had a good impact on their yields. As Bigan concluded: 'Things are changing and improving.'[6] If many farmers did not manage as well, there was at least no actual bonded labour and even landless people had a relative margin for manoeuvre. Several of them raised chickens, goats or pigs for sale. The forest played an important role in their economy. Dry wood was collected for sale, as well as leaves which were dried and used to make baskets.[7]

The area is only twenty-five kilometres away from the plains, where agricultural expansion seems to have proceeded faster than in Muzaffarpur. Small towns and cities are also growing. Both factors enable some people to find small jobs. As far as the future is concerned, the French team rightly emphasizes the crucial role of irrigation. Ground water seems limited but the construction of more reservoirs at the foot of the hills in order to store more water for the dry season could help the expansion of rabi crops considerably.

Where the Plough is Not Yet Used

Other patterns of life and agriculture are typical of isolated parts of the Deccan: tribal (adivasi) areas where burning and shifting cultivation[8] is still practised, sometimes side by side with settled agriculture. In 1954, I visited a few Saura villages of Parlakimedi in Orissa. The people here were living in remote hills covered with jungle, accessible with some difficulty by jeep. There was still a reasonable balance between population and resources: happy and good looking people worshipping natural forces (animist cults), burning forest tracts where they would till the land only with a hoe, getting enough out of the forest and out of their agriculture. The increase in population is today condemning these societies to changing both their activities and their way of life.

In 1978, we visited another tribal area in Phulbani district (Orissa).

---

[6] J. P. Dardaud, op. cit.
[7] They can earn Rs 5–7 a day and occasionally Rs 10.
[8] Called *podu* in Orissa.

The hilly tracts undulate under thick forests, with patches of barren land here and there, where the forest had recently been burnt and the land cultivated. In the valleys, however, a number of people are now tilling their land with the help of bullocks. The average rainfall (1,581 millimetres) enables them to grow paddy, but Phulbani, like other districts in the interior of Orissa, may suffer from drought. In good years like 1978, traditional rain-fed paddy—there is practically no HYV, and no chemical fertilizers—has a yield of 1,200–1,500 kilograms per hectare (800–1,000 clean rice). This declines to 750 in bad years when the rains are scarce or not properly distributed.

There are new roads which made it possible for us to go deep into the hilly areas around Baliguda-Tumudiband. Off the road we walked three kilometres through a few hamlets hidden in the forest. The aborigines (Kutia-Khond) cultivate some mustard and, on the slopes which have been cleared through burning, they grow jowar, bajra, some beans and castor oil on the same plots, each ripening at different times. In the dry season, the villagers go through a difficult time. Their reserves of food are exhausted. They have to go into the forest to collect leaves, dig out edible roots and even go hunting wild game with their bows and arrows. In the hamlet of Ghumargoan, people cultivate and sell some mustard in order to earn at least a few rupees, with which to buy kerosene, salt, and occasionally dry fish. They also raise a few chickens and sometimes a pig.

The overall impression one gathers is one of sadness, as if an old civilization were dying in great moral and material poverty. The aborigines have nothing of the lively cheerfulness of the Sauras we visited in 1954. Since our observations do not apply to the same area, we cannot tell whether the people around Ghumargaon have been in this depressed condition for long. Their lives become doubly difficult because of the hazards of living in the jungle. In Ghumargaon, six families left for an unknown place because they felt they had coped long enough with the damage wrought on their crops by wild elephants.[9] In less remote villages along the roadside, conflict is beginning to occur between aborigines and Hindus. People from the plains often cheat the aborigines, or simply lend them money. When the tribals cannot repay, they have to mortgage their land or their crops. At the initiative of Dr Panigrahi,[10] the very dynamic Director of

---

[9] Such hazards are not confined to this area alone. In other parts of Orissa bears have caused a lot of damage to maize crops, especially in recently reclaimed areas.

[10] The same man is also promoting coconut plantations, as seen in Puri district.

the Horticultural Department of Orissa, a scheme has been started to help aborigines plant fruit trees, in particular mango, jackfruit and guava, which are well adapted to local conditions. Farmers benefit from a subsidy of Rs 140 per 0.4 hectares in the form of different inputs. Five years after planting the seedlings the trees reach full production with a gross return which can amount to Rs 2,500 per 0.4 hectares (Rs 2,000 net). In 1978, in the whole of Phulbani district, 4,400 hectares had been planted with 580,000 fruit trees. In each area of 150 hectares, ten tribal boys are trained for a period of two years (they get Rs 90 per month) on these plantations. Intercultivation is practised within the small plantations, especially with various pulses and, when the trees have grown, with turmeric and other spices. These bring in some additional income.

Along the road, in several villages we stopped to see small plantations recently started. People were clearly better off here than in isolated places. Thus, even in such areas changes and innovations are gradually emerging. This is only the beginning, however, and future development has to face an intricate set of physical, technical and social factors.

In the Northern Part of the Deccan

We paid only a brief visit to Piparsod village in Shivpuri district (Madhya Pradesh) in 1964, but thanks to the most exhaustive study of an Indian village ever made so far, at least to my knowledge,[11] we can follow, through the different visits made by Jean-Luc Chambard from 1957 to 1981, the evolution of the village. This is a typical case of a village where the improvement in the community's living conditions at different levels has been engineered more by activities outside agriculture than by those within it.

Piparsod is located eighteen kilometres from the town of Shivpuri, off a good metalled road in a landscape of gently undulating fields and forests. The first settlers came here in the sixteenth century, though for long the area remained thinly populated. Gradually, from 1951 onwards, the population has been increasing steadily though still slowly in the decade 1951–61: +11 per cent, and +20 per cent from 1961 to 1971, making up a total of 2,222 inhabitants. The soils are not very fertile and irrigation plays but a minor role. In the monsoon farmers grow mainly jowar, and in the rabi—though usually not on the same soils—wheat. The former yielded in the 1960s 700–900

[11] J. L. Chambard, *Atlas d'un Village Indien* (Paris, 1980).

kilograms per hectare, a reasonably good crop because there had 'been better rains than in Maharashtra.[12] The latter, relying on the small winter rains, achieved only a little above 600 kilograms per hectare. Other crops (kharif) were maize, some groundnuts and pulses. The total net cultivated area was 1,100 hectares, plus 100 hectares of pasture land, clear evidence of a relatively low density per square kilometre (116 in 1961). There were also 20 hectares on a small rocky hill which offered some pasture in the monsoon.

Piparsod, unlike so many villages, has two dominant castes: Brahmins and Kirars who together hold the largest part of the land. At the bottom come the Chamars (Harijans). Between 1958 and 1964, the total agricultural production increased by 15–20 per cent. In the next phase until 1977, the increase amounted to 40 per cent. There has been a clear improvement of rain-fed crops. Wheat yields have moderately increased with the introduction of improved—not HYV—varieties. Jowar may have improved, but the most striking change has occurred with groundnuts: both the area devoted to them and the yields have sharply increased because of small doses of chemical fertilizers: 2,000–2,500 kilograms per hectare unshelled (shelled 1,300–1,600). Prices have also increased. Potatoes have expanded so as to cover 60 hectares and give fairly good yields of 15–18 tons per hectare. They are grown partly during the rainy reason and partly with the help of irrigation at other times. Irrigation has increased only moderately because of physical constraints: lack of surface water irrigation, limited resources of ground water. However, 100 hectares are irrigated by wells now fitted with pumpsets. On such plots farmers grow HYV wheat which, with proper doses of chemical fertilizers, gives 3,500 kilograms per hectare. But the farmers are often more interested in richer crops: vegetables, red chillies or, as mentioned above, potatoes.

Already in the late 1950s, the growing number of job opportunities outside Piparsod was bringing much money into the village. Out of 350 families, 80 had one or more member working outside; there were more than a hundred in 1961, out of whom 65 were teachers and 37 petty officials. Most of these jobs were monopolized by Brahmins, but gradually other castes were emerging—for example there were three Chamar teachers. The families of these people remained in Piparsod while the men usually worked within the district, many commuting from the village thanks to the increase in the number of

[12] The average rainfall is around 800 mm.

buses, or going to work on their bicycles. In 1977 there were a hundred teachers and ninety-five officials. Most salaries were around Rs 250–300 per month, which represented a substantial increase in income for the whole family. Since the late 1950s there has been a great deal of construction. A large number of people, especially Brahmins, are building new and bigger houses usually in stone. Now even some Chamars are building new houses.

Chamars, who work as masons, have benefited from this lasting boom in construction. By 1977 they were earning Rs 15–20 per day. Wages for agricultural work have been increased from Re 1 to Rs 5, which means an increase in real terms. From 1956 to 1964 Re 1 was equivalent to 2.5 or 2 kilograms of wheat, whereas Rs. 5 in 1977 are equivalent to 4 kilograms. The wages of permanent labourers have not increased so much in real terms: Rs 100 versus 30. Several Chamars also improved their lot when cultivating, on a share-cropping basis, the lands of Brahmins who had managed to get jobs outside Piparsod. In 1969, electricity reached Piparsod and 150 metres were installed. Seven electric flour mills have been opened, thereby freeing most women of the time-consuming and trying job of hand-milling.

Jean-Luc Chambard also notes much progress in nutrition. Fruit, including apples from Kashmir, and vegetables are sold every day by pedlars.[13] Wheat is gradually replacing jowar as the staple food. The consumption of tea and milk is increasing, whereas twenty years ago tea was considered a rare luxury. No less striking are the changes in the way people dress. Practically no one walks barefoot any more. Brahmin women wear brighter coloured saris. The wide skirt of Chamar women is better, and more often replaced. There is a growing number of men who wear trousers and a bush-shirt, often in synthetic textiles.

There has also been remarkable progress in education. Finally, family planning has gained in popularity without the excesses committed during the Emergency. By 1977, 150 men and 10 women had been sterilized,[14] most of them being Brahmins, followed by Banyas (traders), Chamars and Muslims. These measures have resulted in a clear reduction of the birth rate and the overall rate of population increase. According to Chambard's data, the birth rate is now around or just below 36 per thousand and the death rate 20 per thousand.

[13] Most of them come from Shivpuri. Vegetable plots are also coming up.
[14] Most of the operations took place before 1975–7.

122   *India's Changing Rural Scene*

A last point emerges from this study: the groups who most bene-fited from this diversified process of growth are the Brahmins and the Chamars. The Kirars did not find as many jobs in the tertiary sector as the Brahmins did, hence their condition tended to deteriorate in the 1960s. In more recent years, however, their situation has tended to improve as they have become more involved in the overall process of growth and the diversification of the economy.

This case study shows certain similarities to Mirpur: increase in agricultural wages, construction of new houses (though the latter process is wider in Piparsod), improvements in food and dress. The major difference between them lies in the fact that there has been much more economic diversification in Piparsod, which has compen-sated for the relatively narrow prospects for agricultural growth, especially in the case of foodgrains. In fact, as far as irrigated crops are concerned, the pattern in Piparsod is closer to Karwad than to Mirpur. Here, we also notice the importance of an expanding trade network between villages and district towns.

CHAPTER 12

Arid and Semi-desert Conditions

The approach to these problems differs from the one we have followed so far. Instead of focusing my study on one, or a few, villages, I visited several parts of Jodhpur district in Rajasthan in order to examine a wide range of problems. Some of the technical issues I came across were particularly complex and it is not within the scope of this work to offer a detailed analysis of them. I have, thus, merely identified some such issues.

The so-called arid zone in India occupies over 320,000 square kilometres in Rajasthan, Haryana, Gujarat and some parts of the Deccan. According to the Central Arid Zone Research Institute (CAZRI) in Jodhpur 'the widespread notion that the desert [of Thar] has been advancing at the rate of half a mile per year from the beginning of this century... lacks scientific unanimity'. What is clear, on the other hand, is that the vegetation and land resources are overexploited for two main reasons. The population of the Rajasthan desert has increased from 3.4 million in 1901 to 8.9 million in 1979. The livestock population has gone up from 9.4 million in 1951 to 15.5 million in 1972. Goats and sheep are also increasing fast, an overall trend which is checked only temporarily in times of drought by the large-scale death of cattle. As a result, marginal land is open to the plough and overgrazing has become widespread. The annual rainfall gives only a very rough idea of the situation in view of the erratic rainfall pattern. For the whole of Rajasthan precipitation amounts to 63.6–58.6 centimetres a year, but it varies between 33 and 83 centimetres. The average is much lower in the western districts than in the eastern parts of the state:

	Annual Normal Rainfall in Centimetres	1975–6	1976–7
Jodhpur	32	60	66
Jaisalmer	16	41	36[1]

[1] Directorate of Agriculture, Jaipur.

During these two years the monsoon was very generous (there may also have been very mild winter rains), but frequently the rains are much below normal in Jodhpur and often fail completely in Jaisalmer. High solar radiation, and low and erratic precipitation result in high evaporation and high aridity. The subterranean 'flow of water becomes erratic, ground water lies very deep and is generally brackish and saline and there are no perennial rivers'.[2] All these factors raise complex issues, where development and ecology are closely interconnected with a set of technical and socio-economic problems.

In Jodhpur District

When proceeding from Jaipur to Jodhpur in February 1979 we first drove across a countryside which reminded us of western U.P.—fine wheat fields irrigated by tubewells and properly manured with chemical fertilizers. But further towards the south-west the landscape becomes more severe with rugged hills, undulating and barren plateaux and only small patches of irrigated fields. Beyond Jodhpur, towards Osian or Jaisalmer semi-desert or desert conditions are common with a few sand dunes, shrubs, grass here and there, some fields where bajra has been harvested, herds of cattle, sheep and goats. In Manaklav, a village of 1,500 inhabitants, farmers live on the proceeds of their land and their cattle. In the last few years, the rains have been fairly good and this has pushed yields of bajra to 500 kilograms per hectare. In the rabi some open wells using the mot system irrigate patches of wheat. A farmer explained that he used only farm manure because the water was too saline to enable him to apply chemical fertilizers, and this was why he could not get more than 1,250 kilograms per hectare. In addition to grain all landowners have at least a few cows that yield two to three litres of milk a day, which is more than the yield in the Ganges basin. In semi-desert conditions it is possible to produce different kinds of fodder, except during periods of drought.[3]

Further along the road we stopped and talked to some Mochis (Chamars, shoe makers). Lal Ram, one of them, lived with his three children, his wife and his widowed sister. He earned Rs 3–4 a day making shoes and worked for 20 to 25 days a month. His children looked after his ten goats whose milk they drank. He sold a goat from

[2] See CAZRI, *Research Highlights 1959–77* (Jodhpur, n.d.) pp. 6–9.

[3] In spite of its poor appearance the grass is fairly rich in protein and there are fewer animal diseases under semi-desert conditions.

time to time. The family did not seem to be badly off. They were able to eat three meals a day and even have meat occasionally.

Another group of Mochis included six brothers and their families. Together they owned 9.6 hectares of land. Several parts of their land were fallow every two years. Other plots bore bajra when the rains came. This was not enough to feed such a large group of people and they had to look for other jobs as field labourers. They also made shoes or buckets for the wells. For this they got Rs 4–5 without food. Ten years ago the same work had fetched them Rs 2. Neither the adults nor the children seemed to be badly off. Most of them had three sets of clothes. They also had a few cows and goats. Unlike so many Chamars who had lost their traditional occupation because of the advent of big leather factories and, more recently, plastic goods, in Rajasthan leather goods and handicrafts remained very active. They had benefited from the encouragement given by the government to cottage industry after Independence. The number of people wearing traditional leather sandals was more striking here than in other states.

In Barli village, fourteen kilometres away from Jodhpur on the road to Jaisalmer, we came across a joint family of Kumhars (potters). For six months they worked at their traditional job, each of the two men earning Rs 2.50–3.50 a day, but they had to order earth from elsewhere. This came by truck and took away a sizeable part of their profit. When they could, both men worked as field labourers for Rs 3 a day as against Re 1 ten years ago. They had one cow which gave 1.5 litres of milk a day; this was consumed by the children, some of whom attended school. They used their two donkeys to sell pots in nearby villages. It is difficult to say whether life had improved for them. At best one can say that they managed to make both ends meet. Some other poor people were doing better. Jodhpur city has considerably expanded in the last thirty years. Many new houses under construction still use stones as building materials and this helps quarry work from which workers earn Rs 5 a day as opposed to Re 1 fifteen years ago.

Hari Singh, a Rajput, was the head of a large family of forty people. They could not live on their eight hectares of land, half of which was fallow every two years. However, they had a well which used the *mot* system, and with the help of this they managed to get 400 kilograms per hectare of bajra on the irrigated plots. Others may get less. In winter Hari Singh would sow one hectare of local wheat which gave him 1,200 kilograms per hectare. He rented a tractor for plough-ing.[4] Hari Singh's four daughters and three sons were married. Two years previously, in 1976, he had bought a second-hand truck for Rs 50,000 and, with the help of one son, he used this for transport. Another son worked in a bank in Jodhpur. Hari Singh had five good cows, each of which yielded six litres of milk a day; part of this was sold. Because of all these different activities the whole family was fairly comfortable.

The village faces severe drinking water problems. When the rains are not scarce the local tank and a well supply water for five or six months. During the rest of the year the women have to walk three kilometres away to find water. Further on the same road we stopped at Agolai, forty-five kilometres from Jodhpur. The government had started a drinking water supply scheme here. A deep tubewell had been dug and a network of twenty-two kilometres of pipes had been fitted with taps in each village covered by it. Some people had also benefited from the latest scheme started in Rajasthan, which has also been introduced in some other states in India. This is the Antyodaya scheme by which five of the poorest families in a village are selected and given special assistance in the form of loans and subsidies.

Hari Ram (a Mochi) was a clever young man, married and with three small children. His traditional occupation did not bring in enough money to live by and so he had taken advantage of a loan-cum-subsidy to buy 30 sheep and one mule. He had also received 12 hectares of government land where he grew bajra. He rented a tractor and paid Rs 30–40 an hour. He had plans to gradually sell his sheep. In addition, he worked five months in a year on the Rajasthan Canal Project,[5] where he earned Rs 7 a day. Thus, with government assist-ance and these different activities, his standard of living was improving.

Bura Ram was also young. He belonged to the Bhils, a scheduled tribe, common in Rajasthan. He lived with his wife and his three small children. During the Emergency he was allotted 2.5 hectares of government land. He grew bajra and got 125–150 kilograms per hectare. He also worked as a field labourer for only Rs 2–2.50. However, he got more when he ploughed other landowners' land with his pair of bullocks. He fed seven goats and sold one or two a year

[4] There are 3 tractors in Barli.

[5] The Rajasthan Canal Project plants to irrigate wide tracts of virgin land in the north-west of Rajasthan.

which brougt him Rs 50 per head. He also worked occasionally on the Rajasthan Canal for Rs 5-7, like several other people. He did not complain about his standard of living and except in times of drought, enjoyed several sources of income.

Taking the Pali road in another direction we stopped at Kali Baktashani. The village had several irrigated patches of land covered by two tubewells which belonged to the former *jagirdars* (landlords). Kumar Rup Singh, a landlord, was one of them. He had just inherited sixteen hectares after the death of his father. He had sold his bullocks and bought a tractor. Three cows supplied milk to his family. Rup Singh used new seeds of wheat which, with some urea, yielded about 2,000 kilograms per hectare. In the kharif he grew bajra. Another Rajput sowed only local wheat on his irrigated land. Wages for labourers varied between Rs 4-5 with some food. Both tubewells were near the river bed so that an ample supply of water could be ensured. Ground water was too saline to be used.

We do not have enough data on wages and yields to make the sort of comparisons we have made in other surveys. The growth of bajra is so heavily dependent on the rains that a definite upward trend of yields is by no means certain. Any increase in the sown area also depends closely on the rains. There has been some progress in wheat production in so far as wells and tubewells do not dry up. Wages are far from uniform. In cases when they reach Rs 5 one can talk of an improvement in real terms. In those cases where very small farmers and landless labourers are not victims of acute poverty, this is only because of the wide range of their activities, as for example handicrafts for the Mochis, stone quarrying, temporary employment on the Rajasthan Canal and animal husbandry.

The Expansion of the Milk Trade

Since 1972, definite efforts have been made to encourage animal husbandry and milk collection. A network of co-operatives covers 170 villages out of the 700 in the district. The villages presently left out are inaccessible, being connected by sandy tracks where trucks cannot go. Every day, 30,000 litres of milk are transported to Delhi. We visited some villages on the 'milk road' towards Barmer. The cattle who give milk are fed on the stalks and leaves of bajra as well as weeds and grass. In addition to animal husbandry, farmers grow bajra which, in good years, has a yield of 400 kilograms per hectare, 100 kilograms when the rains are not heavy and sometimes nothing at all.

For drinking water villagers rely on their local pond which supplies water the whole year round if the rains have been generous, or only for six months if they have not. In 1974, however, the drought was so severe that many cattle-owners had to leave their villages with their animals in search of water.

Fighting the Desert

In 1971, Jodhpur district's population numbered 1,153,000 inhabitants spread over 22,720 square kilometres. Around one million hectares are cultivable, but 60 per cent had been degraded by erosion and overgrazing. Irrigation covered 43,000 hectares, mostly through wells and tubewells and around 60 per cent of the ground water potential had been used. There were no prospects of surface water or canal irrigation. Between 400 and 600,000 hectares were devoted to bajra, with an average yield of 400 kilograms per hectare. Wheat amounted to 40–60,000 hectares, mostly irrigated, though often inadequately, with average yields at around 1,200 kilograms per hectare in good years. Under such conditions it is easy to understand why the consumption of chemical fertilizers had not gone above 300 tons in terms of nutrients in 1978–9. It is obvious that the future of agriculture remains dim.

Created in 1959, the Central Arid Zone Research Institute is looking for ways and means to develop this difficult area. One of its programmes deals with arid land management. Experiments are made to stabilize sand dunes through the planting of trees and grass, so that farmers will be able to meet their requirements in fuel and fodder. After some good showers, seedlings of acacia and juliflora are planted at a ratio of 550 trees per hectare. In between these rows grass seeds are sown. After every ten years farmers will collect 5 tons of wood per hectare and 1 ton of grass per year. The first experiments have been successful but the cost is high. Apart from the purchase of seedlings the dunes have to be fenced in with barbed wire, which costs Rs 2,000–3,000 per hectare. In addition, an attempt has been made to create shelter belts of trees in order to protect the crops. Other schemes aim at grass land development. The Institute deals with water management, terracing, contour furrowing and bunding techniques which permit higher water retention and which may lead to a better bajra crop in the catchment area below. Storage of water in artificial ponds during the kharif enables people to grow different crops in the rabi.

In 1975 sprinkler irrigation was introduced on the farm of a retired army officer. The officer installed three tubewells of 10 HP each with pipes and sprinklers. This system has the great advantage of saving more water than flow irrigation, but its capital cost amounts to a few thousand rupees per hectare. In 1976 the CAZRI installed a drip and sprinkler irrigation system on a private farm. This is even more efficient than a sprinkler, but it is also more expensive: investments per hectare amount to Rs 20,000. The farmers, however, are happy with it. Of their ten hectares, six are irrigated now by a tubewell supplying water to the pipes and drippers. They grow wheat and vegetables and papaya trees. While these experiments are all very interesting, they are not within the reach of the small farmers. Also, they have to be used for the richest crops such as vegetables and orchards in order to be worthwhile. It remains to be seen how such complex systems will be maintained once they become fairly wide-spread. The CAZRI is also promoting a gobar gas plant that is cheaper than the one we saw in U.P.

So far, Jodhpur has done reasonably well. The economy is far from static, and the district administration has several able officers who pay a great deal of attention to development problems. The Institute is becoming increasingly involved in concrete applied research. Yet we must bear in mind the fact that, for several years before our visit, Jodhpur had had no drought. During 1979 the situation deteriorated seriously—after unusual floods in July there was a very severe drought.

Milk production, the slaughtering of sheep, goats and buffaloes offer much greater possibilities of expansion than agriculture. Leather handicrafts also offer interesting development potential. However, will it be possible to curb the overexploitation of the vegetation and land resources in time? The means envisaged so far are, in several cases, too expensive to be implemented on a large scale. Other solutions will have to be found. The problem of drinking water, too, is one that requires attention. A great number of villages are still dependent on bad water or, worse, have no water at all for several months. In the whole of Rajasthan, out of 33,305 villages, 10,411 have no reliable source of drinking water within a distance of 1.6 kilometres, 3,888 have water that is susceptible to disease, and 9,730 have excessively saline water. This makes a total of 24,037 'problem villages' which affect 17 million people.[6]

[6] *Draft Five Year Plan of Rajasthan, 1978–83* (Jaipur, 1978).

Summing Up

At the end of this long trek through the villages it is time to summarize observations. India's countryside has come a long way since Independence and, even in remote areas as in the hilly and tribal tracts of Orissa, social and economic changes have occurred. New techniques are noticeable practically everywhere, social relations are also changing under all sorts of circumstances and in certain areas, there are growing tensions which have often led to violence. Most of these violent clashes have, however, occurred in areas of slow economic growth.

Where there are wide differences it is in the size and speed of the socio-economic changes. Areas which have benefited from an early start in pre-Independence times have moved fast while others are only just awakening under considerable constraints. Several regions still have a large untapped growth potential, while in others the margin is narrower. A second feature is the impact of growth on the poor. Our case studies show how fallacious is the latter part of the slogan, 'the rich get richer and the poor poorer', in the so-called green revolution. Equally wrong is the claim that small farmers are by-passed in the process of growth, because they are supposedly unable to afford new inputs. We also noticed that labourers' wages increase in real terms wherever growth and the diversification of the local economy are sufficiently strong. This leads to more employment opportunities.

The overall policy of rural development has clearly improved through a process of trial and error. Today the sense of priorities and practical tasks is better grasped than fifteen years ago. Supplies of fertilizers and seeds operate more smoothly. Village roads have increased in number. However, the serious shortcomings have still not been overcome. The first relates to water management, there being a serious lack of irrigation and drainage, especially in eastern India; and the second to energy. While rural electrification has grown rapidly, the supply of power cannot cope with the demand, a fact aggravated by poor maintenance operations of the electrical network. The crisis became really dramatic in 1979 when it was aggravated by a new shortage—that of diesel oil. Thus the very severe drought of 1979 was aggravated because a large number of tubewells and pumpsets remained idle for lack of power.

PART II
New Strategies or New Rhetoric?

CHAPTER 13

The All-India Outlook

It is time now to leave the villages and the paddy fields and to see how our observations fit into the overall picture of India's rural development, in terms of both growth and income, especially among the poorer people. We shall deal with each area separately.

The North-West

How would we rate Bulandshahr's performance within the north-west (i.e. Punjab, Haryana and the western districts of U.P., a region of 34 million inhabitants) in 1971? Punjab's achievements are the most spectacular because of the more intensive use of certain factors (which also existed in Bulandshahr district) such as a favourable physical milieu, good irrigation potential for both surface and ground water, a relatively early start (although east Punjab was substantially less advanced in 1947 than the famous canal colonies of west Punjab which became part of Pakistan), first-class farmers, many of whom, like the Sikh Jats, had emigrated from Pakistan and had done their best to make the area prosperous. Simultaneously, the rural infrastructure expanded rapidly—villages were provided with good access roads and electricity. The latter has, by now, reached practically all the villages. In addition, trade and market places grew and became more diversified. A large number of small and medium-sized industrial units mushroomed in the towns and big villages. They made agricultural implements, threshing machines, pumps and motors as well as bicycles, leather goods, food products, electrical appliances, etc. The chart below shows how average crop yields in Punjab rose from 1960 to 1978.

Punjab: Average Yields (in kilograms per hectare)[1]

Crop	1960-1	1964-5	1970-1	1977-8
Wheat	1,237	1,510	2,237	2,500
Rice	1,035	1,222	1,765	2,897
Cotton lint	270	300	n.a.	356
Sugar	3,680	3,640	n.a.	5.440

[1]The selected years enjoyed good, if not very good, weather conditions.

While the area devoted to wheat increased from 2.3 million hectares (5.14 million tons) in 1970–1 to 2.6 million hectares (6.6 million tons) in 1977–8, the changes are even more impressive for rice: 476,000 hectares in 1972–3, 858,000 in 1977–8, producing 1.1 million and 2.5 million tons respectively. These trends have continued: production for 1980–1 was 3.2 million tons of rice and 7.7 million tons of wheat. On the other hand, sugarcane and cotton expanded at a much slower pace. For the former, part of the reason for the slow expansion was that Punjab has cold winters which do not make for an ideal climate for this crop.

Such tremendous growth can be explained by a progress in irrigation (mostly private tubewells),[2] the use of new seeds for wheat and rice and a sharp rise in the consumption of chemical fertilizers.[3] Tractors also helped in this, especially because they made double cropping easier by doing the ploughing more rapidly, but they had, as is well known in most countries, a much smaller impact on yields per hectare.

Not only did the rich get richer, but the poor got less poor. Wages, in real terms as well as employment opportunities, increased to the point where Punjab had to resort to importing labour, particularly from eastern U.P. and Bihar, especially for rice cultivation at which farmers were not so experienced. Daily wages amounted to Rs 2.50 per day in 1961, 8.50–10.50 in 1975, often more than that now. For paddy transplantation the wages were Rs 15 to Rs 20 plus food in 1978–9.[4] There were, however, cases of abuse and exploitation,[5] and wages were not uniformly high. Even in a village not very far from Ludhiana, daily wages remained at Rs 5 or 6 because of the strong hold the Jat Sikhs had over labour. On the other hand it is significant to note that out of 48 Harijan workers, only 20 remain agricultural labourers, 20 are now commuter industrial workers, 6 are soldiers and 2 weavers.[6] This is a typical example of how activities outside agriculture are increasing and improving the lot of the poor.

[2] 77 per cent of the cultivated area is irrigated; cropping intensity is 151, i.e. half of the area is double cropped.
[3] Seventy-three kilograms per hectare in terms of nutrients (1977–8) for the gross cropped area.
[4] *Overseas Hindustan Times*, 6 September 1979.
[5] *Economic and Political Weekly*, 28 April 1979.
[6] See the article by Aminder Pal Singh in *Economic and Political Weekly*, 27 October 1979.

With all these factors combined, the small state of Punjab, with only 1.54 per cent of India's geographical area and 2.47 per cent of its population, was able, in 1977-8, to supply the central pool with 63 per cent (3.2 million tons) of the wheat procured by the central government, as well as 56 per cent (1.9 million tons) of rice. This success story, which is equalled by very few in the Third World, is the result of a relatively smooth process of growth involving a favourable physical milieu, good farmers, a good mix of new inputs and research, and attention to non-agricultural sectors such as roads, electricity, market places and small and medium-sized industries. The small size of the state, the relatively small size of the districts, as well as a good administration inherited from the British must also be taken into account. In addition, Punjab is favoured with a lower density of population than many other parts of India: 268 inhabitants per square kilometre in 1971.[7]

Though less impressive, growth in Haryana has been fairly high for similar reasons. Here, in place of the Sikh Jats of Punjab are the Hindu Jats of Haryana who are of the same stock as our farmers in Mirpur. Average yields of wheat are around 2,024 kilograms per hectare and those of rice 2,500 or above. The expansion of the latter has been fast, both in area and in yields: in 1970-1, the figures were 371,000 tons of rice and 2.3 million tons of wheat; in 1980—1, 1.2 million tons of rice and 3.6 million tons of wheat. Haryana is also an important supplier of wheat and rice to the central pool.

The western districts of U.P.—from Muzaffarnagar down to Mathura—fall in the same category as Bulandshahr, with rather similar growth conditions for the period 1962-5 to 1970-3. The annual growth of their agricultural output ranged between 4.5 and 5 per cent a year (this was as much as 6.47 in the case of Aligar! while in progressive districts in haryana it was around 6.2 per cent.[8] Although we lack districtwise data for the decade 1970-1 to 1980-1 for western U.P., it is clear the the latter made a definite contribution to the overall growth of wheat in the state: production increased during that period from 7.7 million tons to 13.1 million. In western U.P. wheat yields of 2,000 kilograms per hectare or above are now

[7] For all the data quoted above see *Five Year Story of Agricultural Production in Punjab 1974–78* (Chandigarh, 1978).

[8] G. S. Bhalla, Y. K. Alagh, *Performance of Indian Agriculture* (New Delhi, 1979), pp. 42–3.

quite common. As to rice, its expansion has been much slower.

The Advanced Areas on the East Coast [9]

Of the 13 million hectares of irrigated rice in India (*Agricultural Census,* 1971) 3.03 million lie in Andhra Pradesh and 2.4 million in Tamil Nadu. In both states a sizeable area depends on tanks in the interior which makes for inadequate irrigation. The coastal districts in both Andhra Pradesh and Tamil Nadu are the richest rice areas because they enjoy either canal irrigation or open wells-cum-pump-sets, as well as shallow tubewells called filter points. Such regions, however, face dangers such as cyclones which are unknown in the north. The coastal districts account for 12 million people (1971) in Andhra Pradesh and 5 million in Tamil Nadu (not counting Madras which has 2.5 million).

Unfortunately, it is not always possible to isolate slow and relatively progressive areas on a district basis. Some of them, like Thanjavur, are quite homogeneous, while others, as in coastal Andhra, include both properly irrigated deltas and inland areas less irrigated or only rainfed, which brings down the average district data. The total growth in rice production amounts to 68 per cent in Tamil Nadu and 45 per cent in Andhra between the two good years 1960-1 and 1975-6. [10] In both cases this is substantial but it is lower than the wheat increase in the whole of the north-west and the rice increase in the Punjab. [11] This gap is caused by several factors. While, from the very beginning, new seeds of wheat proved well suited to local conditions, new paddy seeds were not so successful. Grown mostly in the rainy season, they are more exposed to pests and diseases than crops that are grown in the dry season. In addition, several of the early HYV were ill-adapted to local conditions. While the situation is improving with the latest seeds, all the difficulties have not yet been overcome.

The quality of irrigation must also be considered. In the north-

[9] We could not include surveys of the west coast in Kerala. As will be mentioned in Chapter 15, statistics are particularly misleading on that area as there is a wide range of opportunities for various activities and sources of food.

[10] In 1977-8 the consumption of chemical fertilizers (nutrients) had reached 64 kilograms per hectare (gross cropped area) in Tami Nadu and 39.4 in Andhra. The averages should be higher in coastal areas since these data include districts in the interior and rain-fed areas where the consumption of fertilizers is low.

[11] Tamil Nadu: 5.2 million tons of rice in 1975-6, 4.2 million tons in 1976-7, 5.9 million in 1977-8, 5.8 million in 1979-80, but 4 million in 1980-1. Andhra: 6.5 million tons in 1975-6, 4.9 million in 1976-7, 5.6 million in 1977-8, 7.3 million in 1980-1.

west, much of the progress in irrigation was due to tubewells which, provided the electricity and diesel oil supply were satisfactory, ensured better irrigation than canals which, especially in the south, could be affected by drought. One must, however, emphasize that there was a sharp rise in the number of tubewells-cum-pumpsets in certain rich districts of Tamil Nadu such as Chingleput and north and south Arcot. As many as 800,000 pumps were energized throughout the state in 1978.[12] Apart from this, increases in yields were already quite substantial towards the end of the 1950s and the early 1960s (i.e. before the advent of the new seeds). Hence the rice areas had a head-start which was bound to affect future growth rates.

Small rural industries did not expand to the same extent as in the north-west for reasons which are not too clear. One of them may have to do with history. Punjabi artisans (particularly Sikhs) were already impressing the British by their technical skills in the nineteenth century by making Persian wheels, bullock-drawn flour mills, metal work, carpentry, etc. As tubewells and other machines proliferated, these same people became mechanics and machine operators.[13] In some parts of the south that were dominated by canal irrigation, the expansion of tubewells was more limited and there were a smaller number of tractors. This affected industries and workshops connected with the production, maintenance and repair of these items.

Electricity has spread quickly into the villages. In Tamil Nadu, practically all the villages are covered by now. In Andhra, a number of the villages located in the interior are not yet electrified; this is also the case in coastal areas where only 70 to 80 per cent of the villages are. As far as wages are concerned, in such prosperous areas there has been some growth in real terms. Employment opportunities have also been positively influenced by rural development.

Central Uttar Pradesh

Between the dynamic districts of western Uttar Pradesh and the slow-moving eastern district lies an intermediate zone of some 36

[12] Open well-cum-pumpset: 3–5 HP, 1.2–2 hectares irrigated, 2–4 hectares in particularly favourable areas. In certain places the replenishment of ground water cannot be relied upon and power troubles are common.

[13] S. Saberwal, 'Status and Entrepreneurship: The Ramgarhia Case', and P. C. Agarwal, 'Some Social Aspects of the Green Revolution in Ludhiana', p. 266 in M. N. Srinivas, S. Seshaiah, V. S. Parthasarathy, eds., *Dimensions of Social Change in India* (New Delhi, 1978).

million hectares (1971) in the Ganges basin.[14] Some districts of this area have been developing rapidly with an annual growth rate of around 4.5 per cent in the period 1962-5 to 1970-3. For most of them the growth rate oscillates between 1.8 and 3.8 per cent, with a few falling in the region of 1.5 per cent. It seems likely that such growth trends have continued in more recent years. The whole area belongs to the transitional zone where wheat is gradually decreasing in the cropped areas, in favour of rice. New seeds and irrigation are progressing and drainage problems are less serious than further east. It seems plausible, though a detailed study would be able to establish this better, that the ratio of agricultural output to population has remained favourable.

The Middle and Lower Ganges Basin, the Plains of Assam and Orissa [15]

Our field studies in these areas are, unfortunately, also representative of socio-economic conditions which affect a considerable part of India's territory and population. The eastern districts of Uttar Pradesh and the plains of Bihar make up 200,000 square kilometres with 70 million inhabitants (according to the 1971 census). To this one must add 132,000 square kilometres and 27 million people in the plains of Assam and Orissa. The common feature of these areas is their enormous untapped growth potential. During the period 1962-5 to 1970-3 the total growth rate in agriculture was 1.5 to 3 per cent per year in the less economically backward districts, and below 1.5 per cent in others. In many districts there has even been an actual fall. Except in a few places, the growth in population has either been overtaking that of agriculture or just falling short of it. Progress in rice has been particularly slow, except in West Bengal. For the period mentioned above, it varied between an average annual growth rate of often below 2 per cent and a negative one. From 1973 onwards, we lack precise districtwise data but rough indications point to only a very moderate improvement, and that too, not everywhere.

For Uttar Pradesh, during the period 1962-73, out of the fifteen eastern districts, only five had an overall annual agricultural growth rate above 1.9 per cent. In Bihar, rice increased by an average of 9 per

[14] We have left out of our study the Himalayan districts: 2.26 million inhabitants.
[15] For 1962-3 to 1972-3 the data are derived from G. S. Bhalla and Y. K. Alagh, op. cit., and for later years from the *Economic Survey*.

cent between 1970–3 and 1975–8; and even less when we compare two good years: 1971–2 with 5.3 million and 1977–8 with 5.5 million. For all foodstuffs there was a total (not annual) increase of 9 per cent between 1971-2 and 1977-8, two good years. In both states, the population increased faster during the decade 1970–1 to 1980–1 than during the previous one: 25.5 per cent versus 19.8 for U.P., 23.9 versus 21.3 for Bihar. It is obvious that the overall food to population ratio is getting worse in many districts.

Foodgrain and population trends are even more unbalanced in Assam. The latter grew by 35 per cent during the decades 1961-71 and 1971–81,[16] while the output of rice was 2.25 million tons in 1968-9 and, in two other good years, 1977-8 and 1980–1, it touched 2.3 and 2.5 million tons respectively. The picture is no more encouraging in Orissa: The peak production figure of 4.7 million tons of rice in 1968-9 has never been touched again. In 1977–8 it came fairly close with 4.3 million tons. It fell to 2.9 million in 1979–80 and rose again to 4.3 million in 1980–1. The population increased by 25 and 19 per cent during the last two decades.

How can we explain such a slow growth in agriculture in spite of very favourable natural conditions? Soils are, on the whole, good or very good, rainfall is relatively high, though sometimes too high. There is plenty of ground and surface water available for irrigation.

The major constraint is poor water management. Irrigation is progressing much too slowly. With an increasing population irrigation is becoming more and more important as a complement to monsoon delays and failures, and as a decisive factor in order to push crops in the dry season. Plenty of delays affect major, and even small, irrigation projects. If we look at the Son, Gandak or Kosi projects in Bihar, various works in Assam or the improvement of the Mahanadi delta in Orissa, we come across similar defects—the slow pace of construction, lack of field channels, lack of levelling in the fields and sometimes, as in the Kosi area, rapid silting of canals. Commenting on Bihar, Pradhan Prasad writes: 'Even after 10 years of the completion of the Kosi canal system, the utilisation of its irrigation potential remains less than one third. It has also been found that the percentage for major and medium schemes in 1974–5 in Bihar was only 58.5.'[17]

The picture is not very different now. It seems that the Kosi

---

[16] In addition to natural increase there is also immigration.

[17] Pradhan H. Prasad, 'A Strategy for Rapid Development of Bihar Economy', *Journal of Social and Economic Studies* (1977), v(ii).

Command Area Development Agency was granted Rs 870 million for the construction of field channels in 1978-9, but most of this money remained unutilized.[18] In addition there are the factions and caste affiliations between engineers, lack of commitment amongst officers, corruption, etc.[19]

The progress of state tubewells faces other problems. In eight districts of north Bihar there are 900 state tubewells. Their energization was slow and their utilization remains poor.[20] Of the 2,999 state tubewells as many as 1,753 had no channels in 1978.[21] In the same year the Bihar Government started a very ambitious five-year scheme to install 600,000 private tubewells: 200,000 bamboo ones (with one pump and four borings), 300,000 shallow and 100,000 deeper ones. Most of them were supposed to rely on diesel because of the acute electricity shortage which became worse in 1979, but by that time another serious shortage had appeared—the supply of diesel oil.

The widespread lack of drainage was also tackled rather slowly. Out of a total ground area of 17.3 million hectares, 4.3 million are flood-prone,[22] and this figure does not include all areas that are exposed to excess water in normal years.

Similar defects exist in Assam. Only 8 per cent of the net cropped area enjoys reliable irrigation facilities. Only in the last five or six years now has the state government begun to make greater efforts to tackle this problem. Let us look, amongst others, at the World Bank supported schemes that we spoke of earlier. The target, for the scheme in Nowgong district, is 12,500 shallow tubewells and 2,500 small low lift pumps in different districts. However, farmers who would normally be keen to set up a tubewell or buy a pumpset are discouraged by administrative delays as well as delays in energizing pumps and completing canals. Drainage is equally necessary—of the 1.8 million cultivated hectares in the Brahmaputra valley, 245,000 are chronically flood-affected and 90,000 are occasionally affected.[23]

In Orissa, in 1973-4, only 31 per cent of the irrigation potential created at that time by major and medium works was actually utilized, half of it for minor irrigation (lift and well) schemes. As early as

---

[18]*Economic Times,* 6 March 1979.
[19]See *Times of India,* 17 January 1979.
[20]Gandak Command Area Development Agency, Muzaffarpur 1978.
[21]Government of Bihar, *Draft Five Year Plan 1973-83,* p. 29.
[22]Ibid., p. 77.
[23]*Assam World Bank Project* (Gauhati, 1976).

1972 the Irrigation Commission of India had insisted on the speedy construction of field channels.[24] Six years later, a large amount of work remained to be done both in this regard and in respect to drainage. In 1978, when preparing revised estimates on the Mahanadi delta irrigation projects (started in 1957), the Irrigation Department emphasized several types of delays such as those relating to design, supply of cement, increasing costs, etc. The levelling of land, especially in the interior, is also far from satisfactory. The progress of HYV seeds was bound to be limited by water constraints such as the lack of irrigation in the dry season and sometimes drought in the monsoon and, on the other hand, excessive rain which prevents the growth of dwarf varieties of rice. For the same reasons, the consumption of chemical fertilizers remains very low, as the figures below show:

Consumption of Chemical Fertilizers Per Gross Cropped Hectare

Assam	1.9 kilograms (nutrients)
Bihar	16.0 kilograms
Orissa	9.0 kilograms

Source: *F.A.I. Annual Review of Fertilizer Consumption and Production 1977–8.*

The sluggish growth of agriculture is accompanied by equally slow trends in other fields of the economy. The rural infrastructure, in terms of roads and electricity, is not particularly advanced. Local small industries play a minor role and major industries absorb only a very small proportion of the active population. Thus neither the secondary nor the tertiary sector can even partly offset the shortcomings of agriculture. This is evident from the low rate of urbanization: 10 per cent in Bihar, 8.4 per cent in Assam, 8.3 per cent in Orissa (in 1971) and 10–15 per cent or less in eastern U.P. On the other hand, the more advanced areas mentioned above have an urbanized sector of between 20 and 30 per cent.

With such poor growth performances, a stagnant or declining standard of living is bound to affect a sizeable part of the population, as we observed in the field. One must, however, make some rough distinctions. Conditions seem worse in Bihar because of heavier population pressure than in Assam or Orissa. In eastern U.P. some districts are ahead of the poorest districts of Bihar. In addition to these differences, social relations vary. North Bihar, with its big

[24] K. W. Easter, 'Neglected Opportunities in Irrigation', *Economic and Political Weekly,* 6 April 1974.

landlords, represents a rather exceptional case at the all-India level. Here one can really speak of semi-feudal relations on a rather large scale. Yet the conflicts are not confined to landlords versus small farmers and landless labourers. Acute tensions have also marred relations between middle class/caste farmers[25] and dominant castes, and between the former and Harijans. Violent incidents have taken place in several districts of north and south Bihar, particularly in the last few years, in which a number of Harijans have been killed. In Assam and Orissa such tensions are either much milder or have assumed a different pattern. There are few big landlords, and caste competition is, at least for the present, less prominent. Moreover, in Assam, one of the major sources of tension is the conflict between the large number of migrants from other states or from Bangladesh, and the native inhabitants.

In spite of all these shortcomings one cannot say that the economy has been really stagnant. We have come across evidence of changes and improvements in the standards of living, some progress in irrigation, progress in wheat in eastern U.P., and in Bihar, plots of high land sown with HYV paddy. Some landless people are now better off. One finds middle farmers belonging to middle castes who are improving their lot. A few upper landowners are becoming more enterprising, though the number of gentleman farmers *à la* Punjabi remains low.[26] Yet, the overall process of growth and diversification of the economy has not gathered enough momentum to lead to an expansion wide enough to affect a large number of the poor.

West Bengal

Within the vast area of eastern India, West Bengal represents a case *per se*. Most districts in this state have known a growth rate above 2 per cent per year in the period 1962–5 to 1970–3,[27] a trend which has continued in recent years. There has also been a sizeable expansion of minor irrigation which has allowed for more crops in the dry season, as well as the expansion of HYV rice, though the recent fall in the

---

[25] See the agitation for reserved seats in favour of the so-called 'backward classes' who are in fact rising middle classes (Kurmis, Yadavs) struggling against Brahmins, Bhumihars, Rajputs and Kayasths who have tended to monopolize jobs in the tertiary sector.

[26] See the fascinating description of Bihari landlords and Punjabi farmers in Kusum Nair's *In Defense of the Irrational Farmer* (Chicago, 1979).

[27] G. S. Bhalla, Y. K. Alagh, op. cit.

output of wheat is surprising.[28]

	1967–8	1977–8	1980–1
Wheat	71,000 tons	1,051,000 tons	473,000 tons
Rice	5,208,000 tons	7,508,700 tons	7,465,600 tons

The average consumption of chemical fertilizers per gross cropped hectare, though much lower than in the Punjab or Tamil Nadu, is 22.4 kilograms higher than in Bihar.[29] I have no data on wages[30] but, as far as employment is concerned, a study by P. Bardhan indicates for the Hoogly region (a progressive district with 4.25 per cent agricultural growth per year from 1962–5 to 1970–3) that inputs of labour per acre nearly doubled due to increased irrigation, more double cropping and a growing diversification of crops.[31]

One must also bear in mind that West Bengal's economy is relatively well diversified with a large industrial sector including not only big factories but also a great number of small industries. Trade and other services are also important. Both these characteristics are evidenced by a high rate of urbanization: 24.6 per cent of a total population of 44.4 million in 1971. Finally, the agricultural traditions of Bengali farmers are more efficient than those of the Biharis.

The Wide Tracts of the Deccan

As we have seen, peninsular India is far from homogeneous in terms of soils, climates, patterns of crops and overall levels of development. On the whole, population densities here are much lower than in the plains. However, here too, one comes across sizeable differences. Most districts range between 100 to 190 per square kilometre, some districts in semi-desert areas falling to 20 or less, some reaching 200 to 240. Even rough trends of agricultural production are difficult to assess because of very sharp variations in crops dependent on a good or bad monsoon, since irrigation is much less developed than in the north-west or along the south-east coast. Twenty-five districts, mainly in Rajasthan, Gujarat and in the rain-shadow part of Maha-

[28] All years enjoyed good weather conditions.
[29] Such a figure may be misleading, as more fertilizers are applied for rabi irrigated crops than in the monsoon.
[30] Wages may be affected in West Bengal not only by agricultural growth but by the pressures of the Communist Party which is relatively well-rooted in the countryside.
[31] P. Bardhan, 'On Labour Absorption in Asian Rice Cultivation with particular reference to India', in *Labour Absorption in Indian Agriculture* (Bangkok, ILO, 1978), quoted by M. L. Dantwala in *Economic and Political Weekly*, 23 June 1979.

rashtra and Karnataka, have an average rainfall of from 375 to 750 millimetres, with 5–10 per cent of a total net cultivated area of 18 million hectares under irrigation. Elsewhere the irrigated area is between 10 and 15 per cent and, in relatively few districts, above 20 per cent. Practically all large and medium-scale irrigation projects have been, or still are, behind schedule. Considerable delays occurred in the construction of canals down to field channels, land reclamation and levelling. Much of this was due to lack of funds, whether we consider the southern projects like Nagarjunasagar or the northern ones like the Rajasthan Canal. The latter aims at irrigating 1.15 million hectares, an enormous task. The Project should have been completed around 1978. But, by that date, even the first stage of the project (540,000 hectares) was far from complete.[32] No less disturbing is the condition of tanks in the south of the peninsula. Tamil Nadu accounts for 37,000 tanks which command one million hectares. Poor water management and deterioration of works as well as the silting of tanks, disrepair of channels and a general lack of control in water distribution, result in the falling capacity of tanks. A project to remedy these defects was planned for 1979–80.[33]

The main cereals here are coarse grain, jowar and bajra, which do not show a significant upward trend, except under generous rainfall conditions. Fluctuations are thus very sharp. For instance, in Madhya Pradesh, coarse grain production has never again attained the exceptional level of 3.5 million tons achieved in 1967–8. Between 1970–1 and 1980–1, it fluctuated at around 2.4 to 3 million tons. Rajasthan has never succeeded in repeating its performance in the miracle year 1970–1 when the production of coarse grains had reached 4.9 million tons. Since then it has fluctuated between 2 to 3 million tons. Variations are also severe in Gujarat, where coarse grain jumped from 1.15 million tons in a bad year (1974–5), to 2.6 million under the very fine monsoon of 1975–6. In Maharashtra, after the three disastrous years from 1970 to 1972, coarse grain moved upwards. Good weather conditions have played an important role in this. It was only in 1974–5 that total foodgrain production reached 7.8 million tons again, after the comparable bumper crops of 1960–1. Increases in the last few years have been due mainly to a sharp rise in the quantity of coarse grain, which has been helped by the good

[32] In all fairness, one may add that the early provisions on these projects were too optimistic, the difficulties having been underestimated.
[33] Information supplied by the Irrigation Department, Madras,

weather.[34] As far as pulses are concerned, no clear increase is visible—there are fluctuations following a good or a bad monsoon and, in certain cases, an actual downward trend.

When taking all crops into consideration, G .K. Bhalla and Y. K. Alagh (quoted above), show (for 1962-5 to 1970-3) a sizeable increase (2 per cent or above per year) for 24 districts of Madhya Pradesh, 12 of them recording an increase below 2 per cent, and 7 recording an unspecified increase after a previous decrease. The picture for Maharashtra is particularly dark due to the very bad year at the end of the 1970-3 period; it is unduly rosy for Rajasthan because of the miracle year 1970-1, which inflated the growth rate. The hilly and plateaux areas of Bihar, Orissa and Andhra hardly indicate any progress at all. Some districts of Karnataka are expanding fast, others slowly. In Gujarat several districts have moved very slowly. No major change has occurred since 1972- 3 for wheat and rice but there is evidence of some further progress in several districts of Madhya Pradesh. Both cereals have improved their performances in Maharashtra, rice has moved up moderately in Karnataka and trends in wheat and rice are a little stronger in Gujarat. Wheat is definitely on the increase in Rajasthan, especially in the irrigated areas of the eastern districts. On the whole, yields are between 600 to 1,200 kilograms per hectare of clean rice, except in some rich districts of Karnataka which are above 2,000. For wheat, the range is between 600 and 1,500 kilograms per hectare (rarely more) in Madhya Pradesh and Rajasthan where it is an important cereal in several districts.

The Tamil Nadu interior is difficult to assess because of its great diversity. Coimbatore has enjoyed a sizeable expansion of irrigated crops. Plains devoted to irrigated paddy in Madurai and Tiruchirappalli are also moving forward. Other districts face severe constraints such as uncertain rainfall and a low irrigation potential. The prospect for cash crops such as cotton and oilseeds is not bright. Wherever they are rain-fed, as is mostly the case, yields are by and large static. Except in some rich areas like Coimbatore, yields of cotton lint often remain at around 100 kilograms per hectare or less. Wherever irrigation is available, sugarcane production has increased, particularly in parts of Andhra and Tamil Nadu.

In the districts, richer crops[35] grown on small irrigated plots can

[34]Total foodgrain production: 10.4 million tons in 1977-8, which includes 6.1 million tons of coarse grain against 4.6 million in 1974-5 , and 9.7 million in 1980-1.
[35]Usually not recorded in statistics like vegetables and fruit.

partly compensate for the poor yields of rain-fed cereals in terms of income. Another compensation comes from non-agricultural activities and the migration of labour to small and larger towns, as we have seen in Piparsod. In this regard, too, the Deccan offers great contrasts. When driving from the Bihar plains to the hilly areas of the same state and further inland into Orissa, one sees vast tracts of land that are covered with mediocre, rain-fed paddy. In a good year, this land gives 700 kilograms per hectare in terms of paddy. Elsewhere ragi, also under good rainfall conditions, yields 500 kilograms per hectare. Wells and pockets of irrigated land are rare. Even in roadside villages economic activities seem limited. Electricity, however, is more common than it was twenty years ago. There are some garages, but very few small industries. The scene is more lively in Telangana (Andhra) where tanks or wells enable small paddy fields to break, here and there, the dominant pattern of a poor rain-fed jowar. Several parts of Karnataka are clearly expanding in tertiary and secondary activities, especially in the irrigated zones and in big and middle industrial towns. The same can be seen in different parts of Tamil Nadu. Coimbatore has become an industrial city including both large and small-scale enterprises, often agro based. Medium and small manufacturers of pumps for irrigation are particularly prominent. The advanced districts of Gujarat give a similar impression.

Several district towns of Maharashtra have, like Satara, undergone substantial development and compensate for some of the shortcomings of agriculture. Such features are also noticeable in Madhya Pradesh and Rajasthan, but in these states the process seems much less advanced. In the western part of Madhya Pradesh there are long stretches of rain-fed jowar fields, the monotony of which is only broken by some better agriculture, a few big bazaars and some industrialized cities. Significant in this regard are the rates of urbanization: 28.1 per cent of the total population in Gujarat (1971), 31.2 per cent in Maharashtra, 24.3 per cent in Karnataka, but only 14.3 per cent in Madhya Pradesh, 16.3 per cent in Rajasthan, 10 to 15 per cent or less in many districts in south Bihar, inland Orissa and Andhra. To sum up, peninsular India, without the coastal areas, accounts for about 225 million inhabitants (1971) out of a total population of 547 million (1971). I would be tempted to suggest that the most difficult areas, in terms of poverty and growth potential, are in south Bihar, inland Orissa, several parts of Telengana and Rayalasema in Andhra, as well as very dry parts of Maharashtra and Gujarat.

One must add a final note of concern. The population growth rate has been higher in large parts of the Deccan than in the Ganges basin, or on the south-east coast (as the chart below shows), during 1961–71. Such a trend has been partly altered in the following decade by an increase in the rate of population growth in U.P. and Bihar.

Percentage of Population Increase in 1961–71 and 1971–81

	1961–71	*1971–81*
Gujarat	29.3	27.21
Maharashtra	27.3	24.36
Madhya Pradesh	28.7	25.15
Karnataka	24.1	26.43
Rajasthan	27.6	32.36
Orissa	25.0	19.72
Uttar Pradesh	19.8	25.49
Punjab	21.0	23.01
Bihar	21.2	23.90
Andhra Pradesh	20.6	22.76
Tamil Nadu	22.0	17.23

The case studies mentioned in the previous two chapters give us an idea of the incomes of the poor. As we have noticed, these increase in real terms wherever the process of growth is wide and diversified enough. Standards of living either remain stagnant or deteriorate in isolated villages where neither agriculture nor other activities move forward. It is not really possible to estimate the amount of bonded labour. In a recent article, the figure of two million was mentioned for the whole of India. This includes specific, and most distressing, cases of women sold for prostitution, some of whom come from the poor villages in the Himalayas.[36] The Labour Minister mentioned an estimate of 2.2 million according to a recent sample survey. Identification and rehabilitation have been tardy: 105,180 bonded labourers have been identified in twelve states; of these 104,749 have been freed and 31,844 were being rehabilitated.[37] It is important to remember also that there are areas of serious tensions which have led to violence and killing, particularly in the economically slow-moving districts of Telengana.[38] This is the region where open guerilla warfare was attempted by the Communist Party (CPI) in 1948 and continued until it became necessary for the army to intervene in 1951. Today, such

[36] *Overseas Hindustan Times*, 6 December 1979.
[37] *Hindu*, 9 December 1978.
[38] Karimnagar district, still less advanced than the Telengana region, has also been badly shaken by violence. In the period 1962–5 to 1970–3 its agricultural production was not only stagnant but falling.

agitation is revitalizing itself. Labourers are reacting against exploitation by landlords. Activists of the CPI (ML) group are inducing the poor to have the Minimum Wages Act for Agricultural Labour implemented. In recent years there have been several incidents of actual fights involving death casualties and heavy police intervention.[39]

National Data

It is time now to present the main all-India data on agricultural production and inputs.

	1949–50	1960–1	1970–1	1977–8	1978–9	1980–1
Rice	25.1	34.6	42.3	52.7	53.8	53.2
Wheat	6.8	11.0	23.8	31.3	35.5	36.4
Jowar	6.9	9.9	8.1	11.8		10.5
Bajra	3.2	3.3	8.0	4.7		6.3
Maize		4.1	7.5	5.9	30.4	6.8
Other cereals	8.6	6.7	6.9	7.3		6.3
Pulses	10.0	12.7	11.8	11.8	12.2	11.2
Total foodgrains	60.6	82.3	108.4	125.6	131.9	129.9
Oilseeds	5.2	6.4	9.3	8.9	9.35	8.3
Sugarcane in terms of raw sugar	6.1	11.4	13.0	18.8	15.73	15.4
Cotton lint	0.47	1.0	0.86	1.28	1.35	1.29

Source: *Economic Survey,* 1969–70 and 1981–2.

The selected years enjoyed good to rather good weather, unlike 1979–80, when production fell to 109.7 million tons of foodgrain. In 1981–2 production was 134 million tons. Such trends explain why India stopped importing grain during the calendar years 1977 to 1980 (inclusive). For the financial year 1981–2 imports of about 1.5 million tons took place in order to replenish government stocks. These are no mean achievements when one remembers that the average net annual imports of grain amounted to 3.9 million tons for the period 1971 to 1976 (inclusive) and to 6.6 million tons for the period 1965 to 1970.

The picture that emerges from this table fits well with our field and general observations: an extraordinary expansion in wheat, mostly in the north-west; rice production which is gradually accelerating, mostly in the already advanced areas. Maize is not doing particularly well. Jowar expanded largely because new lands were opened to the

[39] *Economic and Political Weekly*, 8 November 1978, 17 November 1979; *Hindu*, 8 December 1978.

plough in the 1950s. Bajra also expanded through land reclamation. Pulses are scarcely progressing—the area under them, and yields, are continually fluctuating. Progress is also disappointing with regard to oilseeds, and somewhat better but not outstanding for cotton. The picture for sugarcane is better.

Such data are difficult to interpret as they hide the enormous differences in growth trends and yields observed in this book. For wheat and rice we get the following distribution: out of 31.3 million tons of the former that were produced in 1977–8, 9.5 million tons came from Punjab and Haryana, and the same quantity from Uttar Pradesh, especially the western part. Thus nearly two-thirds of India's wheat comes from three states. For rice, in the early 1970s, out of 36 million hectares of land sown in paddy in the whole of India, 13 million were irrigated. Eastern India, including part of Madhya Pradesh, accounted for 25 million hectares, of which 5 million were irrigated. In the south-east there were 5.9 million hectares, 5.5 million being irrigated.[40] In 1977–8, out of 52.7 million tons of rice, 15 million were produced in four states: 3.8 million in Punjab and Haryana, 5.3 million tons in Andhra, 5.9 million in Tamil Nadu. Data on secondary crops such as vegetables, potatoes and other root crops such as tapioca are either lacking or not too reliable. Here, however, are a few figures: the output of potatoes has increased from 1.8 million tons in 1970–1 to 7.3 million in 1976–7. Tapioca, grown mostly in Kerala, amounts to 5 million tons. It is quite clear that substantial progress is taking place. Thirty years ago even in a big town like Poona (Maharashtra), vegetables and fruit were not abundant. Today, not only is the supply to big cities increasing, but it has also reached district towns and many smaller towns.

The increase in milk production is confirmed at the national level. One of the most dynamic schemes has been Operation Flood One which achieved the following results:

	1970–1	1975–6	1977–8
Milk zones	4	28	39
Number of co-operative societies	1,238	4,359	8,936
Number of producers	245,480	502,158	928,761
Milk collected (in million litres)	176	300	485

The total production of milk has increased from 21.7 million litres in

[40] *Agricultural Census 1970–71.*

1970–1 to about 27.5 million litres in 1977–8. Poultry has moved faster, the number of eggs per year reaching 10 billion in 1977, i.e. four times the 1961 figure .

Supply of Inputs

The figures below show the gross area under irrigation (in million hectares) during the period 1950–1 to 1979–80.

Surface water:	1950–1	1960–1	1968–9	1977–8	1978–9	1979–80
Major and medium works	9.7	13.1	16.9	21.2	22.0	22.6
Minor works	6.4	6.5	6.5	7.5	7.8	8.0
Ground water	6.5	8.3	13.0	19.8	21.0	22.0
TOTAL	22.6	27.9	35.9	48.5	50.8	52.6

Source: *Ministry of Agriculture, Department of Irrigation.*

While major and medium works (canals) are proceeding relatively slowly with a gap between the potential created and the actual utilization, there has been, after 1960–1, a very rapid expansion of tubewells, mostly private. This has more than doubled the irrigated area relying on ground water.

The net cultivated area increased from 119 million hectares in 1950–1 to 133 million in 1960–1. Since then, the pace of growth has slowed down, less and less land remaining available for reclamation. By the mid-1970s the net area had reached 142 million hectares. As to the gross area, under the impact of more multi-cropping per year, it increased from 132 million hectares in 1950–1 to 153 million hectares in 1960–1 and 173 million hectares in 1977–8.

The evolution of the supply of chemical fertilizers is no less significant. The increase had been very slow until the mid-1960s. Then, because of the introduction of HYV and the expansion of irrigation, it rose considerably until 1973–4. It fell in the following years under the influence of price increases and picked up sharply from 1975–6 to 1978–9 (inclusive). During 1979–80, consumption grew by 2.7 per cent only because of drought. In the following year the increase amounted to 6 per cent only because supplies were short, and prices increased by 38 per cent.

Consumption of Chemical Fertilizers

The chart below is self-explanatory and shows the consumption of chemical fertilizers in terms of nutrients N, P_2O_5, K_2O, in million tons.

	N	P_2O_5	K_2O	Total in tons
1950–1	55,000	7,000	—	62,000
1960–1	193,000	20,000	25,000	288,000
1970–1	1,480,000	540,000	240,000	2,660,000
1973–4	1,830,000	650,000	360,000	2,840,000
1974–5	1,770,000	470,000	330,000	2,570,000
1975–6	2,140,000	470,000	280,000	2,890,000
1976–7	2,460,000	630,000	320,000	3,410,000
1977–8	2,910,000	870,000	520,000	4,290,000
1978–9	3,420,000	1,110,000	590,000	5,120,000
1980–1	3,710,000	1,230,000	600,000	5.540,000

Data on irrigation and chemical fertilizers and the trends in these, like production figures, seem to mask considerable differences, as we have seen earlier.

CHAPTER 14

Rural Development, Agrarian Reforms, Management and Planning

Towards the end of the nineteenth century the British became increasingly concerned with rural development. This is evident from the creation of district boards, and agricultural, health and education departments. In 1904 the first All India Cooperatives Act was passed in order to promote co-operative credit. Relief works were organized in times of famine to offer employment to the poor. Some isolated community projects were started under the initiative of different people: that of Rabindranath Tagore in Bengal, Dr Spencer Hatch of the Y.M.C.A. in Kerala, F. L. Brayne, the Deputy Commissioner in Gurgaon and, later, V. T. Krishnamachari in Baroda.

After Independence

One of the first issues to be tackled immediately after 1947 was land reform. Following the guidelines set by the Central Government, the states passed legislation on this. The zamindari system was abolished. While this did not alter the status and rights of the occupancy tenants (which had been protected by different acts under the British),[1] the disappearance of the system took away from the zamindars various rights of a semi-feudal nature, such as *begar* (compulsory unpaid labour for a certain number of days, special fees, etc.). It therefore helped reduce the power of the landlords, albeit in an uneven manner. We have seen, for example, how in Bihar landlords still remain powerful. Various laws were adopted in favour of share-croppers and

[1] Most of the land was already under occupancy tenants, i.e. farmers whose rights were entered in the land records and who could not be ejected unless they failed to pay rent to the zamindar. Such rights had become hereditary. With the new laws such farmers could acquire, under payment, full property rights.

farmers renting land from others, but they could not be thoroughly implemented. The competition for land was and is too great to induce share-croppers, for instance, to complain about the owner's lack of respect for the law—for they fear being ejected. Laws imposing a ceiling on land property did not produce any remarkable results either (16 hectares according to the Act of 1960 in U.P.) because big landlords had managed to split their holdings among relatives.

We have seen, in Chapter 2, how the consolidation of holdings paved the way for private tubewell irrigation, a situation typical of the whole north-west of India. In Punjab and Haryana such operations were completed during the 1960s and they did contribute to the overall growth of the region. Consolidation is making headway (as mentioned in connection with Varanasi district in Chapter 5) throughout U.P.

Progress is much slower in most other states. In certain cases this may be due to some kind of inertia. However, in general, there are certain practical aspects to be considered. In lowlands exposed to floods or simply to excess water, farmers often prefer to own plots located in different places in order to minimize their risks. Hence the consolidation of holdings is, in such cases, directly linked with drainage and flood control. Apart from this, wherever there are filter points or pumpsets on open wells, fragmentation of holdings is less of a hindrance than in tubewell areas because the command area of a pumpset or a filter point is smaller than that of a tubewell. This explains the expansion of such minor irrigation techniques in non-consolidated areas such as, for instance, Tamil Nadu or Maharashtra. In addition, as explained earlier in Chapter 8, in a plain criss-crossed by canals, tributaries and field channels, many canals would have to be realigned in order to consolidate holdings. Thus while such operations are highly desirable, there are several areas where they face greater difficulties than in the north-west.[2]

A final issue in connection with land reform is the updating and revision of old land records, which has not been fully done. This could have helped to clarify many cases of litigation and to give better protection to small landowners.

In spite of all that has been said in recent times on the so-called neglect of agriculture, an enormous effort to help the rural sector was initiated immediately after 1947. A number of institutions were gradu-

---

[2]In 1979–80, about 45 million hectares had been consolidated. This was about one-fourth of the consolidable land (*Sixth Five Year Plan*, 1980–5, p. 115).

ally created or expanded; community development throuh 5,000 blocks covered practically the whole country, together with a wide network of primary co-operative societies in villages and district banks. Panchayati Raj introduced a three-tier system of local councils at the village, block and district levels. Education and health measures also expanded considerably. All this yielded mixed results from both the social and economic points of view. In fact, to speak of failure, as is often done, is grossly unfair. The truth is simply that the original expectations or hopes were much too optimistic because of unrealistic assessments of rural societies and because of practical difficulties.

In the sphere of social justice the main criticism has been that these institutions hardly helped the poor, most of the benefits being cornered by more prosperous farmers. This is a statement which needs qualification. It is true that landless labourers and small landowners were too often left out of the process, but a sizeable number of medium farmers did benefit from the extension of services and co-operative loans which helped them to increase their production and strengthen their position *vis à vis* the big landowners. We came across two types of situations: in certain places like Mirpur or Kila Ulur local institutions were in the hands of medium farmers, among whom were to be found the local leaders (*neta*). In Kalpi and Karwad such institutions were controlled by large landowners.

The position of the poor has been weak from the very beginning. Within the power structures of Indian society any local institution is bound to be controlled at least by the medium, if not the upper, farmers. This is why the late Dr Ambedkar, one of the main architects of the Indian Constitution (who, as a Harijan, was well aware of such facts) did his best to reduce the power of the Panchayats; this attempt was defeated through the introduction of Panchayati Raj in the late 1950s. As far as the achievements of concrete goals are concerned the shortcomings are conspicuous; but we cannot condemn them without looking more closely at the situation.

In its early phases, community development opted for a multipurpose (socio-economic) approach in order to cover all aspects of village life. This resulted in very limited agricultural achievements, and consequently, by the end of the 1950s, priority had to be given to agricultural production. In this field again, hopes were not in keeping with the facts. One could not expect from the 50 to 70,000 extension workers and officers an ability, competence and dedication commensurate with the needs of rural society. Limited qualifications cannot be overcome simply by conducting training programmes. Added to this is the fact that small and medium civil servants in the districts work under much more difficult conditions than do their counterparts in the big towns and cities. Easy-going attitudes, a lack of a sense of responsibility and possible corruption were bound to occur, and to expect the contrary reveals a limited grasp of the working conditions of such people. The fact that such bureaucrats have been sympathetic to upper-caste farmers should also have been foreseeable in view of the social and caste background of these civil servants which is similar to that of most well-to-do farmers.

In spite of these defects inherent in the system, and common to many other developing countries, there were some positive achievements. In the past, government and administration did not filter down below the district level. Villages were reached mostly through land revenue and major irrigation works (as in old China), and, in a very limited way, by other administrative departments. Today government and planning reach the village level much more thoroughly and, among other things, help to promote minor irrigation, loans for tubewells, the use of chemical fertilizers, new seeds, etc.

In the field of credit, success is no less mixed. Credit co-operatives were originally meant to help agricultural production and in many cases they did. However, loans were often used for marriages instead of to purchase fertilizers. The poor recovery of loans, and malpractices on the part of farmers and co-operative officers are well-known facts. Added to this, the institution of Panchayati Raj is far from having achieved its original goal of stimulating greater participation by the masses in development activities. Panchayati Raj has often been nonexistent or has served to provide a springboard for the ambitions of local politicians.

These broad comments require qualification because conditions vary from state to state. A first major difference is in the role of the IAS district officers. In certain states (Andhra and Tamil Nadu for instance), the Collector is much more directly involved in district planning and development than in U.P., Bihar or Orissa. In Maharashtra, the district is run by the Collector, while most local development activities are under the Chief Executive Officer (CEO), an IAS officer of the same rank as the Collector. The more direct involvement of IAS officers helps to improve the system and its operations; in other states the officers most directly responsible belong to the state cadre and are usually not of the same calibre as the IAS officers. They are also more susceptible to influences and pressures from local politicians.

The achievements of co-operatives are no less diverse. In certain states like Assam and Bihar their performance has been very poor, while in Tamil Nadu or Maharashtra the results have been better. The same can be said of Panchayati Rāj, which has been more or less dormant in U.P., Bihar, Assam and Orissa and definitely more active in Tamil Nadu, Gujarat or Maharashtra. It would be beyond the scope of this study to explain these differences, but one of the factors may be traceable to the different historical backgrounds of the states. In the north, local affairs were attended to by the local zamindars, and their abolition has created a vacuum which is not easily filled. In areas which previously had the *rayatwari* system, on the other hand, there has been, for centuries, some tradition of self-management among the people.

The above conclusions, which we had reached in our surveys in the 1960s, were confirmed by a number of official reports and books dealing with the period 1950–70.[3]

Rural Development Strategy After 1970: Land Reforms Again

A number of factors induced the government to alter the rural development strategy it had followed so far. Some of them were of a political nature and were connected with the relatively weak position of the Congress Party after the elections of 1967 and the split within the party in 1969. Others had to do with the growing—or renewed—concern for poverty,[4] the need to do more for the poor while, at the same time, strengthening the position of Indira Gandhi and her followers. Practical lessons were also learnt from the experiences mentioned above and from a better knowledge of technical problems as well as the progress of research.

All these factors combined to lead to a wide range of measures, some of which were beginning to be implemented from 1970 onwards, others after Indira Gandhi's sweeping victory in the 1971 general

[3]See, among others, Reserve Bank of India, *Report of the All India Rural Credit Review Committee* (Bombay, 1969), and *Agricultural Development of India*, edited by C. H. Shah and C. N. Vakil (Bombay, 1979). The latter work goes beyond 1970 and is one of the most comprehensive books on the subject.

[4]Such a trend was not confined to India alone. It was spreading in other developing countries and in international organizations such as the World Bank.

elections fought under the slogan of 'garibi hatao' (remove poverty). In July 1972 new national guidelines on land reforms were issued following the conference of chief ministers. Different ceilings were fixed on land—6.3 hectares (18 acres) was the recommended ceiling on good, irrigated land allowing double cropping; on land which had assured irrigation for only one crop the ceiling was 10.8 hectares (27 acres). For all other types of land it was not to exceed 21.6 hectares (54 acres) except in special cases such as desert and hilly areas. For families which had more than three minor children, additional land could be granted and every major son was treated as a separate entity.

Most states enacted the new ceiling laws and, by the middle of 1976, the estimated surplus land amounted to 1.76 million hectares according to official figures, while the actual total declared was 800,000 hectares, out of which half was taken possession of by the government. According to Charan Singh, in his book *India's Economic Policy* (New Delhi, 1979), 'Of this area only 280,000 hectares have been distributed amongst 354,000 persons, 162,000 belonging to scheduled castes and tribes.' By March 1980, 956,000 hectares had been taken possession of by the states, and 679,000 hectares had been distributed to 1.15 million landless persons (Sixth Five Year Plan, p. 115).

In an essay on 'Agricultural Policy in India since Independence',[5] M. L. Dantwala adds: 'According to the National Sample Survey, out of 100 million households in the country, 19.6 million do not own any land'; 35.6 million owned less than 0.4 hectares and 15 million between 0.4 and 1 hectare. In order to provide each household with one hectare, one would require 58 million hectares, 'a large portion of which', says M. L. Dantwala, 'is in regions characterized by semi-arid conditions'. Since 1971–2 the number of households has increased due to further division of holdings following inheritance practices. Pursuing this argument other Indian observers point out that, with the passing of time and the further division of holdings after the death of the owner, any new ceiling law will become increasingly meaningless.

What is worth emphasizing is that 'the proportion of irrigated land is larger on smaller holdings', although, as Dantwala adds, this may change with the increasing use of tubewells, since nearly 50 per cent of the area dependent on tubewells consisted of holdings of four hec-

[5] M. L. Dantawala, 'Agricultural Policy in India since Independence', in *Agricultural Development of India,* op. cit.

tares and above by 1974. This hypothesis is, however, open to question as it is common for tubewell owners to have a surplus of water which they sell to neighbours.

What is the impact of the size of holdings on yields? In traditional agriculture yields are often inversely proportionate to the size of holdings. With the advent of new inputs, the picture becomes more complex. According to a survey conducted in Haryana, landowners with between 2 and 8 hectares were getting higher yields than either the smaller or larger farmers.[6] Following a broader survey it appears that, in the less developed states, small farmers cultivate land more intensively than large farmers.[7] In Bihar, for instance, when a farmer who has less than one hectare of land applies chemical fertilizers, the yield amounts to 65 kilograms per hectare as opposed to 45 for farmers with between 2 and 10 hectares. In more advanced states the differences, if any, are much smaller. The percentage of farmers using fertilizers tends to rise with the size of holdings but, in advanced states, the proportion of farmers with below one hectare using fertilizers is much higher than in others—up to 71 or 75 per cent in Haryana and Punjab, only 5.5 per cent in Assam and 10 per cent in Orissa.

One can conclude that in progressive areas most farmers (including the small ones) manage one way or another to use new seeds, chemical fertilizers and occasionally pesticides as well. Many small farmers also improve their irrigation facilities.

Tenancy problems were raised again with the aim of reducing the rent in cases of fixed rent arrangements or in order to increase the share of the tiller under share-cropping. Here again, achievements have been no better than in previous decades. As long as means of strict implementation are lacking, the usefulness of legislation on the subject will necessarily be limited. Secondly, the magnitude of the problem cannot easily be assessed. About 90 per cent of the cultivated land is owner-operated and 10.6 per cent is leased, but, as Dantwala says, tenancy may be under-reported or seem to have been reduced, simply because there has been an eviction of tenants. In addition, the system works both ways—not only do small farmers lease in land from

[6]G. S. Bhalla, 'Transfer of Technology and Agricultural Development in India', *Economic and Political Weekly,* Review of Agriculture, December 1979.

[7]Unpublished study by the National Council of Applied Economics, quoted in *The Economic Times,* 6 March 1979.

bigger farmers, but often large landowners lease in land from small farmers.[8] One must also bear in mind that the pattern of relations between landlords and tenants is far from static. P. Bardhan and A. Rudra show that there is 'some evidence of a higher share for the tenant positively associated with higher yielding varieties of grains'. They also give a number of examples of landlords taking 'a lot of interest in productive investments on the tenant farm' including cost sharing arrangements.[9] It is obvious, thus, that land reforms will remain a blind alley or, at best, a very limited remedy, unless radical political changes occur. One could envisage collectivization as in China, but for long the influence of medium and upper farmers will remain strong enough to prevent such a solution. And political leaders are too well aware of these facts to propose such drastic solutions.

Two exceptions should be pointed out. Under strongly leftist governments Kerala and, more recently, West Bengal have been able to achieve more for the protection of tenants and landless labourers. This is particularly so in Kerala which succeeded not only in adopting minimum wage regulations but also in implementing them.

Is it possible to imagine growing agrarian unrest leading to more drastic reforms? The answers are not simple. Such unrest, as we have seen, occurs generally in areas where rural development has been very slow, for example, in eastern U.P., Bihar and parts of Andhra. In these cases, the internal conflicts are much more complex than in a classic class struggle. As seen in Bihar, there is conflict between high caste landlords and medium rising castes and classes, conflict between the latter and Harijans, between landlords and Harijans. In addition, small landowners, especially in rice-growing areas, employ labourers to work on their lands while working as labourers themselves. This often creates a tricky situation. In many states and, more particularly, in the villages, the forces of the left are not well organized. All these factors put together would lead one to conclude that a gradual shift from agrarian unrest to a real revolution is unlikely, unless something unforeseeable happens.

[8] M. L. Dantwala, 'Agricultural Policy in India', *Indian Journal of Agricultural Economics*, no. 4, 1976.

[9] P. Bardhan and A. Rudra, 'Terms and Conditions of Sharecropping Contracts: An Analysis of Village Survey Data in India', *The Journal of Development Studies* (April 1980).

New Agencies and Institutions

The government and the administration have considered other types of activities: target group-oriented as well as area-oriented schemes, and occasionally a combination of the two. In the first category (Small Farmers' Development Agency, SFDA) the idea is to concentrate on giving assistance, loans and grants to small farmers (usually those with below two hectares of good land) and marginal farmers (with below one hectare). In the second category is the Drought Prone Area Programme (DPAP) where attention is given to districts particularly exposed to drought. Another type of agency has been created to speed up the development of large irrigation projects where, until recently, many works remained uncompleted and consequently the irrigation potential had not been fully tapped. Each Command Area Development Authority (CADA) is in charge of a large project,[10] and looks after land levelling, field channels and other infrastructural works. The programme also looks after extension services, crop demonstration and the consolidation of holdings. By 1978 as many as 340 districts had been covered by one or more of these special schemes which involved 2,950 blocks out of a total of 5,100. While a nucleus staff devotes itself to these programmes, the implementation of these projects is also heavily dependent on regular department lines. Most of the funds devoted to these programmes come directly from the Central Government.

The principle of emphasizing area-oriented schemes is sound and fills an important gap in planning. As far as the results are concerned, we lack overall reports. We did, however, notice some useful steps being taken in the Gandak project in Bihar. The impact of the CADA approach did not appear to have been striking in the Mahanadi delta in Orissa. When driving through the Nagarjunasagar CADA in Andhra and after meeting the head of the project in Guntur, on the other hand, we felt there had been some definite improvement. However, there is still a wide range of taks involved which need to be implemented. In their context, it is important to take cognisance of the calibre of the senior officers whose job it is to get the bureaucratic machinery moving. Where the officers in charge are smart and

---

[10] About sixty major irrigation projects with a total cultivable command area of fifteen million hectares. The CADA would benefit about five million small and marginal farmers. Between 1974 and 1978, 37 CADAs covering 47 projects and 14 million hectares were set up (*Draft Five Year Plan 1978–83*, p. 139).

efficient—for instance in the CADA of the Chambal project—things move faster.

The target group approach, which is becoming increasingly popular in many developing countries and within international organizations, raises more complex issues. To quote Professor Raj Krishna, the SFDA approach aims 'at special preferential arrangements for the supply of inputs to small farmers', whereby loans are granted with a 25 to 32 per cent subsidy component. 'The present definition specifies 2 hectares (5 acres) of dry land (unirrigated land) as the cut-off point for identifying small farmers and 1 hectare (2.5 acres) of dry land for identifying marginal farmers.'[11]

Between 1971 (when the scheme began) and 1978, 16.3 million people had been identified for inclusion in the scheme, 2.4 million of whom belonged to scheduled castes or tribes, and 7.1 million of whom had been enrolled in co-operatives. In 1978 the number of beneficiaries under minor irrigation schemes was 728,000; under dairying it was 461,000; under poultry 18,203; under animal husbandry 199,000 and under improved agricultural practices 5,197,000. The total value of co-operative loans distributed since the inception of the programme was Rs 1,152 million while loans from commercial banks totalled Rs 964 million. The funds released by the centre for intensive block development totalled Rs 265 million, to which should be added the Rs 1,743 million released by the centre on normal SFDA schemes.[12]

Two major questions must be raised. First, can such a scheme gradually reach all small and marginal farmers? The precise number of farmers to be reached cannot be gauged because data on landholdings do not give us a detailed break-up of dry and irrigated land. According to the 1971 Agricultural Census, 70 per cent of rural households (i.e. 49 million) had below 2 hectares. As we have seen, an increasingly large number of landowners with 1-2 hectares of adequately irrigated land can manage reasonably well without special assistance. But how many such landowners are there? To avoid any over-optimism one can say that at least 25 to 30 million holdings out of the 49 million are not so favourably placed. This gives us an idea of the magnitude of any scheme which aims to cover the majority of the small and marginal farmers. In addition to heavy investments, can

[11]Raj Krishna, 'Small Farmers' Development', *Economic and polictical Weekly*, 26 May 1979.

[12]*Times of India*, 12 March 1979.

credit institutions attend to such an enormous number of loan-cum-subsidy applications? However, by raising these questions I do not mean to question the value of the limited efforts that are being made presently. But it is important not to overlook the size of the problem.

The second question deals with the content of the programme. The operations of the SFDA have suffered from serious shortcomings and malpractices. Commenting on them—as well as on the DPAP—M. L. Dantwala notes that 'there is a widely shared view that most of the benefits under the scheme have been diverted and appropriated by better off farmers with political influence'.[13] Such a judgement is severe and it is debatable whether it is warranted. Malpractices are widespread and it is possible that in the process of identification big landowners, through an artificial division of their holdings, get benefits reserved for small farmers. The latter may have other undeclared assets, which would not entitle them to special assistance.[14] In other cases an influential landlord gets a buffalo with a loan-cum-subsidy through an application formerly made by a genuine small farmer who then receives only a part of the subsidy. Such cases were mentioned in some districts. The *Hindu* (5 March 1979) cites examples of even more questionable cases where the loan-cum-subsidy is granted to a big landowner through the application of a small one, but the actual purchase does not take place.

In all fairness, however, one must mention genuine cases of help to small and marginal farmers which we noticed, for example, in Mirpur and other areas during our last survey. Then there are cases where the target group can work—if there is fallow land that is available for distribution, or on loan-cum-subsidy schemes for milch cattle, poultry or fishing—and these do lead to more positive results. But in view of all the above-mentioned factors, it is best not to expect too much of any such scheme.

In 1977 the Rajasthan Government introduced a new scheme: Antyodaya or the uplift of the last man. Under the programme it envisaged, the village assembly was called upon to identify the poorest families, and the identification was carried out under the supervision of an officer nominated by the Collector. Help was then provided in the form of pensions for old people without means of support, job opportunities (such as work on the Rajasthan Canal), a

---

[13] M. L. Dantwala, op. cit.

[14] Reserve Bank of India, *Small Farmers' Development Agencies, A Field Study, 1972–73* (Bombay, 1975). The Report contains many other cases of faulty identification.

loan-cum-subsidy to buy a camel and a cart, or a cow and, when possible, an allotment of land. After one year of this scheme 160,000 families had been identified and nearly half this number provided with some help.[15] Since 1978-9 a number of states have adopted this scheme, and here and there in the field, we could see that it had had some results. The idea is to take in five more families each year. It will be interesting to see how the scheme works.

Since the 1970s the concept of integrated rural development has regained popularity in many developing countries and in international organizations.[16] This is emphasized in the Draft Five Year Plan 1978-83 where we read that 'a sectoral approach is not adequate to lead to an overall development of the area', and that it is therefore necessary to plan integrated programmes dealing with development tasks, the infrastructure and social services. 'A major effort will be made to formulate area specific plans' based on 'comprehensive block level planning' (op.cit., p. 155). The same effort should be made at the district level, the different departments of which should be strengthened in order to supply the block with adequate support. In addition, the various agencies referred to above can become part of the integrated approach and can maintain a bias towards small and marginal farmers.

The Benor System (Training and Visit System)

Towards the mid-seventies, Daniel Benor, an officer of the World Bank from Israel, introduced a new approach to extension.[17] This approach, which came to be known as the Benor system, had, in its experimental stages, been associated with World Bank loans for projects, particularly in the field of irrigation. The basic idea behind this scheme is to improve production, particularly among small farmers who use 'low level technology and usually traditional methods'. Agricultural extension workers are under the control of different subject matter specialists (fertilizers, pest control, minor irrigation, etc.) and the whole system depends on the district agricultural office through a 'single line of command'. The system aims at better extension and a greater co-ordination of work among the many agencies and departments operating within the district.[18]

Each village level extension worker (VLEW) is in charge of about

[15] Antyodaya (Jaipur, 1978).

[16] See my *Bangladesh Development in Perspective* (New Delhi, 1979).

[17] D. Benor, J. Q. Harrison, *Agricultural Extension* (Washington, 1977), p. vii.

[18] The same system has been advocated and introduced in several other countries.

800 families which are divided into eight groups. Within every group the VLEW selects, with the advice of the village headman, about ten families as contact farmers (each family is supposed to have ten followers). The system is called 'training and visit'. The VLEW advises the farmers on simple technical improvements involving little expenditure, for example better soil preparation, better timing for sowing, seed selection or treatment, use of new seeds, proper use of chemical fertilizers, spacing of seeds, weeding, new crops, etc. The VLEW must visit each of his groups every fortnight for a full day, and always on the same day. This makes it easier to control his work from above. On two days each fortnight he receives training from his superior officers and attends to official work. Six to ten VLEWs are supervised by one Agricultural Extension Officer. On three days a week this officer superintends the work of the VLEW. He spends a day on his own training (which is conducted by subject matter specialists), a day on training the VLEW and one Saturday every fortnight on office work.

Actively promoted by the World Bank in several of its projets in India, this system has found favour with a number of senior officers associated with rural development as well as with members of the Planning Commission. It was introduced in 1975–6 in the CADA of the Chambal project in Madhya Pradesh and Rajasthan, in Burdwan district in West Bengal and Nowgong district in Assam. During 1979–80, the Government of India decided to introduce the system in ten states. It will be adopted by all the remaining states during the Sixth Plan period. In 1981, the World Bank supplied IDA credit of over a hundred million dollars for this purpose.

What has the programme achieved so far? A World Bank booklet claims it has been successful in the three areas where it was initially introduced in 1975–6. For my part, I cannot comment on the first two regions but as far as Nowgong district is concerned (see Chapter 7), the results observed in the field are not impressive but limited. This may, however, need qualification, for we visited the area two and a half years after the introduction of the system, while the World Bank evaluation was made soon after it began.[19] An evaluation report by the Director of Agriculture in Assam (dated April 1978) offers similar conclusions to ours. According to this report the training of VLEWs and agricultural officers remained unsatisfactory in 40 per cent of the

[19] *Internal Evaluation Report on Intensive Agricultural Extension Service in Nowgong subdivision* (Gauhati, 1977).

the cases. 'Only three subject matter specialists out of the six required were present more than one year after the inception of the programme. The selection of contact farmers had not been done properly. The regularity of attendance of the contact farmers ... was also not observed.' Finally, 'the self assessment reports of the VLEW appear to be much exaggerated as they indicated high achievements in all respects', as could be gathered from their diaries. About 7 to 8 per cent of paddy areas benefited from new technologies. The report considers this number a 'low performance'.

In fact, it is quite possible that after an early and high start the scheme lost momentum. The programme started when one of the most able IAS officers in Assam (R. Dutta) was Deputy Commissioner of Nowgong district, and received active encouragement from him. Later he was transferred to the Assam secretariat in Gauhati. In the cases of Chambal and Burdwan personal factors came in. The project officer of the CADA in Chambal was a man of high calibre, like his predecessor. In Burdwan, much work had been done under a particularly able Collector, K. R. A. Menon, before the system was introduced.

Before 1978 and 1979 the Benor system was debated in several state capitals. Pressures from the centre and the World Bank met with mixed reactions. While in Assam and Orissa reactions were, on the whole, favourable, we met with a great deal of reluctance in other states. Some very experienced officers admit that in newly reclaimed areas which require a new cropping pattern, or in remote tribal regions, the training and visit system can be useful, but in many other areas the VLEWs are at a loss as to what to tell contact farmers every fortnight. In many cases, as we have seen, the key problem is not really extension and, contrary to what the World Bank assumes in its booklet, many farmers have already altered their 'traditional methods' where necessary. The idea of a 'single line of command' is certainly a good one and has been advocated time and again for the last thirty years. But is the district agricultural officer the right man for the right post? Unfortunately, the answer is no. During my latest trip, as in previous ones, I have been struck by the rather low calibre of district agricultural officers. In terms of technical qualifications, dynamism and actual leadership, they range from mediocre to fair. Other officers underline the cost of a new system. Such costs may, in the early stage, and for certain projects, be covered by World Bank assistance, but what about the long-term future? Some officers argue that, instead of starting new systems again, it would be better to improve the existing one.

There is also a fairly major risk involved. In their booklet, D. Benor and J. O. Harrison underline the fact that 'without dedication and particularly the enthusiasm which initially depends very much on the inspiration of the key personnel selected to put the system into operation, one might question whether it can be expected to succeed.'[20] For the reasons explained above, it is not possible to expect such enthusiasm and commitment from the lower and medium agents involved. Only a small group of highly talented and motivated cadres leading the operations within each district can do this work. This explains the success stories mentioned in the World Bank booklet. On the other hand, in most cases, district agricultural officers and subject matter specialists remain, we have said before, very much below standard.

To conclude, in spite of the questions which we have raised, one must agree with some of the supporters of the Benor system that in order to diversify Indian agriculture it is necessary to have more sophisticated techniques and, *a fortiori*, new extension efforts. This is why the discussion should not focus on the system *per se* but on its practical aspects.

Panchayati Raj, Co-operatives and Commercial Banks

In its efforts to speed up rural development the Janata Government concerned itself with ways and means of strengthening Panchayati Raj institutions. The report prepared by a committee under the chairmanship of Ashok Mehta[21] summarized conclusions so often drawn on the subject: 'meagre activities, weak resources, political factionalism, corruption, inefficiency, dominance of oligarchic elements'. The authors nevertheless added that 'such a pessimistic appraisal is not shared by all. The basic soundness of the system with necessary correctives, is strongly emphasized by many'. The committee recommended a substantial transfer of power from the State Government to local bodies. It favoured a two-tier system, instead of the three-tier system at present,[22] with a district level council (Zila Parishad) and a Mandal Panchayat covering a group of villages.

[20]Op. cit., p. vii.
[21]*Report of the Committee, Panchayati Raj Institutions* (New Delhi, 1978) called the Mehta Report.
[22]Village, block and district councils.

The reactions to these proposals were not too enthusiastic. State politicians hesitated to strengthen local bodies, several civil servants were not too enthusiastic about new changes in the framework of these institutions. Another committee responded rather negatively by raising two basic questions—'except in a few states there is hardly any worthwhile set-up of Panchayati raj institutions. ... They have either withered away or are lying in a moribund state. Secondly, the weaker sections of villages have too little influence in these institutions to benefit from them, which is hardly surprising in the given context of the inegalitarian structure of the rural economy.'[23]

It will be interesting to see what the position of the new Indira Gandhi government will be on this. What is clear, however, is that Panchayati Raj has only limited scope. Moreover, let us remember that the system has been in existence for more than twenty years. While it might be difficult to write it off, one could, as is being done in some states, assign to it certain subjects which concern the whole population: possibly some school buildings, drinking water supply, family-planning propaganda. These matters could also perhaps be supervised by some state officials.

Co-operatives are another long-standing issue. For more than ten years now there has been an attempt to get rid of dormant village societies[24] and improve the efficiency of the others which are working with greater or less degree of success. However, the same shortcomings remain. 'The main constraint in the credit flow has been low recoveries, high level of overdues and consequent ineligibility of a large number of cooperative institutions for refinancing. Therefore it will be imperative to improve upon the management of rural credit.'[25] Besides, credit is spread very unevenly, since nearly 52 per cent is reported by five states—Andhra, Gujarat, Maharashtra, Punjab and Tamil Nadu. As we have seen, co-operative credit is particularly weak in states like Assam and Orissa.

The Draft Five Year Plan proposes to have larger societies covering several villages and dealing with several activities on the lines of

[23] *Report on Block Level Planning* (New Delhi, 1978), p. 9. Working group under the chairmanship of M. L. Dantwala.

[24] The number of primary village societies came down from 208,000 in 1965–6 to 135,000 ten years later, while the membership rose from 24 million to 40 million. *Indian Express*, 6 December 1978, quoting the Reserve Bank review for 1975–6.

[25] *Draft Five Year Plan 1978–83* (New Delhi, 1978), p. 151. For 1977–8 about Rs 16.5 billion for short-term loans, 2.35 for medium-term loans and 4.1 for long-term ones.

the Farmers' Service Societies or the large multi-purpose societies that are created in certain areas. Each society should have a paid manager with adequate training. The goal to reach more people is reaffirmed. As we have seen, one comes across more cases of loans to small farmers and even landless labourers today than twenty years ago, but nonetheless one cannot say that the balance of power within the co-operative set-up has been fundamentally altered.

Another development in the field of rural credit is the growing involvement of commercial banks which have opened a large number of branches in the countryside. From 1,833 branches in 1969 the number went up to 11,053 at the end of 1977.[26] In some states banks fill part of the gap that co-operatives cannot fill. They contribute by bringing in more money to the villages. Yet commercial banks often lack experience in rural credit, and loan recovery has become a serious problem. There are some states like Maharashtra and Gujarat where local politicians do not favour the expansion of banks, because, unlike co-operative banks and primary societies, commercial banks are not so easily controlled.

The Food for Work Programme

For many decades, including the British period in India, it has been the practice to organize various types of schemes for the unemployed, such as relief works in period of drought. In 1978, a programme called the Food for Work Programme was launched. Under this programme the centre allocated to the states a certain amount of grain which was to be used to pay workers engaged in public works such as road building or repairing, water conservation, anti-erosion activities, etc. For 1979–80, 1.5 million tons of foodgrains were allotted out of which more than half had been released by July. The programme envisages providing 50 to 80 days of work to some eight million people (this is twice the figure for 1978–9).[27] For lack of recent detailed information, it is difficult to assess precisely the impact this programme has had. The *Statesman Weekly* of 18 April 1981 refers to a 'highly damaging report by the Programme Evaluation Organization of the Planning Commission', which mentions various defects and shortcomings. On the other hand, grain supply to the programme met with difficulties in 1980–1. One would be tempted to conclude tentatively that while such programmes do help, they will probably

---

[26] *Statesman*, 24 November 1978.
[27] *Hindustan Times*, 19 February 1979.

not become a major part of the rural development strategy because of the many practical and organizational constraints they face, witness the experience of the last thirty years.

Private Voluntary Organizations

As we have seen, since the beginning of this century if not earlier, a number of private organizations, Indian, foreign or mixed, have been working in rural India, a movement which was greatly influenced and encouraged by Mahatma Gandhi. While such activities went on in the 1950s and the 1960s, there is now a renewed interest in them. One of the most well-known recent experiences is the one in Rajasthan: the Social Work Research Centre based in Tilonia, a village near Kishangarh. As Marcus Franda notes, 'Significant and unusual is the project's leadership which is composed exclusively of young professionally trained experts of various kinds.'[28] They attend to the various aspects of village life which 'impinge on growth', and are also devoting their attention to research. Led by Bunker and Aruna Roy, the team is most remarkable in that its members belong to the elite and are often from high-class urban families. All of them could have got better jobs and salaries but have preferred to work in the villages. For instance, Aruna resigned from the IAS, while her friend, Dr Sawny, could have gone abroad for advanced medical studies and perhaps set herself up independently later. This is one of the most striking examples of young urban people going back to the villages and combining their technical and practical abilities with a desire to help the poor.

CHAPTER 15

The Attack on Poverty

The questions we will look at here are how rural development can be
improved, and the main economic sectors which must be considered
in order to widen the growth process and its impact on the poor.

The Conduct of District Operations and the IAS

In spite of the defects in the increasing number of rural institutions
introduced or expanded in the 1950s, there has been a further proliferation of agencies and programmes since 1970. 'At the field level ...
multiplicity of functional departments and agencies has led to virtual
balkanisation of the field', writes Mohit Bhattacharya.[1] Despite the
many efforts to stimulate development from below, 'there is a lot of
spurious decentralisation all around such as looking to sanctions and
approvals upward, almost at every step.' Often, during our survey, in
state capitals and district towns we heard similar comments from
experienced civil servants. As a senior IAS officer told me, 'What we
need are some simple ideas upon which to build rural development.'

Let us try to look at some of the possible improvements. To begin
with, the size of districts varies a great deal,[2] although it has considerably increased everywhere in terms of population. There has been, in
states where districts are particularly big (in terms of population, as
in Bihar), a trend to bifurcate them. This needs to be systematically
encouraged, in almost all states, as a number of officials pointed out
to me both in Delhi and in the provincial capitals. The whole process
of rural development is becoming increasingly complex in every
sense of the word: social, economic and technical. Thus it is necessary
to work with a unit which is really manageable and controllable from

[1] M. Bhattacharya, 'Administrative and Organisational Issues in Rural Development', *The Journal of the Indian Institute of Public Administration*, No. 4, 1978.
[2] Total number 405 in 1980–1.

district headquarters.[3] At the same time it would be better to have smaller states. For decades, it has been suggested that the enormous state of Uttar Pradesh should be bifurcated. I remember some leading officers in Madras (in 1964), saying that the smaller size of their state after the 1956 changes had proved helpful for planning and management. While there is much good sense behind such ideas, the issue is so heavily loaded with politics that it may not be possible to implement such a change in the near future. District bifurcation, though by no means simple from a political point of view, is less difficult to realize.

The next step deals with district leadership. As we have observed, wherever a good IAS Collector is in command, the district administration works more swiftly. In many states, however, the Collector is not directly involved in developmental tasks. Perhaps the ideal solution would be to have a District Magistrate or Collector who is directly and primarily concerned with developmental tasks, and is a generalist in development, seconded by a first class agricultural officer, well trained, well paid and with enough prestige attached to his rank. Both these officers could directly control and run the main agencies. This is very different from the present situation in which the Collector has five types of responsibilities: law and order, revenue, distribution of certain commodities, development, and relief operations in cases of emergency like floods and drought. In addition, he is the chairman of various committees involved in development. He also acts as a co-ordinator for the different departments engaged in development. He could perhaps be relieved of some of these functions (law and order, and land revenue, for instance) handling only the occasional serious and important matter in these areas, other activities being left to his subordinates.

While our conclusions remain the same today as they were in the 1960s, one must raise several questions with regard to the future. Are the new generations of IAS officers of the same calibre as their predecessors? I do not have enough direct evidence to answer this, but in the opinion of one of the most senior and experienced officers, the best candidates joining the IAS are as good as ever; however, between the top people and the average he thinks there is a wide gap. The latter are of poorer calibre than their predecessors, for several young people today are less attracted by the IAS. They prefer to enter business,

[3] Among the many factors which explain development in pre- and post-partition Punjab and later, was the relatively small size of the districts.

scientific research and other professions. There is also the question of seriously falling standards of university education. The IAS does not train its officers sufficiently in economic, financial and banking problems. On the other hand, with the recent sending of probationers to villages, the service has improved as far as training in rural development is concerned. The Planning Commission has recently decided to adopt another method (this was adopted by Maharashtra in 1962) by which, in addition to the Collector or District Magistrate, another IAS officer of equal rank and status should have 'complete authority and responsibility with respect to development work'.

The efficiency of the administration is also highly dependent on the political leadership. At present, the quality of the local politicians in several states is fairly low because of a number of factors: poor qualifications and lack of experience,[4] intrigues and rivalries. All in all, political leaders often do not demand enough from their officials and this encourages a lack of rigour at administrative levels. Politicians also sometimes prefer to have a senior IAS officer as Collector because the latter is likely to be more amenable to political pressures. IAS officers also, in certain cases, look down on political bosses in the districts or in the states if they feel the local party leaders are poorly educated. People also speak of a growing tendency among IAS officers towards careerism and opportunism, which is connected with 'the danger of posting and promotions becoming matters of patronage', as B. B. Vohra states in a very critical article. Such a risk goes hand in hand with a 'search for security'.[5] Apart from this, there is also the fact of corruption.

B. K. Nehru, one of the most respected ex-ICS officers speaks of similar problems: 'The forces which erode the efficiency of the administration have been in operation in the States for a much longer time than at the Centre.' He adds that it is necessary to 'remove political influence from the civil service, to improve its economic position to such an extent that it becomes impervious to financial pressures and financial inducements, and thirdly, to restore to it once again its professional integrity'.[6]

In spite of these weaknesses, India still enjoys several advantages

[4] In one medium-sized state, three ministers knew only their native language, which was not Hindi, in 1978.

[5] B. B. Vohra, 'Time for New Norms', *Seminar*, October 1978.

[6] B. K. Nehru, 'The Role of the Civil Services in India Today', Seventh Govind Ballabh Pant Memorial Lecture, April 1980.

in this regard in comparison with other developing countries. A number of IAS officers now in senior positions in New Delhi and in the states are competent, quick-witted and fully dedicated to their country and their work. Besides, a number of them are thoroughly familiar with the basic technical aspects of agricultural problems.[7] On the other hand, there are cases where the generalist approach goes too far. For instance, I know of an ex-Secretary of Irrigation in a state, whose previous experience (in foreign trade in New Delhi) had nothing to do with his job, and of a Secretary of Agriculture who had previously been with the Ministry of Defence.

The reader may well ask why we are emphasizing the role of the IAS so much. We will revert to that matter in the next chapter. Here it is enough to point out the following facts. All attempts at peoples' participation through co-operatives, community projects and Panchayati Raj have yielded disappointing results both in terms of economic development and social justice. The slow rate of economic development has been confirmed by numerous examples, while that of social justice is unavoidable since such institutions are bound to remain in the hands of medium and upper farmers.

Some dedicated and able cadres (and these do exist)[8] can 'have things done' and more effectively protect the interests of the poor. Among such people are civil servants who constantly tour their districts, meet the villagers and listen to them; we have seen a number of such officers during our surveys and subsequent visits. Of course, even an able Collector supported by a first-class agricultural officer will not achieve miracles, mainly because the tasks are so enormous, but such a team would nonetheless bring about a definite improvement. One would not then hear the frequent complaint made by farmers who, after expressing some grievance, add the usual *koi nahin sunta* ('nobody listens').

As we have seen, district planning is becoming increasingly complex. The earliest attempts to improve it go back to the preparation of the Third Five Year Plan (1961–6). Nearly twenty years later, the

[7] This of course does not mean that they can replace agronomists, but that they know and understand enough to design and implement suitable policies with the assistance of specialists.

[8] Some people object that too many IAS officers are not interested in district life and prefer to be in a state or in the central secretariat. There are certainly cases like that, but one still finds a number of young cadres who are prepared to spend several years away from big towns and paper work.

question has still not been solved. There are comparatively well-run districts such as Thanjavur, but too often district officers are of relatively low calibre and are given no lead by the Collector. The Dantwala Committee on block level planning recommends 'pooling together the available planning skills at the district level instead of scattering this scarce resource in several blocks'.[9] Such a team should visit the blocks at frequent intervals to help them prepare their own plans. It is clear that these guidelines will be easier to implement by means of a small hard core of officers as outlined above. These officers could, by dint of their ability and character, compensate for at least some of the shortcomings of their subordinates. The improvement of district planning, which also requires similar efforts at the state and central levels, would, of course, boost economic growth. But, what is less obvious, it will also have social implications and value for the poor, as will be emphasized below.

Indirect Versus Direct Attacks on Poverty

It is obvious that a direct attack on poverty through collectivization leading to a greater equalization of incomes and power remains a very remote hypothesis, unless some unforeseen events occur in the not-too-distant future. Also, the target group approach can be expected to contribute only in a limited way to the eradication of poverty. Should one, therefore, talk as some Indians do, of the 'lack of a political will? I would be more inclined to say that politicians are simply aware of the balance of power within villages and that it is in their interests not to upset this drastically.

When considering an indirect attack on poverty there seems to be more scope for strengthening trends observed in relatively progressive areas where growth favours the poor as well as the rich. With a stronger district organization, a wide range of measures can be pushed through. We have already dealt, in the previous chapter, with the social value of updating land records and consolidating holdings, wherever possible.

Proper water management is one of the priorities in terms of irrigation and drainage. As far as the farmer is concerned, considerable progress has been achieved. Gradually minor irrigation and quick result-oriented schemes have been encouraged with outstanding results in several regions. Efforts are being made to speed up major irrigation works. A number of very alert senior civil servants like

[9] *Report of the Working Group on Block Level Planning* (New Delhi, 1978), p. 7.

B. B. Vohra have played a highly positive role in this.[10] In the draft of the present Five Year Plan (1978–83), Raj Krishna, as member of the Planning Commission, has had the opportunity of implementing the ideas he has been advocating for many years. The problem is to go even faster and provide more assistance, particularly in terms of qualified personnel, to states like Bihar, Assam, Orissa and parts of U.P. where progress remains slow. Drainage is equally needed and, in this connection, I wonder whether the extreme urgency of a more massive effort is always understood by policy-makers.

Such a water-oriented policy has an obvious economic value, but its social consequences are no less important. As we saw in many districts where the untapped potential for irrigation remains considerable, a farmer with even 0.5 hectares of land properly irrigated and drained can, with the help of additional inputs, considerably improve his income. At the same time he becomes less vulnerable to pressure or exploitation by big landowners. Besides, having more work to do on his own land, he creates employment opportunities for landless labourers.

Then comes the supply of other inputs. Before thinking of credit and subsidies to small and marginal farmers, the most urgent goal is to ensure an ample supply of appropriate seeds, chemical fertilizers and pesticides at a reasonable price. This automatically wipes out many malpractices and other cases of abuse, the victims of which are always the small, and marginal farmers. Since they carry little weight in rural institutions, in times of shortage they are the first to suffer. Shortages leading to black marketing compel them to pay high prices if they can afford them, or prevent them from buying at all. During our last survey, we found substantial improvements in the supply of chemical fertilizers and seeds, with the result that, unlike in 1963–4, we rarely registered complaints. The same could not be said of cement, which was rationed,[11] and for which, too often, a bakshish had to be paid. In other cases the cement delivered was mixed with sand.

Agronomic research and adequate seed multiplication need further improvement, although much has already been done. This involves research institutes and agricultural universities. The latter, created in practically every state during the 1960s, often with Ameri-

[10] For over a decade he has been advocating a stronger water policy. See B. B. Vohra, *Land and Water Management in India* (New Delhi, 1975).
[11] There have been ups and downs in the supply of cement since the 1960s.

cans support, have uneven records. The positive role of the Punjab Agricultural University of Ludhiana is well known. The same can be said of Pantnagar U.P. Agricultural University. Its research, seed multiplication and extension activities were boosted by one of the finest IAS officers, D. P. Singh.[12] Unfortunately the situation has deteriorated in the last few years and in some states one hears that these universities have become a hotbed for politics or that research is not sufficiently oriented towards local problems. Certain researchers also tend to seek assignments abroad, especially in U.N. agencies.

The problem of improving seeds supply also needs to be considered[13] and here again conditions vary from state to state. In fact, the whole of India must get used to what has happened in the Western world, namely, a continuous process of releasing new seed varieties and multiplying them.

Research in wheat has made a fair amount of progress; the situation is now improving for rice, but the same cannot be said of pulses and oilseeds. As regards the former, some new and better varieties (green gram, *mung* beans), which mature in sixty days instead of ninety, could play an important role as a third crop between the rabi and the kharif. Experiments conducted with farmers have yielded 500–700 kilograms per hectare, which is usually higher than traditional varieties. Besides, such crops enrich the soil in fixing nitrogen from the atmosphere. They do not need chemical fertilizers if phosphate has been used for the previous crop. Maize, which is a kharif crop, could be sown with greater profit in the rabi in several parts of Karnataka or Maharashtra, if not in the north-west. Some very encouraging success has been achieved in eastern U.P. and Bihar in the last few years.

Sorghum and bajra grown in poorly rain-fed areas face difficulties, yet there is room for some progress[14] through the use of new seeds, treating them against pests and sowing them early. It is surprising that so little has been done so far for oilseeds (particularly groundnuts) especially when there is a deficit of vegetable oil at the all-India level due to which oil imports are growing. Attempts to introduce soyabeans have not yet produced any striking results. On the other

[12] D. P. Singh later dealt with the National Seeds Corporation until December 1976.
[13] The National Seeds Corporation has been going through various troubles since 1977.
[14] Indian research institutes as well as the U.N. International Crops Research Institute for Semi-Arid Tropics (ICRISAT) at Hyderabad, are active in these fields.

hand, sunflower seems to be rather promising in Maharashtra. Cotton needs increasing attention. Research in new varieties is moving ahead, but one major problem is that the rains are often very poor and there is a lack of irrigation; yields are therefore bound to remain low. Today, they are often around 100 kilograms per hectare in Maharashtra, while the highest yield in the country was 360 kilograms (lint) in Punjab (in the year 1978–9).

Sugarcane, another cash crop, has not been greatly helped so far with new varieties. It is true that the relatively cold winter of northern India does affect yields negatively, but more can be done as, even today, in many districts of eastern U.P., farmers are not yet using the better varieties of sugarcane introduced in the 1930s in western U.P. (Special mention must be made, however, of a new variety—COJ 64—released by Dr J. C. Kanwar of the Punjab Agricultural University, which has pushed the average yield for Punjab from 39 tons per hectare in 1971–2 to 56 in 1977–8, with a sugar recovery rate of 10.8 versus 8–9 per cent with old varieties).[15] Tapioca has known a sharp expansion in Kerala under a very suitable climate, but its potential has not been fully exploited elsewhere. In other areas, we have seen how potatoes are progressing. Here again, the next steps are not so simple. The bumper crop of 1977–8 led to the crisis of a surplus, which, because potatoes are a perishable commodity, was aggravated by the lack of cold storage facilities. Prices fell sharply and this discouraged farmers from pushing potatoes further.

Then come the new crops. In the hills of Orissa, they are experimenting with wing beans, a plant cultivated in Papua and Burma. The pods, leaves, seeds (which contain 17 per cent oil) and roots are rich in protein and in vitamins. Aquaculture and fish enjoy a large untapped potential. Interesting schemes such as the raising of prawns in brackish ponds near the sea in Thanjavur have been started. Vegetables have expanded considerably in the last thirty years, first around the big cities[16] and then in the vicinity of district towns. Today smaller towns have begun to be surrounded by a vegetable belt, but much more can be done deeper in the countryside, provided it is well connected by road to enable quick delivery to markets. The same applies to milk promotion and sales as well as to fruit. All these subsidiary activities are of particular importance for small or very small farmers. They all require a good water supply management.

[15] M. S. Gill, 'Punjab—The Continuing Miracle', *NCDC Bulletin,* Nos 3–4, 1979.
[16] Even in 1950, a town like Poona, in Maharashtra, had a poor supply of vegetables.

The question is not to innovate, but to speed up existing trends, or encourage them wherever they are still sluggish.

Intermediate, Alternative and Low Cost Technologies

Indian farmers are engaged in a process of semi-technical change, combining several old techniques with key new inputs such as pumps, chemical fertilizers, pesticides and, less frequently, tractors. Like other Asian peasants, they are trying to follow a new road towards agricultural progress which is neither the traditional pattern nor a copy of some Western blueprint. In this process there is scope for further innovation in the field of intermediate technology. Biogas plants can help but, as we have seen in several places, they are too expensive and only medium and upper farmers can afford them. Cheaper devices are being introduced, but small farmers will find even these too expensive.[17] In addition, the smaller farmers lack enough cattle to feed the biogas plants, and social relations in the villages are such that we cannot expect much from collective and jointly-owned units. It is also important to note that what is left from biogas in terms of manure, though better than normal manure, cannot replace chemical fertilizers. And such devices can very seldom be used for energizing tubewells. The biogas unit cannot be built in the midst of the fields since this would mean that farmers would have to transport their cattle manure, which is usually near their houses where the cattle are kept. Bamboo tubewells, though promising, are not always an answer to steel pipes. Bamboo pipes have been a success in certain regions (as in parts of Bihar) but not in others.

Research is progressing in solar energy but often, as in the case of engines and pumps, the present models are still too expensive. No large-scale application of solar energy looks promising for the immediate future but, according to Dr Ved Prakash, 'There is no reason why direct use of solar energy cannot be undertaken exclusively within the next fifteen years.'[18] Another interesting field of research is being opened, particularly in Tamil Nadu, which seeks to reduce the quantity of inputs like chemical fertilizers or pesticides while increasing their efficiency. For instance, when steeping sprouting seeds of

[17] The investment cost for some of the devices used earlier varied from Rs 4,000 to Rs 5,000. The latest devices cost Rs 2,000–3,000. In both cases 5 head of cattle are required to make the plant economical. More than 80,000 biogas plants were operating in India in 1980–1 (*Nouvelles de l'Inde* No. 214, October 1979).

[18] *Kurukshetra*, June 1977.

paddy in Carbandazim (Banstin) solution for fifteen minutes, 'the control obtained is equal to spraying twice with chemicals against bacterial leaf-blight'. The cost of treating one hectare drops from Rs 250–575 for field spraying to Rs 9. By applying di-ammonium phosphate at the rate of 2–3 kilograms for 40 square metres, it is possible to either cease applying chemical fertilizers to the main field or to reduce them to 30 per cent, while getting the same or higher yields as with full applications to the main fields. The costs are cut to nearly half. The placing of nitrogen fertilizers five centimetres below ground level can also save half of the chemical fertilizers normally recommended for the same yield.[19]

These examples give us an idea of what can still be done in all these matters, and of the enormous social content of this research. The first problem is one of initiative—which is still seriously lacking in several states (here again I wish to emphasize the high calibre of a number of senior officers I met in Tamil Nadu). The second problem is to find new devices or new techniques which are so cheap that small, or at least medium, farmers can afford them.

Small Industries and Trade

In spite of all that has been written of the bias in favour of large-scale industry, there has been a tremendous expansion of all sorts of medium, small and tiny industries, including workshops equipped with only one or two machine tools. Here again progress is extremely uneven, as we observed when travelling through the country. The growing emphasis on the small sector is welcome, but where it is just starting, as in eastern U.P., Bihar, Assam, Orissa and wide tracts of central India, it may take time to gather momentum because the Punjabi model cannot be transplanted so easily in a different set-up. Trade is also penetrating deeper, beyond roadside villages to others less well-connected, especially in the progressive areas. This needs more encouragement, just as the promotion of growth centres does. Both sectors help diversify the rural economy, increase the total volume of production and widen employment opportunities.

Roads and Electricity[20]

Compared with many developing countries, India had a relatively

---

[19] J. H. S. Ponnaya, *Low Cost High Efficiency Technology for Rice* (Madras, 1978).
[20] All data come from Tata Services, *Statistical Outline of India, 1980* (Bombay, 1980).

good start at the time of Independence and the progress achieved, in terms of road construction, has been impressive. People who have covered around 40–50,000 kilometres by road since the early 1950s, as we have done, are struck by the growing density of roads and the increasing number of asphalted roads leading to villages. Yet this is not enough, as the economy is becoming more demanding than ever. Typical are the villages around Mirpur which, like many others, are still a few kilometres away from a good road, and consequently put to a fair amount of inconvenience regarding transport. Then, as we saw in Palamau, there are areas which are even more isolated.[21]

Rural electricity did not cover even one per cent of the villages at the time of Independence. By the beginning of 1981, 250,000 (45 per cent of all villages) had been electrified; and as many as 4.1 million pumps, tubewells and pumpsets were relying on electricity. In some states such as Punjab, Haryana and Tamil Nadu, practically all the villages are electrified.

These data represent remarkable achievements and yet, power crises and shortages have assumed really dramatic proportions since 1979.[22] Irrigation suffers a great deal and tractors and pumps relying on oil engines have been hit by the lack of diesel oil. The whole small industries sector—flour and rice mills, threshing machines, engineering workshops, small pump manufactures, etc.—has either had to operate at less than optimum strength or has often even ceased operations altogether. As will be explained below, the crisis has several causes and affects practically all sectors of the economy.

The National Process of Rural Development

The different sectors of rural economic life reviewed so far present us with the basic framework of the national process of rural development. In addition to major crops, secondary agricultural activities (vegetables, fruit, fish, animal husbandry, milk) play an increasing

[21] *Road network:*	1950–1	1975–6
	(in thousands of kilometres)	
surfaced	157	533
unsurfaced	243	843
	400	1,376

Railways 53,200 kilometres in 1950–1,60,700 in 1977–8.

[22] Although serious problems have always existed, they reached a peak in 1979 and after. During the summer of 1981, tubewells in parts of Bihar were getting electricity for only one hour a day. The situation improved in the latter part of 1981–2.

role. Trade and small industries are expanding. Agricultural and non-agricultural activities require an increasingly wide and efficient network of transport and communications as well as electricity. To these priorities are to be added social programmes such as those for family planning, drinking water supply, health and education.

It is clear that the present stage of India's rural life is already miles ahead of the stereotyped image of closed and isolated villages which Charles Metcalfe described in the early nineteenth century: 'Village communities which are little republics, having nearly everything they want within themselves and almost independent of any foreign relation.'[23] It is beyond the scope of this work to discuss the validity of Metcalfe's statement (which has been contested by certain historians) even for the nineteenth century, but it is clear that, in spite of the renewed popularity of the concept of self-reliance under the Janata Government and international influences, the ideal of the self-sufficiency of the village is totally unrelated to the actual facts of life. As we have seen, with the population pressure being so heavy, the only way out is to have an increasingly open village economy, linked with the outside world: a fast growth of yields per hectare involving the proper selection of new inputs (and not the copy of some Western or Soviet model), and the active promotion of non-agricultural activities, some relying on the advanced technologies of large factories, others on the various intermediate technologies used in small factories.

In order to achieve a relatively harmonious development of these interdependent factors of growth, one needs to plan and manage the district economy better, and to make sound use of government and private forces. Yet this is not the end because these goals are closely connected with planning at the national and state levels.

National Planning in Electricity

Since our intention is to study rural development, we will consider here only the sectors which have a direct impact on the process described above.[24] As regards infrastructure, especially road building, the use of trucks and buses, no new measures seem necessary.

[23]Quoted by B. Cohn, 'Structural Change in Rural Society', in R. E. Frykenberg (ed.), *Land Control and Social Structure in Indian History* (Wisconsin, 1969).

[24]Many publications have dealt with national planning and agriculture. See, in particular, the fine analysis by John W. Mellor, *The New Economics of Growth, A Strategy for India and the Developing World* (Ithaca, 1976).

Electricity, on the other hand, is a major concern, requiring, as many Indians emphasize, extraordinary and drastic efforts. In several respects, this is a typical crisis of growth since India's progress has been enormous: consumption has increased from 6.6 billion kilowatt hours in 1950–1 to 76 billion in 1977–8, capacity from 2.3 million kilowatts to 26 million. One must, however, underline that the growth rate has been falling from a yearly average of 11.1 per cent for the decade 1960–1 to 1970–1, to 6.6 per cent for 1970–1 to 1977–8.[25] For many years there has been a power shortage, but it took a really dramatic turn for the worse in 1979. Climatic factors have affected hydro-electric plants negatively in periods of drought as in 1979, or positively as in 1978 when the monsoon was very heavy. On the other hand, the same 1978 monsoon adversely affected thermal power stations that year, due to the flooding of coal mines.

Other major factors can explain the crisis too. Coal[26] is still supplying many electric plants but production is far from satisfactory: management, labour troubles, ageing equipment and shortage of rail transport, all explain why production has stagnated at around 105 million tons from 1976–7 to 1979–80, though in 1980–1 it increased to 119 million tons. Shortcomings in planning and constructing new electrical plants are no less responsible for the crisis. The Second and Third Plans (1956–66) achieved two-third of their targets for installed capacity, the Fourth Plan of 1969–74 only 47 per cent. Performance improved to 75 per cent in the following years. Other troubles, such as the increases in oil prices and the several months-long embargo on oil transport from Assam, have made the situation worse.

State electricity boards and the management of power plants are facing similar difficulties which have been aggravated by strikes and other troubles since 1976. For instance, in Uttar Pradesh, thermal generation fell by 50 per cent in December 1979 due to an agitation provoked by power engineers. In Bihar—and the case is not exceptional—the existing installed capacity of the Electricity Board is 730,000 kilowatts, but since several units are old and subject to frequent breakdowns, the present capacity varies from 350 to 400,000 kilowatts, while the peak demand is 600,000. When it can, the Elec-

[25]The rate seems to have risen again in 1978–9 by about 10 per cent; installed capacity 29 million kilowatts. Further improvements in 1982–2.

[26]Coals mines were nationalized in 1973. Thermal power stations (including oil and gas) supply more than 50 per cent of the country's electricity, hydro below or above 40 per cent, nuclear around 2.8 per cent.

tricity Board receives assistance to the extent 100,000 kilowatts from the neighbouring states. This assistance is not regular and is inadequate.[27]

The total network relies on over one million circuit kilometres of transmission and distribution lines, including 28,000 kilometres of transmission lines at 200 kilowatts or over. Here again expansion has not been smooth. Management and operations face several short-comings as observed in the field: malpractices, falling voltage, break-downs, etc. Several networks have expanded gradually instead of being planned from the beginning, so that high voltage transmission lines are lacking—which leads to heavy losses of power over long distances. To remedy this situation would require considerable rede-signing of systems. There is also a tendency, on the part of able officials and engineers, to concentrate more on increasing the existing capacity instead of improving maintenance and operations.

One can thus say that the present crisis is due to a number of factors such as lack of discipline, mismanagement and labour trouble in the coal mines at certain times as well as the price of oil and the unrest in Assam. As a result, many industries were affected and had to work at less than optimum capacity. Several key industries such as chemical fertilizers, cement and steel were hit. In 1980-1, the production of cement was 18.5 million tons as against a potential production of 22.66 million tons; nitrogen factories produced 2.15 million tons instead of the potential 2.84 million; steel ingots were 9.12 million tons as against a potential 11.4 million. Part of this deficit had to be made up by additional imports, thus eating into the country's foreign exchange reserves.

The Renewed Debate on Agriculture and Industry [28]

With the advent to power of the Janata Party in 1977, the old debate which had arisen just after Independence—namely, should one give priority to agriculture or industry—was revived and the Five Year Plans were criticized for laying excessive emphasis on industry at the cost of agriculture.

In fact, the problem is not one of a choice between the two but of

[27] *Overseas Hindustan Times*, 6 and 14 December 1979. On the whole, the crisis is worse in northern India than in other parts. One factor may be the poorer management of state electricity boards here than in other parts of the country.

[28] For the following data, see *Economic Survey*, 1981-2, and *Statistical Outline of India*, 1980.

proper interdependence or linkage. We have seen how agriculture has become dependent on several key industrial inputs. On the other hand, a large sector of industry depends for its survival on agricultural goods, which it processes. Finally, in terms of incomes and the demand for consumer goods, there is a close link between an expanding agriculture and industry. In this context, what is to be criticized is not industrialization *per se*, but its content. Greater emphasis should have been placed on certain industries directly supporting agriculture. The most glaring example is chemical fertilizers. Starting practically from scratch in 1950–1, production reached 344,000 tons in 1965–6 and 3 million tons in 1980–1.[29] In one sense this meant a substantial rise, but India still imports more than one million tons of nitrogen fertilizers and a substantial quantity of phosphate fertilizers. The performance through the Five Year Plans has been as follows:

Percentage of Targets Achieved in the Production of Chemical Fertilizers

1951–6	71
1956–61	18
1961–6	19
1969–74	24
1974–8	71

In addition to power shortages, other difficulties delayed the construction of new plants. The situation is only partly improving[30] and several new plants are under construction, but one can imagine how much easier things would have been if greater efforts had been made between the mid-fifties and the mid-seventies.

The picture is not very different for cement, which is urgently needed in all fields of economic life. From 2.73 million tons in 1950–1, output reached 10.8 million in 1965–6. It went up to 18.8 million in 1976–7 and then levelled off at 19.3 million during the next two years and fell to 18.5 million tons in 1980–1. Steel follows a similar trend: 1.1 million tons (finished steel) in 1950–1, 4.8 million tons in 1965–6, 7.1 million in 1976–7 and then a decline over the next two years down to 6.6 million in 1978–9. Here also, the power shortage is not the sole factor inhibiting production.

It is also important to look at industries that depend on agricultural goods. There are too many 'sick mills' in the textile and sugar

[29] In terms of nutrients, N (nitrogen), P_2O_5 (phosphoric acid).

[30] Although utilization of the existing capacity remains rather low—57 per cent in 1970, 58 per cent in 1978.

industries. This does not stimulate agricultural growth and leads to low industrial productivity and high prices. In certain cases the mutual dependence between farmers and mills affects the farmers negatively.[31]

Several more examples can be given of the need for greater efficiency and linkage between both sectors. All these problems explain why manufacturing industries declined by 2 per cent during 1979–80. Over and above all this, and related to it, was large-scale deficit financing and the return to a high rate of inflation (about 20 per cent in 1979) which, in previous years, had been considerably controlled.

Since 1980–1, the situation has improved. Industrial production increased by 4 per cent, and in 1981–2 it went up by 8 per cent. There was some improvement in the supply of electricity and rail transport, but it will take several years to overcome the present shortages. Agriculture picked up in 1980–1, as well as in 1981–2.

Price Factors

Money plays an increasing role in rural development: more wages in cash, greater use of cash inputs, a growing share of agricultural production entering the market, rising investments and increasing purchases of goods. Thus the relationship between monetary production, costs, and prices of agricultural produce has become a very sensitive issue, which requires constant watching. We have seen cases where farmers need more or better price incentives to induce them to push certain crops. Apart from this, the situation is fluctuating—a glut of sugar brings prices down, a sharp increase in potato production is followed by a fall in prices. Farmers know how to raise their voices, but the task of the government is not easy and it continues to grow with the increasing diversity of the monetized sector in rural life.

These observations, made during our field study in 1978–9, were amply confirmed in the following two years, which shows how complex these issues have become today. For decades, traders in grain, cotton, sugar and oilseeds were the main pressure groups, lobbying at the local and national levels with politicians in power. Today, while this set of factors remains, others have appeared: direct action or agitation by farmers, not only the big ones (who may, at the same time, be traders as well), but also medium and small farmers. The initial movement began under the leadership of Sharad Joshi, an

---

[31] Farmers in U.P. may have to wait six months, if not more, before they are paid for their work by certain co-operative sugar mills.

ex-international civil servant posted in Geneva, who later returned to India. From Maharashtra the movement spread to the north-west and the south[32] where several serious incidents occurred. This new situation is, in itself, a sign of the advance made by Indian agriculture. Similar problems were faced by farmers in Europe—even in a country like Switzerland, agitating farmers took to direct action and created several 'incidents'.

To set up proper price relationships between inputs and outputs is an extremely complex technical task. If political interference is added to such a situation, it becomes still more difficult to find solutions. Thus India will have to learn how to live with such problems. One cannot expect instant and correct answers in all cases.

Towards A.D. 2000

The first question I would like to look at here is that of population. The 1981 census has counted a total of 684 million people. The decennial rate of increase of 24.75 per cent over the 1971 figure is hardly below the rate for 1961–71, which was 24.8 per cent. It is, however, interesting to note that in several states with more than 200 million inhabitants, the growth rate is coming down. In most cases this is due to a fall in the birth rate. At the national level the birth rate is estimated at 36 per thousand (41 in 1971). As to the death rate, it is clear that it remains fairly high (14–15 per thousand) compared with several other Asian countries. It can be expected to fall in the coming decades. Drastic efforts are therefore required in the field of family planning in order to compensate for the fall in the death rate and to bring down the rate of population increase.

It is interesting to note that, although the idea of birth controls is much more widespread in towns and villages today than it was years ago, implementation varies greatly from state to state. In Maharashtra, Tamil Nadu, parts of Andhra and Kerala, progress is obvious. In U.P., Bihar, Rajasthan, Orissa and some other states propaganda has never been very active except during the Emergency. Today a growing number of town-dwellers understand the logic behind family planning in view of the overall cost of living, the cost of educating their children and the problems of finding jobs.

---

[32] Barbara Harriss studied these problems in a very fine paper entitled 'Agricultural Mercantile Politics and Policy—A Case-Study of Tamil Nadu', paper presented at the Seventh Conference of European and South Asian Studies, London, July 1981. See also G. Deleury, 'Societe traditionnelle en Inde, le poids des castes', Paris, *Croissance des Jeunes Nations* (May 1981).

In villages a large number of medium and relatively small farmers understand that when their holdings are divided between several sons, the latter will face all kinds of hardship. On the other hand, it is true that tiny landholders and landless people may find an advantage in having a few more children, since labour is the sole source of income in such families and the more children there are, the more the potential labour power. However, as we have observed in the field, the fertility of these couples is rather low and infant mortality is still very high. It is highly desirable, thus, to speed up family planning programmes without committing the excesses of the Emergency. This is a problem the seriousness of which cannot be underestimated. According to the Census Commissioner, if much greater efforts are put into family planning than have been done so far, it is possible that the population will not exceed 950 million in the year 2000. If this is not done, reaching the billion mark is not an impossibility.

It is obvious that India's rural economic potential is far from being fully tapped; consequently, even without drastic political and economic changes, growth can expand further and affect a larger number of the poor. In this connection the first question is that of water management. The old canal systems need substantial improvement in order to increase water supply, prevent loss through seepage and possibly increase the time period over which irrigation is provided when water supply and water sources are not perennial. In the mid-1970s, B. B. Vohra estimated that 16 million irrigated hectares could be improved thus.[33] There are also areas where the replenishment of ground water is not reliable, which could lead to decreased irrigation. In certain cases deeper tubewells solve the problem, but this cannot be the answer everywhere.

There is also the important question of additional irrigation. From 20 million hectares (gross) so far, the ultimate potential of ground water is assessed at 35 million hectares. But one must bear in mind the fact that, at the beginning of 1975, 63 per cent of the territory was not yet covered by systematic hydrogeological surveys. It is significant to note that differences ranged from 75 to 80 per cent in Bihar, Orissa, Maharashtra, Madhya Pradesh; they came down to 9 per cent in Haryana and 17 per cent in Punjab.[34] It is amazing that in a developing country as advanced as India, such an elementary and crucial task has not yet been completed.

[33]Op. cit., p. 40.
[34]*Fifth Five Year Plan 1974-79*, p. 95. The situation is worse in many other developing countries.

These data confirm that there is still a large untapped irrigation potential in the eastern region, in many parts of which poverty is particularly acute. Most of these areas have good, if not excellent, alluvial soils which can easily hold two crops a year of wheat and paddy, or two of paddy, the wheat yielding 2,000 kilograms per hectare and the paddy 4,000. For several years discussions have been held about the creation of a national water grid to connect the Ganges basin (which has an excess of water) with the Deccan rivers which are more susceptible to a low flow of water. One of the biggest obstacles in this is to take the grid across the Vindhyas. The latest proposal envisages pumping at a maximum height of 130 metres instead of lifting the water to 400 metres as earlier planned. Such a grand scheme, if achieved, could further enlarge the irrigation potential. However, it will take several decades for it to be completed.

No less urgent a problem is that of drainage. At present 25 million hectares are flood-prone, but as many as 20 million of these can be protected. These data, given in the Draft Five Year Plan 1978–83, probably exclude many tracts of lowlands suffering from excess water even under normal rainfall conditions. Then there are 6 million hectares which are affected by waterlogging, and 7 million which are saline or alkaline due to various factors such as the 'capillary rise from subsoil bed of salt, indiscriminate use of canal water, ingress of sea water'.[35]

On the basis of present achievements, it is clear beyond doubt that progress in water management can pave the way for progress in other inputs such as new seeds for cereals, chemical fertilizers and, when required, pesticides. The National Agricultural Commission has made the following forecasts for the year 2000:

	1971	2000
	(in million hectares)	
Cultivated area (net)	140	150
Cultivated area (gross)	165	200
Irrigated area (net)	31.3	61
Irrigated area (gross)	38.5	84
Foodgrain area	123	123
Cash crops	28	45
Horticulture	5	13
Plantations	2.3	2.8

Source: *National Commission on Agriculture*, pp. 304–5 of their report.

[35] National Commission on Agriculture, *Abridged Report* (New Delhi, 1977), p. 209.

Present conditions confirm these national assumptions: wherever grain yields go up, farmers tend to reduce the area devoted to grain in favour of cash crops. The acceleration of progress in irrigation implies that the targets envisaged for 2000 can be achieved. In 1980, they reached 52.6 million hectares gross. The Commission assesses the supply of chemical fertilizers at 14 million (nutrients) in A.D. 2000, nearly three times the 1978–9 level of 5 million. This implies that there will be a tremendous effort to build new plants, and to operate old and new ones more efficiently than is being done now, because imports can cover only a very small part of the total supply that has been forecast. The target seems rather difficult to attain, unless very exceptional measures are taken and implemented over the long term. But it deserves consideration as one of the top priorities for the country.

Losses due to rodents, insects, diseases and weeds have never been scientifically assessed on an all-India basis. Following one of the most conservative guesses, such losses represent 20 per cent of the crops, particularly food crops. Though the use of pesticides is progressing, especially in advanced areas, more has to be done to include other methods such as biological control and the eradication of rodents with simple traps, as is being done in the Krishna delta. On the whole, the complex tasks needed for a sound control programme require more efforts than have been made so far.

The Commission envisages a production of 230 million tons of foodgrains for the year 2000 (132 million in 1978–9, a good year). Practically all the increases are to be achieved through higher yields.

Forecast for the Year 2000

Main Foodgrains	Yields (tons per hectare)	Area (in million hectares)
Wheat (irrigated)	3–4	15
(unirrigated)	1.5–2	3
Rice	2.8–3.5	32 (24 million irrigated)
Maize	2.6	9
Jowar	1.2	17
Bajra	1.2	12
Pulses	1.5	25

Source: *National Commission on Agriculture*, pp. 242–51 and 304 of their report.

The targets, in terms of yields, seem too high. For wheat the already advanced irrigated areas can perhaps reach these targets. Late starters will not. The estimates for non-irrigated wheat appear fairly doubtful. For rice, what has been seen in the advanced areas of south India makes 3.5 tons per hectare (about 5 tons per hectare in terms of paddy) appear plausible. Even if water management improves drastically in eastern India, an average figure of 2.8 tons (4.2 in terms of paddy) as given for U.P., Bihar, Madhya Pradesh, seems far too high, especially as today these states have not even been able to attain one ton of rice per hectare in many areas.

For jowar and bajra, which are bound to remain largely rain-fed, the target seems very optimistic if we keep in mind that today they range from 200 to 700 kilograms per hectare. An average yield of around 700 kilograms per hectare seems reasonable. To treble, if not more, the present yields of pulses, seems extremely ambitious, although we must wait for the results of the new varieties that are presently being released. It may be safer to expect not more than 1,000 kilograms per hectare.

To sum up, the targets set for wheat and rice can certainly be attained with irrigation, but they may take longer than expected. For rain-fed crops in dry areas, such high average yields do not seem practicable for biological reasons, unless new scientific discoveries take place.

Could one reach the 230 million ton target by devoting more area to foodcrops at the cost of other crops? Even if the latter were done, it seems that the target is too high. In the last few years, the growth trend has tended to level off, partly because of already high yields in advanced areas and partly because of slow progress in poor but potentially rich districts of Eastern India. It seems that to reach even 200 million tons in AD 2000, considerable efforts would be needed in the overall agricultural policy and in the support of industries.

To produce is one thing, to consume is another. India managed to have a surplus of 22 million tons of foodgrains in 1979, in spite of malnutrition in several parts of the country. The main reason is that in areas of slow growth, the income of the poor has hardly improved; hence they cannot buy and eat more, thereby absorbing the surplus of the advanced areas. To avoid or discourage such trends, it is imperative to bring about, at least in areas opened upto irrigation in the future, a more balanced pattern of growth. As we will see below, this is by no means easy at this stage.

In the field of cash crops the Constitution envisages sharp increases in areas and yields:

	Area (in million hectares)	
Crop	*1971*	*2000*
Oilseeds	16.3	25.5
Sugarcane	2.6	5.0
Cotton	7.6	11.5

Source: *National Commission on Agriculture*, p. 304 of their report.

According to the National Commission on Agriculture, average groundnut yields should increase from 0.7 tons per hectare to 1.5, sugarcane from 42 tons to 82, cotton lint from 120 kilograms per hectare to 460. Here again, targets seem too high in terms of areas and yields,[36] though one can expect substantial increases in both. Any forecast on the expansion of horticulture is very risky since actual figures are even less reliable than those for the main crops.

Even if we assume that the birth rate will fall more rapidly in coming years, it is obvious that the fairly large number of farmers who live reasonably well now on 1.5–2 hectares of irrigated land will in the coming generation, have to manage on half that amount, if not less. Those plots which are already small will become smaller, which means that not only will their owners need to increase their yields, but they will also have to work harder in non-agricultural pursuits.

What will happen in dry, semi-arid zones that are not fit for irrigation? (These cover around 47 million hectares in 84 districts.) A clear answer is difficult to give. No matter what can be achieved with better dry farming techniques, yields beyond 500–1,000 kilograms per hectare are very doubtful and double cropping is, of course, out of the question. These areas are less heavily populated but, compared with land resources, the balance is tight. This underlines the greater need for efforts in better communications and non-agricultural activities.

Finally, we must consider the political leadership. A great deal has been written on its impact on development and the needs of a strong and stable government. Such statements are much too sweeping. As many Indians have pointed out, it is doubtful whether, in the near future, India can enjoy a government which follows absolutely clear-cut and rational policies. The network of forces and interests at the centre and in the states compels her to make compromises, untidy bargains which hinder a smooth economic policy. At the same time,

[36] The yields of the table correspond to a total of 250 million tons, while the Commission takes 230 million. Yet even that quantity involves very high yields.

this type of political life has thus far kept India out of major and dramatic crises whereby the future of the nation is at stake, unlike countries such as Iran, Afghanistan and Pakistan.[37]

'We finally muddle through', remark some Indians, and a friend went even further: 'We have become like Italy, we can manage even with a poor government.' Such statements need some qualification. As the collapse of the Janata Government demonstrated, there are limits to 'muddling through'. The deterioration of law and order, the growing labour unrest, the student disorders[38] and lack of decision-making, had, at that time, assumed dangerous proportions. Secondly, in the case of rural development, we can broadly consider two kinds of problems. As confirmed in western U.P., even political instability has not prevented a widespread process of development because local conditions have been favourable. These areas have had a relatively good start, enterprising castes, and minor irrigation that relies on tubewells. In Punjab also, the breakthrough in new seeds occurred at a time of great political instability.

On the other hand, in many parts of India, especially in the region that extends from eastern U.P. to Assam and Orissa, individual farmers and private trade cannot overcome the most fundamental obstacles to development such as water management (which requires major and medium works of irrigation), drainage and flood control. Unstable governments, political leaders who are more interested in local feuds than in public works, as well as a weak administration have a grave and negative impact on such schemes. Such conditions have existed in U.P., Bihar, Assam and Orissa for nearly two decades now. Unless some exceptional local leaders at last take over, how can things really improve? Fortunately, a number of other states, especially in the south and in Maharashtra and Gujarat, have faced much better conditions so far.

Towards New Horizons

Not only is India changing but so also is its image abroad. At last a growing number of foreigners are realizing that it is not only a

[37] Each of these countries faces a different type of crisis, but all the crises are extremely serious.

[38] The growing deterioration of the educational system (which becomes worse every year) is not felt too strongly in certain circles since senior jobs are still in the hands of people who were educated in the early years after Independence. But the impact will soon be more noticeable. In the long term, this is a matter of major concern.

country of sadhus, holy cows and beggars. What is becoming increasingly clear is the will to use the socio-economic forces of the country more efficiently, the economic assets developed so far, the large stock of available talents.

Such aims, which fit well with the perspective of this book, face severe obstacles. A number of warnings have been issued in recent times about existing and future dangers. As L. K. Jha, an experienced civil servant, has emphasized in his book *Economic Strategy for the 80's:* 'We are passing through not just a bad patch in our economic progress, but a deeper social, political and moral malaise, the seeds of which lie in the malfunctioning of the economic system as a whole. Indeed the very quality of individual and national life is in jeopardy.' B. K. Nehru, a man of great calibre, like L. K. Jha, issued another warning in *The Roots of Corruption* (1981) in which he spoke of the deterioration in the political scene. Many similar opinions could be quoted, which give us an idea of the challenge faced by India's government.

Several positive factors may gradually counteract these defects. Mrs Gandhi has gathered around her a number of very competent civil servants, who do not believe in dogmas but in efficiency. After thirty years of red tapism, economic controls, an inefficient public sector, which together hindred the economy and led to all kinds of malpractices and corruption, definite steps are being taken in order to stimulate productive forces in the well-founded hope that they will also affect the conditions of the poor. Mrs Gandhi has given the first indications of changes being made in the right direction, as an increasing number of Indians acknowledge, but these may need further efforts if they are to make a greater impact on the economy.

Such a down-to-earth policy belongs to the art of the possible. In the socio-political and economic context of India, one does not see any other way out.

CHAPTER 16
The Other Side of the Picture

Having met the farmers let us now look at what is said about them in discussions relating to them both in India and other Asian countries, particularly in China. Since the beginning of the 1970s, themes such as 'self-reliance', 'absolute poverty', 'poverty line', 'basic needs' have been flooding speeches, reports, conferences in international organizations and universities that are concerned with development in the West, as well as in the developing countries. The same concerns are reflected in plans and discussions within the Third World.

The Arguments on Poverty

The claim that development strategies in the 1950s and 1960s overemphasized growth and increases of the GNP at the cost of social progress is a surprising one.[1] Social progress was, in fact, stressed in the First Five Year Plan: 'Economic planning has to be viewed as an integral part of a wider process aiming not merely at the development of resources in a narrow technical sense, but at the development of human faculties and the building up of an institutional framework adequate to the needs and aspirations of the people.'[2] In a number of developing countries planning was not so different—as we can see from the multi-purpose approach to community development attempted in Asia. The First Five Year Plan of Pakistan (1955–60) refers to the 'spirit of self help' and 'the rapid economic and social improvement' (p. 30), and the Second Five Year Plan (1960–5) of the then Federation of Malaya speaks of a 'big push' in order to 'provide for the social and economic needs of the

[1] It has become increasingly recognized that rural development cannot be viewed as a narrow technical problem or increasing production through modern inputs', write the editors of a recent study by the International Labour Organization (ILO), Dharam Ghai, Azizur Rahman Khan, Ed Lee, Samir Radwan, in *Agrarian Systems and Rural Development* (London, 1979), p. 1.

[2] Government of India, *The First Five Year Plan* (New Delhi, 1952), p. 7. The words are similar to those used in the ILO study under the subtitle 'Alternative Agrarian Systems'.

nation'. It lays particular emphasis on providing the rural sector with 'a higher level of living and stable economic growth'.

Equally peculiar is the so-called discovery of the problem of poverty. Already in 1870 Dadabhai Naoroji had expressed his concern in an article on 'The Wants and Means of India'. This was followed, in 1876, by his book *Poverty and Un-British Rule in India*.[3] In 1888 Lord Dufferin, Governor-General, ordered an enquiry which was to determine whether 'the greater proportion of India suffers from a daily insufficiency of food or not.'[4] One hardly needs to remind the reader of the campaign of Mahatma Gandhi in favour of the Harijans. Later, soon after Independence, the situation of landless labourers was carefully studied and such problems were tackled by the First and subsequent Five Year Plans. This trend was strongly encouraged by V. M. Dandekar and N. Rath's study on *Poverty in India*, the influence of which went beyond India's borders. The following year, Rath's and Dandekar's findings were quoted by Robert McNamara, President of the World Bank. McNamara spoke of the poorest 40 per cent of the population of the Third World and mentioned that 200 out of 500 million people in the subcontinent had an income of no more than 40 dollars a year.[5] In 1973 he went further and spoke of about 800 million people, i.e. 40 per cent of the two billion inhabitants of the Third World (not including China), who suffered from 'absolute poverty'.

How valid are these assumptions? No matter whether we confine ourselves to India or whether we consider other countries whose statistics are even more unreliable, serious doubts have been expressed about such data. P. G. K. Panikar has questioned *Poverty in India* which, in the case of Kerala, claims that 90 per cent of the rural population is below the poverty line. The authors have not given due recognition to several food items such as tapioca, fish and other products that are difficult to measure. While Dandekar and Rath take, as a minimum requirement to cross the poverty line, monthly food expenditures of Rs 34 to Rs 43 in villages and Rs 43 to Rs 55 in towns, Panikar gives an estimate of Rs 20.72.[6] In an excellent

---

[3] See M. L. Dantwala, *Poverty in India Then and Now—1870-1970* (New Delhi, 1973).

[4] B. M. Bhatia, *Famines in India, 1860-1945* (London, 1963), p. 145.

[5] R. McNamara, *Address to the Board of Governors* (Washington DC, 1972).

[6] P. G. Panikar, 'Economics of Nutrition', *Economic and Political Weekly*, annual number, February 1972.

study, Wolf Scott has demonstrated the arbitrary nature of the so-called poverty line in several countries. It is difficult not to agree with his conclusion that 'Poverty need not always be measured; it needs to be prevented and abolished.[7]

Data on nutrition are also open to doubt. P. V. Sukhatme criticizes S. Reutlinger and M. Selowski's book *Malnutrition and Poverty* (Washington, 1976) as well as *Poverty in India*. The FAO and the WHO take an average of 2,450 calories per day for a male weighing 65 kilograms and a female weighing 55. Since the actual requirements of two individuals of the same weight, age and occupation may vary by approximately 300 calories above or below the average, this gives a range of 2,000 to 2,500 calories as the cut-off point.[8] There is, however, a more serious reason for questioning these data. As observed in the field, the poorer a man, the more difficult it is to measure his income. Nonetheless, it is possible to gather fairly accurate figures for medium farmers whose income comes entirely from their own farms. But it becomes impossible to measure, even approximately, the total income of small landowners and agricultural workers who have several sources of income which vary a great deal from each other.

The same applies to nutrition. No survey or statistics can take into account certain types of food such as the grain retrieved from rats. More so, data about people eating rats, water snakes, field crabs or roasting rain insects. 'Our dieticians and nutritionists who sit in the cool of their urban offices must go out to the fields and study the diet of the ordinary people', over a one-year cycle. 'This kind of study', concludes M. N. Srinivas, 'cannot be left to the tip and run method of an inferior class of investigators who commute from the cities to the nearby villages.'[9] Louis Dumont, the well-known French anthropologist, reaches similar conclusions: 'It is difficult to give global estimates on yearly consumption, especially among the poor, because their diet is irregular, they buy and live from hand to mouth.'[10]

Another weakness of large-scale surveys is that they too often club together areas with different levels of productivity and wages, so that average figures lose much of their validity. We have seen in the case of Guntur district that it was difficult to consider the district as a unit

[7] W. Scott, *Concepts and Measurement of Poverty* (Geneva, 1981) p. 1.

[8] P. V. Sukhatme, 'Incidence of Undernutrition', *Indian Journal of Agricultural Economics*, no. 3, 1977.

[9] *Economic and Political Weekly*, 5 June 1976.

[10] L. Dumont, *Une sous-caste de l'Inde du Sud* (Paris, 1957), p. 110.

because of its diversity (dry land and irrigated area). In a recent study C. T. Kurien has dealt with the 'dynamics of rural transformation' in a case study of Tamil Nadu.[11] National data on growth trends indicated 'a new dynamism unknown in the past', but the small farmers were tending to become 'progressively pauperized and real wages of labourers are declining'. In a discussion with Professor Kurien in Madras, I asked him what kind of national data he had, especially on wages as the trends in wages may not be the same in progressive districts as in others. Apparently, such disintegrated data had not been taken into consideration.

Thus, these calculations are too uncertain to be of much use when designing a planning policy. Should we, then, reject the conclusions reached in these discussions and these sophisticated reports on poverty and basic needs? It is difficult to give a clear-cut answer. Underlining the problem of poverty may help to make people more conscious of such problems, but direct evidence would be more useful than mere 'armchair studies'. Finally, no matter how many poor there are, we know that in countries like India the problem is so grave that, for a long time to come, no efforts made to solve it can be superfluous.

Old and New Dogmas

In the 1950s debates on development strategies were plagued by two sets of dogmas: on the one hand Marxist economists advocated a concentration on heavy industry with a bias in favour of nationalization, whereas, for others, free enterprise, priority to agriculture and light industry were the key factors. For the latter the very word 'planning' raised suspicions of leftism. However, when both points of view touched upon practical experiences it was found that rigid attitudes did not fit the concrete situation. The value of planning was now realized and promoted by several Western agencies of co-operation. A number of Marxist economists realized that heavy industry and nationalization were not the panacea. Indian planners who had, since the beginning, refused to make such a dichotomy, aimed at better intersectoral linkages. Dogmas reappeared during the 1970s, but assumed a different pattern. They did not have the backing of a definite ideology but relied more on populism. They are, however, rigid and quite uniform, as can be seen in several U.N. reports, academic discussions and books, in Western as well as developing countries and in the exchange of views within the Third World.

[11] *Economic and Political Weekly*, annual number, February 1980.

The So-called Development Failures of the Past Decades

Here is a summary of the mood of disenchantment which emerged around 1970: 'Literature is overburdened with post mortem critiques of development history which are unanimous on the appalling results and generally candid on the causes of the failure...'[12] An ILO study came to similar conclusions: 'The number of rural poor in Asia has increased and in many instances their standard of living has tended to fall. Perhaps, surprisingly, *this has occurred irrespective of whether growth has been rapid or slow* or agriculture has expanded swiftly or sluggishly.'[13] The Asian Development Bank echoed this: 'Rural poverty is thus particularly widespread...and there is a general consensus that the problem has worsened considerably in the past decades.'[14] Similar statements can be found in the report prepared by the FAO for the Conference on Land Reform and Rural Development held in Rome in 1979.

It is not possible to quote all the books and articles which have played the same tune. Some of them have become particularly popular in Europe and America; for example, Susan George's *How the Other Half Dies* or *Food First* by Frances Moore-Lappe and Joseph Collins. Newspaper articles also had much the same thing to say. Thus an article in the *Far Eastern Economic Review* (13 July 1979) mentioned 'islands of prosperous capitalists in an ocean of impoverished small farmers and landless labourers' in Asia, In a particularly strange comment (in the light of what has been seen in India), Ajit K. Ghose and Keith Griffin claim that 'It is not the lack of growth but its very occurrence that led to a deterioration in the conditions of the rural poor.'[15] In a textbook that is widely advertised in the USA, Europe and the Third World, Michael P. Todaro, while speaking of South Asia refers to 'the further impoverishment of the masses of rural peasants' as a consequence of the green revolution.[16]

The basic dogma of the so-called green revolution is that the rich get richer and the poor get poorer. This is supported by several publications, as we have seen. However, while painting a gloomy

[12] W. Haque, N. Rath, Anisur Rahman and P. Wignaraja, 'Towards a Theory of Rural Development', *Development Dialogue*, 2, 1977.

[13] ILO, *Poverty and Landlessness in Rural Asia* (Geneva, 1977), p. 1. Italics mine.

[14] *Asian Agricultural Survey* (Manila, 1977), p. 11.

[15] A. K. Ghose and K. Griffin, 'Rural Poverty and Development in South and South-East Asia', Nyon (Switzerland), IFDA, Dossier 9, 1979.

[16] M. P. Todaro, *Economic Development in the Third World* (New York, 1981), p. 227.

picture of the socio-economic achievements of most Asian countries, several publications emphasize the performance of the Chinese. The late Barbara Ward wrote in her introduction to *Learning from China* by Sartaj Aziz: 'The Chinese have found solutions to virtually all the major problems posed by the first stages of modernization.' Aziz follows with, 'In many countries rapid growth has further aggravated the problem of poverty', while in China 'the acceptance of a basic needs approach to development can be regarded as something of a breakthrough.'[17] M. P. Todaro has more or less repeated what Sartaj Aziz had stated (op. cit., pp. 280–4).

The New Strategy

What remedies can be proposed? 'Of all the new values to be created, self-reliance is the single most important,'[18] as a national policy and, more specifically, for rural development. There are also severe criticisms of foreign technology which has led developing nations to neglect 'their own research capabilities and innovativeness'. Appropriate or intermediate technology is advocated along the lines of E. F. Schumacher's book *Small is Beautiful*. Reluctance, if not mistrust, of modern inputs for agriculture (new seeds, chemical fertilizers, pumps, pesticides) is common to several publications, because the latter are supposed to increase the developing countries' dependence on the developed. Greater use of manpower for hydraulic works is also emphasized. 'People's participation', 'creativity of the people', 'co-operation' are some of the key words used to describe this 'new process' as P. Wignaraja, among others, calls it. The Fifth Five Year Plan of Pakistan (1978–83) states that 'community participation in the development effort is essential' as also the need to 'channelize the creative energies of the rural populace... . Local democracy will have to be the cornerstone of the new institutional framework.'[19] These currents are also reflected in international organizations and have had some influence on national planning. Charan Singh's book *India's Economic Policy—The Gandhian Blueprint,* and the policy statements of the former Janata Government, reflect this thinking. Often, in reports or statements China is cited as an example in

[17] Aziz, *Rural Development—Learning from China* (London, 1978), p. xvi. The author is one of the most senior officers of the FAO. The organization published similar reports on China.

[18] W. Haque *et al.,* op. cit.

[19] Islamabad, 1978, p. 435.

self-reliance, intermediate technologies, mass mobilization for rural works and people's participation. It is interesting to see the remarkable unity of views on this subject from people of many different nationalities, and with various intellectual and ideological backgrounds. It is more difficult to understand this than the previous uniformity of the old dogmas repeated in pure Marxist circles or among diehard advocates of liberalism. What is, however, more embarrassing is to ask whether or not these analyses and intonations of populism correspond to what is actually happening in the villages.

Words and Facts

The gap between the direct evidence presented in this book (which has been confirmed by many scholars and officials) and the statement that 'the rich get richer and the poor poorer' is puzzling. It is not, of course, correct to generalize from the Indian case[20] but, in itself, India represents about one third of Asia (not including the Middle East) and one fifth of the Third World. The relationship between relatively fast growth, rising wages in real terms, and increasing job opportunities is not confined to India. One finds indications of it in Pakistani Punjab as confirmed by Dilawar Ali Khan in a very interesting paper.[21] In Jhang district Michael Mordasini noticed that during years of rising production, wages also rose, while in more recent years, due to agricultural stagnation and steep inflation, wages, in real terms, fell.[22] In Malaysia, where rice output increased sharply, U. N. Bhati reports improvements in income for small farmers and more employment opportunities for landless labourers.[23] In Java we cannot say whether the real wages and incomes of the poor have improved,[24] but it is clear that even very small land-owners (0.2 hectares) are now increasing their yields because of new seeds and chemical fertilizers, and, in certain cases,

[20] In Mexico, for instance, the green revolution has occurred under very different socio-economic circumstances and has had different social implications.

[21] Dilawar Ali Khan, 'Employment and Occupational Change in the Rural Punjab: Consequences of the Green Revolution', Islamabad, Conference on Employment Planning and Basic Needs in Pakistan, May 1978.

[22] Forthcoming Ph.D thesis on *'Rural Development in Pakistani Punjab'*, Geneva, Graduate Institute of International Studies.

[23] U. N. Bhati, *Some Social and Economic Aspects of the Introduction of New Varieties of Paddy in Malaysia* (Geneva, 1976), p. 80.

[24] We must bear in mind that population pressure is worse in Java than in most densely populated parts of India. A Javanese medium farmer has often no more than 0.5 hectares.

pesticides, as Jean-Luc Maurer observed during several field studies in the 1970s.[25]

Let us try to find some explanations for these differences. Too many studies are not based on direct field observations. For instance, the Asian Bank has worked mainly from secondary sources, books, reports, official statistics, 'visiting each country for an average of a week or less'. The ILO study has by and large followed a similar approach with surprising results in some chapters. Rohini Nayyar writes of Bihar that 'the per capital income of agricultural labourers was the second highest in India', and that the distribution of income was 'somewhat less inegalitarian than in many other states'. Anyone who is even slightly familiar with rural India should know that such statements are totally wrong. The author seems to rely on the National Sample Survey and its twenty-fifth report (1970-1) on agricultural labourers' wages. The said report presents the following data:

Daily Wages of Labourers (NSS)

Coastal Andhra	Rs 2.03
North Bihar	Rs 2.01

Data Collected in Our Surveys

	1967	1978
Guntur	Rs 3.00	5.00–6.00
Muzaffarpur	Rs 1.50	3.00

These differences have been best summarized by M. N. Srinivas when he says that 'As things are, courses in methodology usually concentrate on survey techniques, elementary statistics and the like. Further *the importance of honesty and of contrary instances becomes devalued* [italics mine] when it is argued that since the social sciences are not value-free, the pretence of objectivity should be discarded and social scientists should use their knowledge to promote worthy causes usually interpreted as progressive causes.' He adds:

the general tendency among post-independence economists has been to rely on data collected through the various agencies of the Planning Commission, the Reserve Bank ... the National Sample Survey, the reports of the U.N. agencies ... while economists have been diligent in extracting every ounce of information [from such sources], the idea that they themselves undertake field work does not seem to occur to them ... . This is indeed perplexing, as they are anxious to end exploitation of the poor and oppressed. But these

[25] Forthcoming Ph.D thesis, Geneva, Graduate Institute of International Studies.

laudable aims have not created in them a desire to come into close human contact with the objects of their concern and sympathy.[26]

These observations go much beyond the Indian case. Indeed, they summarize perfectly the attitudes and work methods of a large number of scholars in rich and poor countries and of many experts belonging to international organizations, as well as those of a number of policy-makers and other high officials. Robert Chambers, who has done excellent field work in Africa and Asia, reviews with a witty pen other shortcomings of what he calls 'rural development tourism', which has a high number of addicts ranging from government officials, academic researchers, the staff of voluntary agencies, to journalists and diplomats. 'Differing in race, nationality, religion, age, sex, ... they have three things in common: they come from urban areas; they want to find something out; and they are short of time.' Another defect is that often too many people visit the same places and the latter turn into show pieces or exceptional cases. There is also a definite preference for travel during the dry and cool season, while often more useful observations can be made during the rainy, but less comfortable season.[27]

An anonymous article in the *Economic and Political Weekly*[28] criticizes the 'tribe of seminarists [who] know no geographical boundaries ... no color bar'. They indulge in conferences, seminars where they 'formulate strategies and targets for alleviating poverty [thanks] to a continuous refinement of econometric models'. The whole game is supported by scholarships, grants and other expenditures from various sources in order to hold conferences, while 'seminarists from the Third World and their enlightened brothers from the developed world ... lash out at exploitation by capitalists, traders, the bourgeoisie ...' There is an additional problem. A number of Indian scholars and civil servants (some of whom have been quoted in this book), can give us a more realistic picture of rural development, but their work does not generally get known outside their country—except, of course, by foreign specialists on India. These people hardly appear in bibliographies and reports such as those mentioned above. On the other hand, certain books such as Francine Frankel's *India's Green*

[26] M. N. Srinivas, 'Village Studies, Participant Observation and Social Science Research in India', *Economic and Political Weekly*, special number, August 1975.

[27] R. Chambers, 'Rural Poverty Unperceived: Problems and Remedies' *World Development*, January 1981.

[28] Client Intellectuals', 25 May 1980.

Revolution,[29] or the ILO report are widely quoted in many publications in spite of their shortcomings. It remains but to say—as the article in the *Economic and Political Weekly* hinted—and as my friend Ashok Mitra, former Secretary of the Planning Commission, has said, 'There are at least some people who know how to make money when talking on poverty.' Clearly, this network of vested interests is not to be easily dislodged.

The Chinese Case[30]

Coming to the actual reading of China brings us miles away from the claims of many foreigners. First of all, the self-reliance strategy and the massive efforts in intermediate technologies have proved a mixed blessing due to distortions and imbalances in implementing the concept of 'walking on two legs'.[31] For about fifteen years now, a large part of the additional industrial output has come from the small or indigenous sector relying on intermediate, or rather rough, technologies.[32] Since the death of Mao Zedong the Chinese press and all political leaders have admitted to many shortcomings and defects. At the same time, even the large industrial sector is relying too much on obsolete and outdated techniques. This is why, between 1972 and 1974, under the influence of Zhou Enlai, the Chinese imported 3 billion U.S. dollars worth of turnkey factories or full units of production,[33] a trend that is picking up again at the present time. This alteration of the development policy does not mean that the Chinese are being inspired by a Western or Japanese model. Simply that, after a period of emotional and unreasonable behaviour, they are now once more dealing with things with common sense and lucidity.

As an example, let us look at chemical fertilizers. Chinese farmers have always made the most thorough use of farm manure, human

[29] Apart from being premature, the conclusions of Francine Frankel are questionable on several points. Her understanding of tensions in Thanjavur is partly misleading (Chapter 9). On the whole she fails to show that most agrarian unrest had occurred, even at that time, in areas where one could, and can even now, hardly speak of a green revolution or of a rapid growth process.

[30] The following comments are taken from my book *La Chine fait ses comptes* (Paris, 1980).

[31] Modern large-scale industry versus small indigenous factories and workshops.

[32] In 1978, 70 per cent of chemical fertilizers, 60 per cent of cement, 45 per cent of coal, 11 per cent of steel, many machines, tractors, trucks, etc., were produced by the 'small sector'.

[33] From 1960 to 1970 similar imports amounted to only 200 million dollars.

excreta, compost, etc.[34] Yet, if they want to increase yields per hectare—and there is little doubt that they do with such an acute shortage of arable land—they need sizeable doses of chemical fertilizers, a point that the advocates of 'biological agriculture' often overlook. Secondly, intermediate technology, used for supplying a growing percentage of chemical fertilizers, produces low quality fertilizers, often at a high cost, and requires too much energy. It was for these reasons that, in 1972–3, the Chinese ordered thirteen plants of synthetic ammonia and urea (500,000 tons of the latter) from American, French and Japanese companies. Today, the Chinese are proceeding further, modernizing and expanding with imported equipment their coal mines, steel mills and their machine industry.

This does not mean that all efforts in favour of small industries and intermediate technology have been given up. Far from that. There has, in fact, been a further proliferation of small units down from district towns to big villages, but at the same time, the Chinese are walking on two legs in a much more balanced fashion than they did during the heyday of the great leap forward (1958–60) of the Cultural Revolution (1966–71), or in the last two years of Mao Zedong. In fact, China is a typical example of a country which, like India, needs a sound combination of small indigenous and large modern industries. And as far as advanced technology is concerned, it is by no means needed in all sectors, but only in some of them. In the early stages such technology cannot but come from the outside.

Other erroneous readings on China should be mentioned. In the early phases, until the mid-1960s, many large hydraulic works (irrigation, flood control) were built in the traditional manner with mass mobilization, picks, shovels and wheel barrows. In many cases such works did not prove adequate, particularly in view of the need for a more efficient system because of increasing population pressure. Gradually, modern inputs, steel, concrete, heavy machinery, sophisticated engineering, and large pumping stations were introduced.[35] The Chinese have grasped equally well the advantages of minor irrigation through tubewells and pumpsets.[36] They are also pushing — though rather belatedly and with difficulty— new high

---

[34] It is worth remembering that the impact of farm manure is greater in temperate climates, as in most parts of China, than in tropical countries.

[35] Already in 1972, 80 per cent of the cost in certain major works was devoted to equipment, machines and steel, as against 20 per cent for manpower.

[36] 2.03 million tubewells (11 million hectares), mostly in the northern plain.

yield varieties of cereals. New pesticides are needed as the old methods of pest control are inadequate.

In addition, the whole jargon of China's success in satisfying the 'basic needs' of the population is questioned and contested by practically all Chinese political leaders, scientists and experienced officials. Foodgrain output per head has remained constant between 1957 and 1977, stated Hu Qiaomu, president of the Academy of Social Sciences. The standard of living of the masses remains very frugal and there are sizeable income disparities between well-run and well-located communes and those that are poorly managed and/or located in areas with poor soils, low and erratic rainfall and low potential for irrigation. It seems that, out of one billion Chinese, around 10 per cent do not enjoy minimum food rations. There is also considerable unemployment.

Some naive foreign observers have given us the impression of a whole countryside that is smoothly led by dedicated and able cadres with active participation on the part of the people. This is true of a number of advanced communes, the ones which foreigners are shown, but, unlike India, China has not so far allowed us to see the other side of the picture and its defects. However, the Chinese press is becoming more and more outspoken about this and many cadres speak freely when properly questioned. During my last visit in 1978, after seeing some wonderful paddy fields (5,000 kilograms per hectare of paddy per crop, and two crops) around Canton, I had a long meeting with several senior provincial cadres. They mentioned that the average yield for the province of Guangdong had risen from 3,150 kilograms per hectare per crop in 1971 to 3,375 kilograms per hectare in 1977. The lower yield here as compared with the advanced communes, was due to various shortcomings not particular to the province, such as bad management of the communes, inefficient, easy-going, sometimes even corrupt officials, delays in the supply of fertilizers, power shortages, lack of transportation, etc. All these are features common to many countries. It is difficult to say whether they are less widespread in China than elsewhere, but there is no doubt that they exist. Besides they are as acutely felt as in India, because in China too district planning becomes more demanding.

When underlining the weaknesses of China one should not minimize its achievements. I still have the impression that acute misery of the kind found in parts of India or Bangladesh is non-existent in China, but, on the other hand, life in China is much harder than one would believe. There is very strong pressure from the Chinese masses for sizeable improvements in the conditions of living, a point fully realized by the new leaders. Also, what is remarkable in China nowadays is the frank and sound self-criticism, and the admission of errors and mistakes, not all of which are attributed to the Gang of Four. Apart from this, other countries have more to learn from the present Chinese experience then ever before. The main senior leaders and cadres are doing exactly the contrary to what is advocated by the dogmatists of the present populist vintage. The limits of self-reliance are amply demonstrated in China as in India, where the only way villages can progress is to interact increasingly with the outside world through a whole network of interdependent links. Besides, even in China, one has some doubts about people's participation when one sees the growing emphasis on material incentives, and on smaller working groups (often a single family) within the already very small basic collective units. The Chinese approach to foreign and local technology is no less reasonable. The same can be said about the combination of old and new inputs in agriculture. In other words, the most valid lesson of China today is the rejection of 'empty words', to quote the hard-headed Deng Xiaoping!

Other Asian Countries

Most of Asia is engaged in a tough fight against poverty in which rural development, no matter what the size of the urban large-scale industrial sector, is crucial. Several Asian countries such as Bangladesh, India, the island of Java, and China suffer from severe shortage of land. Pakistan is slightly better off in its land-man ratio. Thailand and Burma are more at ease, but population pressure has begun to be felt in the former (if not also in the latter) where not much land is now left for reclamation. In spite of these relative differences, all these countries are 'condemned' to increase their yields per hectare, as they will otherwise become too dependent on foreign grain or lose all export possibilities (as in Thailand and Burma). As seen in the advanced parts of india, such growth induces an increasingly wider process of agricultural and non-agricultural activity which, provided the growth is sufficiently strong, has a positive impact on the real wages of the poor and on their employment opportunities.

Taking into account local differences it is possible to say that all these countries still enjoy a sizeable untapped growth potential which should enable them to avoid—at least in normal years—large imports of grain, and to gradually improve living conditions. In order to achieve these goals, irrigation, new seeds and fertilizers must be actively encouraged wherever possible. We have seen that this is a complex process. Some countries fall behind India. For instance, in Pakistan seed research and multiplication is moving slowly; in Afghanistan, even before the war, very little had been done in either field. Things are improving in Bangladesh but constraints of all types are so severe that it will take time to ensure self-sufficiency in food.[37] It is perfectly possible to irrigate most of the land in the dry season; this would produce fine crops which would not be exposed to floods and would be much less susceptible to pests than monsoon crops. Yields of paddy in the Burmese and Thai plains are still extremely low, due to very poor water management which prevents the proper use of new seeds and chemical fertilizers. The island of Java is not far from reaching its upper limits in terms of yields per hectare because it has one of the best farming populations in the world, as well as a fair amount of new seeds and a widespread use of chemical fertilizers even among the smallest landowners. Nevertheless, there are many parts of the island which could be improved.

A shortfall in the supply of chemical fertilizers and other inputs can occur in practically any of these countries (though in differing degrees), together with malpractices and corruption. It is also not unusual for governments to subsidize inputs for which there is a shortage, with the result that the more well-to-do farmers, who control the rural institutions, get their requirements at the official price, while small farmers have to buy on the black market or not buy at all. Such a situation is both anti-economic and anti-social. Thus, it is necessary, in practically all parts of the region where a sufficient water supply can be made available, to reach yields of 2,000–3,000 kilograms per hectare of wheat and 4,000–5,000 of paddy per crop, in order to compensate for yields in areas which, because of a lack of water, cannot expand very much beyond 1,000 kilograms per hectare of grain, and that too not uniformly. In addition, in the latter areas there can be only a single crop while the others permit double cropping.

In order to attain these goals in the next twenty years so that production outpaces the increase in population, there is no other method than the package of new inputs combined with traditional techniques, as outlined above. What has been said of India can also

[37]See my *Bangladesh Development in Perspective* (New Delhi, 1979).

be applied to other Asian countries, particularly those that are already in one way or another following a similar track.

Also to be taken into consideration are ecological factors—a favourite subject with those who criticize the green revolution. Risks and actual problems do exist, as we have seen in India and elsewhere, and hence it is necessary to pay more attention to them. Yet, on the whole, the dangers are relatively small in areas that are properly irrigated and drained and where balanced and careful use is made of chemical fertilizers and pesticides. To understand these elementary conclusions one needs only to exercise one's common sense and have some knowledge of the technical problems involved. Yet a surprising number of scholars, experts and officials have failed to grasp these problems. The solutions they propose would lead either to enormous grain deficits or to a recurrence of the terrible famines of the past.

Income Disparities

Another criticism levelled against the green revolution is that it encouraged income disparities between the rich and the poor. Though this should be carefully verified, it certainly does happen. However, this is not the main issue; at this stage what matters is that the poor become less poor, less vulnerable to pressures from the rich or to the hazards of nature. Perhaps at a later stage it will be possible to think otherwise. In the same perspective, increasing regional income disparities are criticized and proposals are made to concentrate investment in backward areas.

A number of countries have known uneven development similar to India's and have faced growing income disparities. Particularly striking is the case of China, one of the very few countries which has followed an 'egalitarian' way. Yet, today advanced communes and districts enjoy much higher yields and a better standard of living than many other areas. For instance, the value of a normal 10 point labour day can go up to Yuan 1.0 or 1.50 in rich places, fall to 0.30–0.50 or worse, and even down to 0.10–0.20, in others. (The value of the point depends on the overall production of the collective unit and on the number of people. 1 Yuan=0.55 US dollars). Such disparities are unavoidable wherever a country aims at increasing its foodgrain production as fast as possible. It needs the surplus from rich rural areas to feed the urban population and the districts with a deficit. If, on the other hand, one decided to concentrate on the backward areas, growth and the emergence of a surplus would be slow and, quite likely, insufficient. The consequences would be either large grain imports or famines.

One can conclude that the most urgent task is to reach a kind of minimum safety level in terms of foodgrain availability and reserves at the national level. In times of scarcity, the government could then release stocks on the market to prevent sharp rises in prices. When one takes these different aspects of the green revolution into account, their social content is clear because in times of shortage and rising prices it is not the rich who suffer.[38] At a later stage, when areas fit for rapid growth have already expanded, one can begin to concentrate more on the poorer regions, starting with those, such as eastern India, which offer the greatest potential.

Self-reliance and the Village Community

A question we may ask ourselves is whether in order to reach these goals, it was necessary to place a greater emphasis on rural institutions, or whether there are other means. We have seen how the old ideal of Indian villages being little republics is obsolete with reference to self-reliance, community participation and the community spirit. This applies to other Asian countries as well. It is through a growing process of exchange between the villages and towns (leading to the global process of rural development in the field of agricultural and non-agricultural activity, to rising wages and employment opportunities) that poverty will gradually be reduced. This is happening in advanced areas of India as well as in rich Chinese communes. Once again, it is worth repeating, a population growth of 2 per cent or more makes impossible any self-reliant approach too heavily centred on intermediate technology.

Secondly, the words 'village community' are grossly misleading. The greater the population pressure on land, the greater will be the antagonisms and rivalries between classes. For the same reasons co-operatives and local councils are bound to remain in the hands of upper farmers—this is an almost universal phenomenon in Asia, as pointed out in countless enquiries.[39] Reviewing new rural institutions

---

[38] I am hesitant and uneasy about making such obvious and elementary observations. Yet a number of experts on development have not grasped even such basic points.

[39] For instance the U.N. Research Institute for Social Development, Geneva, made a comprehensive study on co-operatives in Asia, Africa and Latin America. The latter had but a limited impact on the poor. See Vol. vii, *Rural Co-operatives as Agents of Change* (Geneva, 1975).

in the Philippines, Malaysia and Indonesia, Ingrid Palmer concludes: 'In none of these experiments...have there been indications that democracy has taken root....' Further, she speaks about 'the poor prospects for any real democratization of emerging village units'.[40] In spite of the brave words of the latest Pakistani Plan quoted earlier, the scattered attempts to set up rural institutions have not been successful as a democratization process, nor can be in the future, since large landowners remain more powerful than in India. As far as Bangladesh is concerned, we have stated a number of facts which point to similar conditions, though, in that country, a big landowner rarely has more than 5 hectares, while Sindhi or West Punjabi landlords may own a few hundred hectares if not more.

Back to a Better Administration.

The need for better planning and management both at the macro and micro levels is felt in all countries, but too often, even after twenty or thirty years, there is a reluctance to take decisive measures to improve the administrative framework. In some countries, especially in Malaysia which is both small and rich, the administration is relatively sound. The same cannot be said of other former British colonies like Bangladesh and Pakistan. The former inherited a weak administration in 1947 (then it was known as East Pakistan), a defect denounced in many report during British rule but still not remedied. In Pakistan, there has been a growing demoralization of the civil service under the pressure of political instability. Besides, the gap between the rural masses and the senior civil servants is more acute than in India or Bangladesh. In Indonesia the system remains weak.

In all these countries it would help to have a hard core of well trained, reasonably well paid and dedicated senior officers in charge of the districts. When making this plea, we must clear up a gross misunderstanding. The Indian Civil Service of the British was far less alien to India than it has been accused of being. It borrowed much from previous Indian systems as well as from the Mandarin system of China.[41] In other words, it followed a long tradition of administration as practised in several Asian civilizations for centuries. Under present socio-economic conditions the IAS may help rural develop-

[40]Ingrid Palmer, *The New Rice in Asia, Conclusions from Four Country Studies* (Geneva, 1976), pp. 43–6.
[41]See my book on Bangladesh.

ment more than the creation or expansion of rural institutions. Ingrid Palmer reaches rather similar conclusions: 'Monitoring supplies, especially against monopoly practices can be performed by a small number of dedicated and well-briefed civil servants' (op. cit., p. 36).[42] Such people—a few generalists in development, helped by some really able district agricultural officers—would promote better planning and ensure ample supplies of inputs. This does not mean that the government should control all activities; on the contrary, there is room for a better combination of the private and public sectors. Private trade in chemical fertilizers and other inputs is often more appropriate than the use of government agencies, as the latter are susceptible to many abuses and may be less efficient as well.

The role of the government is to devise a policy which avoids shortages through adequate macro-planning. In addition it has an active and more direct role to play in other fields such as improvement of soils and water surveys, basic agricultural research, promotion of road building and rural electrification, market centres, etc. These tasks are fairly advanced in Malaysia but much less so in Pakistan, and worse in Bangladesh. Much remains to be done in Thailand in spite of the considerable progress, especially in road building, and more should be done in the Philippines and Indonesia. While advocating better rural development we are well aware that it will not achieve miracles. But at least it offers more hope than does the repetition of past mistakes, and harbouring illusions about village institutions—which only amounts to changing labels on old bottles.[43]

[42] For instance, the large paddy Muda scheme in Malaysia has 'been controlled by civil servants with no vested interests in the rural locality' (Palmer, op. cit., p. 124).

[43] The Bengal Cooperative Societies Bill of 1936 points out the main classical defects of co-operatives which remain as much a problem today as earlier. These are poor management, defaulting members, incompetent officers, the influence of upper farmers, etc. (E. Tepper, *Changing Patterns of Administration in Rural East Pakistan* (Michigan, 1966).

Conclusion

The content of this book may surprise readers not too familiar with rural problems. Instead of clear-cut conclusions, easy to define and to grasp, one finds a world full of nuances. In practically all regions of India one can perceive indications of economic and social change, but the great problem is that conditions are so diverse. To describe the last thirty years as those of total success or failure would be equally wrong. One would, nevertheless, be inclined to emphasize the positive aspects of these years because, too often, pessimistic and overcritical assessments are made, especially among people who live at several removes (both mentally and physically) from the villages.

The progress to be made in the last two decades of this century can now be speeded up, and can involve more and more poor people, because the period of trial and error of the early phase of post-Independence India is clearly over. If the lessons of the large stock of experience accumulated in all fields—economic, social and technical are taken seriously, overall development policy should continually improve.

At this point one comes up against the question of political leadership. The argument that 'we finally always muddle through' contains some element of truth but, as shown by the fall of the Janata Government, it has its limits. The increasing complexity of socio-economic life makes a sounder leadership a growing necessity. For this reason the more down-to-earth approach followed by the present government is to be welcomed, promising as it does an acceleration of economic and social progress. Such a trend, if sustained, could also help reduce or curb the erosion of the political system, a serious threat for the future.

Keeping these factors in mind, we have also to take into account the balance of power in any rural society and its implications at the national level. It is high time that international organizations and intellectuals in particular, stop proposing 'drastic reforms', which, translated into plain language, mean a revolution. This is all the more objectionable in view of the fact that the likelihood of such an event is remote or uncertain of realization in the face of the weakness of revolutionary forces in many Asian countries, not to speak of other parts of the Third World. To talk of income redistribution when there is still so little to redistribute, as in many Indian or Bangladeshi villages, is equally unsound. Besides, contrary to the slogan of 'the green revolution turning red', we have seen that in India the worst and most violent clashes have occurred in precisely those areas where there has been no green revolution to begin with.

The diversity of farmer's behaviour within castes and or local communities as found in India and in most other developing countries deserves more attention. Attitudes towards agricultural work have never been static, but changes or innovations may be either slow or rapid and may consequently require a greater or smaller effort by way of extension work.

The *social* value of more efficient planning and management has, I hope, been made clear. No doubt a direct attack on poverty (special schemes for the poor) may help, but the path to improvement appears to lie in an indirect approach, i.e. better economic policies. Such policies involve a number of crucial factors which are valid no matter what the ideology. These are, improving soils and, more important, carrying out thorough water surveys—a basic task which has not yet been completed in most Asian countries, including China and India—and further efforts in research. An even more drastic water management policy (irrigation and, when necessary, drainage), is also essential, for as we have seen, in addition to providing economic benefits, it has considerable social value for the poor.

A plentiful supply of inputs is more essential than credit and automatically reduces corruption and other malpractices, the victims of which are usually the small and medium farmers. A sound infrastructure in terms of roads and electricity, small industries and trade is also essential. Other programmes such as family planning and an adequate drinking water supply are no less important. Added together, these factors would lead to a *global process of rural development*, which has obvious economic advantages but also sizeable social ones in terms of wages and employment opportunities.

Such an outlook, which is based on a fair amount of concrete evidence, meets with considerable opposition in favour of alternative solutions (as we have seen in the previous chapter). If the new dogmatism spreads further, it cannot but have a serious effect on the understanding of development and on the design of adequate policies. New labels on old bottles, the rhetoric of armchair planners and armchair revolutionaries—perhaps more common in certain U.N. agencies and universities than within the governments and administrations of the countries themselves—will lead to further disillusionment. As for the poor, they are not fooled by such rhetoric. Often, in India and Pakistan, when talking with some of the poorer people about the new strategies I was given the same answer: 'Arre Sahb, nam, nam hain.' ('Oh Sir, these are just words.')

Let us be clear on another point. Anybody has the right to prefer one ideology to another, but what is unacceptable is the gross distortion of facts, the lack of knowledge and judgement which become apparent in a number of the books and reports mentioned in our last chapter. Such a trend is particularly distressing because we have now reached a point where it is becoming possible to see development issues in a clearer light than at the beginning of the 1950s. Instead of looking for inspiration from Western ideas, liberal or Marxist, it is now possible to gradually evolve development theories based on actual practice in a manner which best suits conditions in a country like India. The links between economic growth and social progress are also more clearly evident.

'Koi nahin sunta' ('nobody listens to us') is a complaint not confined to India. We have recorded the same words in Pakistan near the new dam of Tarbela and in the canal colonies of the Punjab downstream, and their equivalent in Dari (Persian) in Afghan villages. Even in China, where so much has been done to reduce the gap between urban intellectuals and villagers, several reports bring to light cases of policies being imposed on the farmers from above, and proving highly damaging to them. The same is true, and considerably more so, among Western circles interested in the Third World or agencies of bilateral and multilateral co-operation—they simply don't listen.

It is in this context that a major change of attitude is needed. Let us repeat what should be obvious, and what has already been said in our quotation of M. N. Srinivas earlier in this book. Can this message be heeded?

The history of Asia contains a number of cases of enlightened rulers and high officials who used to tour their country, get in touch with villagers in order to grasp their problems and help solve them.

This is what the Chinese used to call the Mandate of Heaven, a concept found also in Hindu and Muslim civilizations. Obviously such a spirit remains as valid today as it was in the past.

Let us raise a final issue: the impact of modernization on Indian traditions. According to several pandits, humanity is coming perilously close to the end of the Kali Yuga (Dark Age), the last of the four ages of a single cycle for mankind as per the Hindu tradition, a point of view shared by other great religions. Everybody agrees that the values of Indian civilization (Hindu or other) are being eroded. And yet, a number of people remain true to them, combining efficiency in practical tasks with their spiritual inheritance, often ignoring the kind of vulgarity so typical of mass consumption societies. The list of such people whom we have met during a period of nearly thirty years would be too long to elaborate. Some of them are dedicated civil servants, businessmen who have not forgotten the genuine Vaishya line of the past, scholars of great integrity, and, most important, villagers who still maintain some harmony between the earth and the sky, intelligently increasing their output, following their rites and customs.

What a sight, in November or December, when the hard work on the soil is temporarily put aside, to see long processions of bullock carts going to the Ganges for the sacred bath. The men lead the bullocks, the women, wearing bright saris, sing to Gangaji, symbol of fertility and purification.

Bibliography

I. OFFICIAL PUBLICATIONS

Government of India, Planning Commission:
The First Five Year Plan, 1952.
Fourth Five Year Plan, 1969–74.
Fifth Five Year Plan, 1974–79.
Draft Five Year Plan, 1978–83.
Sixth Five Year Plan, 1980–5.
Government of India, *Economic Survey*, for the years 1965–6 to 1980–1.
Ministry of Information, *India, a Reference Annual 1977 and 78* (1978).
Registrar General and Census, *Census of India 1971*, part I of 1971.
—— *Census of India 1981*, papers 1 and 2.
Ministry of Agriculture:
All India Report on Agricultural Census 1970–71, by I. J. Naidu, 1975.
National Commission on Agriculture 1976, Abridged Report, 1977.
Report of the Committee on Panchayati Raj Institutions, 1978.
Government of India, Planning Commission, *Report of the Working Group on Block Level Planning*, 1978.
Department of Personnel, Cabinet Secretariat, *Land and Water Management Problems in India*, by B. B. Vohra, 1975.

II. BOOKS AND ARTICLES

Population

Bose, A., P. B. Desai, A. Mitra, J. N. Sharma (eds). *Population in India's Development 1947–2000*, New Delhi, Vikas Publishing House, 1974.
Cassen, R. H., *India: Population, Economy, Society*, London, Macmillan, 1978.
Mitra, A., *India's Population* (2 vols), New Delhi, Abhinav Publications, 1978.

Political, Economic and Social Problems

Bhattacharya, M., 'Administrative and Organizational Issues in Rural Development', *The Indian Institute of Public Administration Journal*, no. 4, 1978.

217

Bhagwati, J. N., and P. Desai, *India, Planning for Industrialization*, London, Oxford University Press, 1970.

Dandekar, V. M., and N. Rath, *Poverty in India*, Poona, Indian School of Political Economy, 1971.

Dantwala, M. L., *Poverty in India then and now 1870–1970*, Delhi, Macmillan, 1973.

Ghosh, A., *Indian Economy* (19th edition), Calcutta, World Press, 1975.

Janata Party, *Statement on Economic Policy*, New Delhi, 1977.

Jha, L. K., *Economic Strategy for the 80's*, New Delhi, Allied Publishers, 1980.

Mellow, J. W., *The New Economics of Growth: A Strategy for India and the Developing World*, Ithaca and London, Cornell University Press, 1976.

Nehru, B. K., 'The Roots of Corruption', Madras, G. L. Mehta Memorial Lecture, December 1981.

Singh, Charan, *India's Economic Policy*, New Delhi, All India Kisan Sammelan, 1979.

Srinivas, M. N., *Social Change in Modern India*, Berkeley, University of California Press, 1971.

Srinivas, M. N., S. Seshaiah, and V. S. Parthasarathy (eds), *Dimensions of Social Change in India*, Bombay, Allied Publishers, 1978.

Viet, L. A., *India's Second Revolution*, New York, McGraw Hill, 1976.

Vohra, B. B., 'Time for New Norms', *Seminar*, October 1978.

Weiner, M., *Party Building in a New Nation*, The Indian National Congress, Chicago, The University of Chicago Press, 1967.

—— *India at the Polls, 1977*, Washington D.C., Amerian Enterprise Institute for Public Policy Research, 1978.

Rural Development

Alexander, K. C., *Agrarian Tension in Thanjavur*, Hyderabad, National Institute of Community Development, 1975.

Bhalla, G. S., and Y. K. Alagh, *Performance in Indian Agriculture, a Districtwise Study*, New Delhi, Sterling Publishers, 1979.

Bardhan, P. K., A. Vaidyanathan, Y. K. Alagh, G.S. Bhalla, and K. Bhaduri, *Labour Absorption in Indian Agriculture: Some Exploratory Investigations*, Bangkok, International Labour Organization, 1978.

Bardhan, P., and A. Rudra, 'Terms and Conditions of Sharecropping Contracts: An Analysis of Village Survey Data in India', *The Journal of Development Studies*, no. 3. April 1980.

Bhatia, B. M., *Famines in India 1850–1945*, Bombay, Asia Publishing House, 1963.

Benor, D., and J. Q. Harrison, *Agricultural Extension*, Washington, World Bank, 1977.

Beteille, A., *Studies in Agrarian Social Structure*, New Delhi, Oxford University Press, 1974.

Chambard, J. L., *Atlas d'un Village Indien*, Paris, Mouton, 1980.

Dardaud, J. P., *Promotion des Petits Paysans dans la Zone de Lutua*, Paris, Freres des Hommes (mimeo), 1977.

Deleury, G., 'Society traditionelle en Inde, le poids des castes', *Croissance des Jeunes Nations*, May 1981.

Dumont, L., *Une Sous-Caste de l'Inde du Sud*, Paris, Mouton, 1957.

Epstein, T. S., *South India Yesterday, Today and Tomorrow*, London Macmillan, 1973.

Farmer, B. H. (ed.), *Green Revolution: Technology and Change in Rice-growing Areas of Tamil Nadu and Sri Lanka*, London, Macmillan, 1977.

Franda, M., *Small is Politics: Organizational Alternatives in Indian Rural Development*, New Delhi, Wiley Eastern, 1979.

Frykenberg, R. E., *Guntur District 1788–1848*, Oxford, Clarendon Press, 1965.

———— (ed.), *Land Control and Social Structure in Indian History*, Madison, University of Wisconsin Press, 1969.

Gill, M. S., 'Punjab—the Continuing Miracle', *National Cooperative Development Corpration,* nos 3–4, 1979.

Hanumantha Rao, C. H., *Technological Change and Distribution of Gains in Indian Agriculture*, New Delhi, Macmillan, 1975.

Harriss, Barbara, 'Agricultural Mercantile Politics and Policy: a Case Study of Tamil Nadu', Seventh European Conference on Modern South Asian Studies, School of Oriental and African Studies, London, July 1981.

Indian Society of Agricultural Economics, *Role of Irrigation in the Development of India's Agriculture*, Bombay.

Krishna, Raj, 'Small Farmers Development', *Economic and Political Weekly*, 26 May 1979.

Lele, J. J., *Food Grain Marketing in India*, Ithaca, Cornell University Press, 1971.

Mencher, Joan P., *Agricultural and Social Structure in Tamil Nadu*, Bombay, Allied Publishers, 1978.

Mundle, S., *Bonded Labour in Palamau*, New Deihi, Indian Institute of Public Administration, 1978.

Nair, Kusum, *In Defense of the Irrational Peasant: Indian Agriculture after the Green Revolution*, Chicago, University of Chicago Press, 1979.

Prasad, P.H., 'A Strategy for Rapid Development of Bihar Economy', *Journal of Social and Economic Studies*, 1977, V.

Racine, J., *Deux Etudes Rurales en Pays Tamoul*, Bordeaux, Centre d'Etudes de Geographie Tropicale, 1976.

Sen, B., *The Green Revolution in India: A Perspective*, New York, Wiley, 1974.

Shah, C. H., and C. N. Vakil (eds), *Agricultural Development of India*, New Delhi, Orient Longman, 1979.

Srinivas, M. N., 'Village Studies, Participant Observation and Social Science Research in India', *Economic and Political Weekly*, Special Number, August, 1975.

Subramanian, V., *Parched Earth: The Maharashtra Drought 1970–73*, Bombay, Orient Longman, 1975.

Thorne, D., 'Coastal Andhra: Towards an Affluent Society', *Economic and Political Weekly*, Annual number, February 1967.

Hunter, G., A. H. Bunting and A. Bottrall, *Policy and Practice in Rural Development*, London, Croom Helm, 1976.

Moore Lappe. F., and J. Collins, *Food First,* Boston, Houghton Mifflin, 1977.

Palmer, Ingrid, *The New Rice in Asia,* Geneva, U.N. Research Institute for Social Development, 1976.

International Organizations

F.A.O., *Report on Agrarian Reforms and Rural Development in Developing Countries*, Rome, World Conference, 1979.

Asian Development Bank, *Asian Agricultural Survey*, Manila, 1977.

World Bank, 'Another Development and the New International Order: the Process of Change', *Development Dialogue*, no. 1, 1976.

World Bank, 'Towards a Theory of Rural Development', *Development Dialogue*, no. 2, 1977.

I. L. O., *Poverty and Landlessness in Rural Asia*, Geneva, 1977.

Scott, W., *Concepts and Measurement of Poverty*, Geneva, U.N. Research Institute for Social Development, 1981.

World Bank, *Small Farmers and the Landless in South Asia* (prepared by Inderjit Singh), Washington, 1979.

INDEX

Absolute poverty, 194-5
Activities: agricultural, 5, 180-1, 206, 209; extension, 176; non-agricultural, 5, 51, 146, 181, 191, 206, 209; subsidiary, 7, 86-7
Administration, 18, 49, 61, 79, 83, 91n, 135, 155, 160, 172, 192, 210; block, 93, 105, 129, 171; district, 93, 105, 129, 171; rural, 12
Afghanistan, 23, 192, 207
Africa, 202
Agolai, 126
Agra, 45
Agra university, 57
Agrarian reforms, 12
Agriculture, 5, 11, 15, 28, 42, 48, 50, 53, 73, 117, 128, 147, 153, 183-4, 199, 206; growth in, 139, 141
Ahmednagar district, 112
Akkulu, 95n
Alagh, Y. K., 12, 135n, 138n, 142n, 145
Alexander, K. C., 94n
Alfalfa, 23
Aligarh, 135
All India Consumer Price Index, 98
All India Co-operatives Act, 152
Amballakarars, 82, 90
Ambedkar, Dr B. R., 154
Andhra, 5, 7, 103, 136-7, 145-7, 149, 159-60, 167, 186; coastal, 5, 59n, 68, 201; coastal districts, 136
Animal husbandry, 47, 108, 110, 127, 161, 180
Anikut barrage, 84
Animist cults, 117
Antyodaya, 43, 126, 162, 163n
Arcot district: north, 11, 137; south, 137
Areas: arid, 6; catchment, 128;

command, 54, 60, 68n, 79, 100, 111, 153; cultivated, 27, 54-5, 60-1, 66, 74, 100, 102, 120, 134n, 144, 188; foodgrain, 188; irrigated, 13, 52, 55, 60, 102, 111, 144, 150, 188-9, 197; low-lying, 95; non-irrigated, 104; paddy, 165; rain-fed, 92, 136n, 176; rice, 136; semi-desert, 6, 143; slow-growth, 66; slow-moving, 8; sown, 127; wheat, 101
Asia, 10-11, 194, 198, 200, 206, 209; South, 208
Asian Bank, 201
Asian Development Bank, 198
Assam, 4, 6, 66-7, 74, 113, 138-42, 156, 164-5, 167, 175, 198, 182-3, 192
Assam World Bank Project, 140n
Aziz, Sartaj, 199

Bajra, 16, 21n, 22, 31-2, 35, 37-41, 46, 103-4, 107, 110, 112, 118, 124-8, 144, 148-9, 176, 189-90
Balkanization, 170
Bamboos, 69, 75, 81
Bangladesh, 142, 205-7, 210-11
Banks, 43, 67, 126, 168; commercial, 168; district, 154; district co-operative, 43
Banyas, 121
Bardhan, P., 143, 159
Barley, 42, 46, 53
Barli, 125, 126n
Bengal, 154; north, 113
Bengal Co-operative Societies Bill, 211n
Benor, Daniel, 163, 166
Benor systems, 163, 165-6
Beteille, A., 12, 94n
Bhalla, G.S., 12, 135n, 138n, 142n, 145n, 158n,
Bhangis, 15, 17, 29, 32-3

221

D